Counseling Leaders & Advocates

Strengthening the Future of the Profession

edited by
Cassandra A. Storlie
Barbara Herlihy

American Counseling Association
6101 Stevenson Avenue, Suite 600
Alexandria, VA 22304
www.counseling.org

Counseling Leaders & Advocates

Strengthening the Future of the Profession

American Counseling Association
6101 Stevenson Avenue, Suite 600 • Alexandria, VA 22304

Associate Publisher • Carolyn C. Baker

Digital and Print Development Editor • Nancy Driver

Senior Production Manager • Bonny E. Gaston

Copy Editor • Kay Mikel

Cover and text design by Bonny E. Gaston.

Library of Congress Cataloging-in-Publication Data

Names: Storlie, Cassandra, editor. | Herlihy, Barbara, editor.
Title: Counseling leaders and advocates: strengthening the future of the profession / editors, Cassandra A Storlie, Barbara Herlihy.
Description: Alexandria: American Counseling Association, 2021. | Includes bibliographical references.
Identifiers: LCCN 2021019223 | ISBN 9781556204012 (paperback)
Subjects: LCSH: Counseling. | Counseling—Moral and ethical aspects. | Social advocacy. | Counselors—Professional ethics.
Classification: LCC BF636.67 .C68 2021 | DDC 158.3—dc23
LC record available at https://lccn.loc.gov/2021019223

Dedication

To the future leaders and advocates in the counseling profession.

Table of Contents

Preface vii
Acknowledgments ix
About the Editors xi
Meet the Contributing Authors xiii

Part I Perspectives on Leadership & Advocacy in Counseling

Chapter 1
Introduction 3
Cassandra A. Storlie and Barbara Herlihy

Chapter 2
Culturally Responsive Counseling Leadership 9
Cassandra A. Storlie, Christian D. Chan, and Michael Hannon

Chapter 3
Leadership and Advocacy in the Field 25
Michael D. Brubaker and Andrew W. Wood

Part II Leaders & Advocates—Their Stories

Chapter 4
Patricia Arredondo 41
Daniel C. Rosen

Chapter 5
Casey A. Barrio Minton 53
Isabel C. Farrell

Chapter 6
Carol Bobby 63
Emily Goodman-Scott

Chapter 7
Craig S. Cashwell 73
Jodi L. Tangen

Chapter 8
M. Sylvia Fernandez 81
Christine Sacco-Bene

Chapter 9
Samuel Templeman Gladding 93
D. Robert Casares Jr.

Chapter 10
Barbara Herlihy 107
Anita M. Pool

Chapter 11
Gerard Lawson 117
Corrine R. Sackett

Chapter 12
Courtland C. Lee 129
Marja Humphrey

Chapter 13
Spencer G. Niles 139
Patrick Akos

Chapter 14
Theodore P. Remley 149
Alexander T. Becnel

Chapter 15
Martin Ritchie 159
Amber Lange

Chapter 16
Thomas J. Sweeney 169
Michael D. Brubaker

Part III Synthesis & Concluding Thoughts

Chapter 17
Synthesis 183
Devon E. Romero, Madelyn Duffey, and Cassandra A. Storlie

Chapter 18
Concluding Thoughts 197
Cassandra A. Storlie and Barbara Herlihy

Additional Readings on Leadership and Advocacy 201
References 203

Preface

We (Cassandra A. Storlie and Barbara Herlihy), as coeditors of this book, welcome you to *Counseling Leaders & Advocates: Strengthening the Future of the Profession*! As professional counselors, we are naturally drawn to and curious about the stories of our clients. Our curiosity allows us to delve into their worldviews and provides an avenue to better understand how to advocate with and for them. In a parallel way, each of us engages in a form of leadership known as "servant leadership" by ensuring that service is central to the counseling profession and that the needs of others come first (Greenleaf, 1970). This servant leadership philosophy, which is congruent with the founding principles of counseling, fueled our own curiosity about the stories of our current counseling leaders. How do their unique stories help us better understand diverse worldviews and the future of leadership and advocacy in the counseling profession? Part I provides more detailed information about the organization of the book and perspectives on leadership and advocacy; Part II presents the stories of 13 leaders/advocates and is truly the heart of this work; and Part III provides a synthesis and some concluding thoughts. We are excited to offer this book and hope you will find it enjoyable and instructive. For us, serving as coeditors for this work has truly been a labor of love.

Acknowledgments

When any new book appears, hidden behind the curtain are vital contributors without whom the work would not exist. This book is no exception. We are grateful to the five leaders/advocates who served as our Academy of Advisors, participating in a modified Delphi process to select the leaders and advocates who are profiled in Part II. We greatly appreciate the work of the two peer reviewers who read the first draft of this work and provided many insightful comments and helpful suggestions for improvement. Working with our publishers, Carolyn Baker and Nancy Driver, at the American Counseling Association has been a true pleasure. We further thank our family, friends, and colleagues who have encouraged and supported us throughout this process.

About the Editors

Cassandra A. Storlie, PhD, LPCC-S (Ohio), NCC, RN (Illinois) is an associate professor and doctoral program coordinator in the Counselor Education and Supervision program at Kent State University. She earned her PhD in counselor education and supervision from the University of Iowa.

Storlie has held a variety of leadership positions in counseling at the state, regional, national, and international levels. She is a past president of NCACES (North Central Association for Counselor Education and Supervision) where she also served as secretary (2015–2016). Storlie chaired the ACES Advocacy Interest Network (2013–2017), has served as an ACES proposal reviewer/mentor, and served on a variety of ACES task forces. She chaired the ACES Bylaws & Resolutions Committee (2020–2021), serves as ACES secretary (2021–2022), and is cochair of the ACES Strategic Planning Committee (2021–2023).

Storlie served as secretary (2016–2018) and chair of the Counselor Community Engagement Committee (2013–2016) for Chi Sigma Iota International. She is the associate editor for the *Journal of Counselor Leadership and Advocacy* (*JCLA*). She has served on the Professional Advocacy Task Force for the American Counseling Association (ACA; 2015–2016) and cochaired ACA's Awards Committee (2019–2020). Storlie was awarded the National Career Development Association's Diversity Initiative Award (2016), Outstanding Mentor of the Year for OACES (Ohio ACES; 2017), Ohio Counseling Association's Writing & Research Award (2019), and was the 2020 recipient of *JCLA*'s Outstanding Article Award. In 2019, she was awarded Distinguished Faculty Researcher in the College of Education, Health & Human Services at Kent State University. As a Latina, her research is focused on leadership and advocacy and the career development of Latinx/os/as and BIPOC (Black, Indigenous, and people of color) communities. She has authored or coauthored approximately 45 journal articles and book chapters.

Storlie and her husband, Chad, have one daughter, Audrey. She enjoys distance running and playing with her two large dogs, Buddy and Derby. She is beyond grateful for the mentorship she has received throughout her career and especially from Barbara Herlihy, coeditor of this book.

Barbara Herlihy, PhD, NCC, LPC-S, is a professor in practice and doctoral program director in the Counselor Education program at the University of Texas at San Antonio. She is also professor emeritus in the College of Education and Human Development at the University of New Orleans.

Herlihy has served in several leadership positions, most recently as president of the Chi Sigma Iota International honor society (2017–2018). She is a past chair of the ACA Ethics Committee, the ACA Foundation, and the ACA International Committee. She currently serves as associate editor for ethics for the journal *Counseling and Values*. She is a past recipient of the Southern ACES Courtland Lee Social Justice Award and the ACES Distinguished Mentor Award. She is an ACA Fellow.

A prolific writer, Herlihy is coauthor (with Gerald Corey and with Theodore P. Remley) of three current books on counselor ethics, and she has authored or coauthored approximately 100 journal articles and book chapters. Her professional interests include ethics, social justice and advocacy, transcultural counseling, and feminist therapy. She is passionate about furthering the ethical globalization of the counseling profession. She loves international travel and has presented seminars and workshops across the United States and in other countries, including Mexico, Venezuela, Malta, Argentina, and Italy.

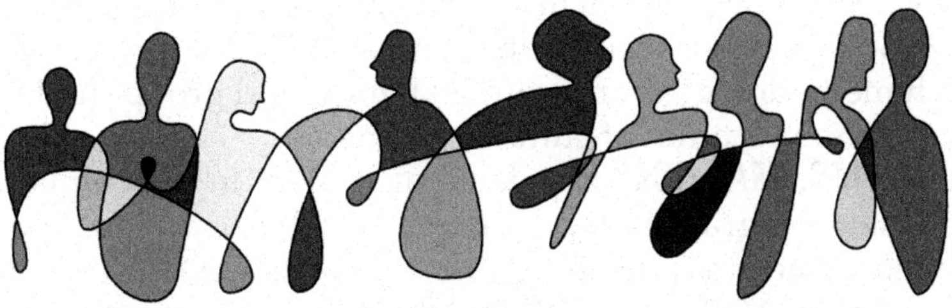

Meet the Contributing Authors

Patrick Akos, PhD, has professional experience as a school and college career counselor that informs his work as a professor in the School of Education at the University of North Carolina at Chapel Hill. His research, teaching, supervision, clinical practice, and leadership are grounded in a strengths-based framework, which is informed by humanistic traditions and empirically supported by contemporary scholarship (e.g., positive psychology). Broadly, he examines how best to support and cultivate thriving, especially during educational and career transitions.

Alexander T. Becnel, PhD, is an assistant professor in the Department of Special Education, Counseling, and Student Affairs at Kansas State University. His research interests include suicide assessment preparation, crisis management and intervention, and counselor leadership. He has also led several trainings and presentations on suicide assessment, prevention, and postvention for school counselors. He has experience as both a school counselor and a clinical counselor specializing in the treatment of adolescents and their families.

Michael D. Brubaker, PhD, is associate professor and associate director of the School of Human Services at the University of Cincinnati. His clinical and research interests have focused on underserved and socially marginalized populations, including those experiencing homelessness; individuals who identify as lesbian, gay, bisexual, transgender, and queer (LGBTQ+); and ethnic minorities. He is past president of Chi Sigma Iota International (2016–2017) and is the editor of the *Journal of Counselor Leadership and Advocacy* (2020–2023).

D. Robert Casares Jr., PhD, is an assistant professor in the Department of Counseling at Wake Forest University. His research interests include creativity in counseling, the clinical and educational utility of podcasts, and boomerang children. He maintains a part-time private practice specializing in couples and family counseling and hosts the International Association of Marriage and Family Counselors' monthly podcast, *The Reframe*.

Christian D. Chan, PhD, NCC, is an assistant professor at The University of North Carolina at Greensboro, past president of the Association for Adult Development and Aging (AADA), associate editor for the journal *Teaching and Supervision in Counseling*, and a proud queer person of color. His interests revolve around intersectionality; multiculturalism in counseling practice, supervision, and counselor education; social justice and activism; career development; critical research methodologies; and couple, family, and group modalities with socialization/communication of cultural factors.

Madelyn Duffey, MS, MA, NCC, is a doctoral student in the counselor education and supervision program at the University of Texas at San Antonio. She has served on the American Counseling Association (ACA) Professional Advocacy Task Force and the ACA Awards Committee, and she is the awards cochair for the Sigma Alpha Chi Chapter of Chi Sigma Iota. Madelyn received the 2019–2020 Sigma Alpha Chi Chapter of Chi Sigma Iota Outstanding Entry Level Student Award and the 2020–2021 Southern Association for Counselor Education and Supervision (SACES) Outstanding Master's Student Award.

Isabel C. Farrell, PhD, NCC, LPC, is an assistant professor at Wake Forest University. Her research is focused on the needs of marginalized populations, specifically immigrant, refugee, and Latinx/o/a clients, in addition to legislative professional advocacy. She was a 2016 National Board for Certified Counselors Foundation Minority Fellow and 2018–2019 Chi Sigma Iota intern. She is currently a committee member of the ACA Public Policy and Legislation Committee (2020–2023), Southern Associaton for Counselor Education and Supervision (SACES) newsletter coeditor (2020–2023), and editorial board member of the *Journal of Counselor Leadership and Advocacy* (2021–2024).

Emily Goodman-Scott, PhD, is an associate professor, graduate program director, and school counseling coordinator at Old Dominion University. Before this, she was a school counselor and worked in multiple mental health counseling settings. She is passionate about research and writing and has published over 30 peer-reviewed articles and two books. She presents across the United States, offering trainings, keynotes, and district partnerships. She co-coordinates the Association for Counselor Education and Supervision school counseling network, was the 2020–2021 president of the Association for Child and Adolescent Counseling (ACA division), and received the 2020 ACA Research Award.

Michael Hannon, PhD, is an associate professor of counseling at Montclair State University. His research focuses on Black men's wellness, with attention to their roles as fathers, leaders, clients, and counselor educators. He has been a contributor to organizations such as Autism Speaks, Thrive Global, Fusion, as well as *The Huffington Post*. His book, *Black Fathering and Mental Health,* will be published in the fall of 2021. He is an associate editor of *The Journal of Humanistic Counseling*.

Marja Humphrey, PhD, NCC, is an assistant professor in the school counseling program at Bowie State University. Her research focuses on counselor preparation, leadership, wellness, and online learning. Her publications have examined multicultural counseling, counselor self-care, and counselor leadership development. She is currently serving as the cochair for the Emerging Leaders program with the Maryland Counseling Association and represents Bowie State University with the Maryland Consortium for Adjunct Faculty Professional Development.

Amber Lange, PhD, LPC, CAADC, is director of external partnerships at Capella University. Her past roles include core faculty and department chair for Capella's CMHC (Clinical Mental Health Counseling) and CES CACREP-accredited programs. She recently sold a mental health practice specializing in sexual health, infidelity, and betrayal. She has been counseling and working in higher education for almost 20 years.

Anita M. Pool, PhD, is an assistant professor in the Department of Counseling at the University of the Cumberlands, where she teaches in the master's and doctoral programs. She serves in various leadership capacities for her department, including director of counseling admissions and doctoral residency coordinator. She has a special interest in qualitative research and serves as a qualitative methodologist on dissertation committees. Additional professional interests include the training and supervision of school counselors and counseling with children and adolescents.

Devon E. Romero, PhD, is an assistant professor in the Department of Counseling at the University of Texas at San Antonio (UTSA). Her research focuses on studying trauma, child development, and integrative and complementary interventions such as neurofeedback and mindfulness. She serves as co-faculty advisor for the Neurofeedback Society of UTSA, chapter faculty advisor for the Sigma Alpha Chi Chapter of Chi Sigma Iota, and assistant editor for the Chi Sigma Iota *Exemplar* newsletter (2019–2022).

Daniel C. Rosen, PhD, is chair and professor in the Department of Counseling and Health Psychology at Bastyr University and was the founding codirector of the Daniel K. Church CENTER for Social Justice and Diversity. His scholarship is focused on applying psychological science to develop interventions that promote culturally responsive clinical care and decrease the racial/cultural biases that underlie existent health disparities. He has a private practice in Seattle, Washington.

Corrine R. Sackett, PhD, is an associate professor of counselor education at Clemson University. She is primarily a qualitative researcher who focuses on topics related to experiences of the counseling process, advocacy surrounding societal issues, and supervision. She has published in ACA journals including the *Journal of Counseling & Development, Counselor Education and Supervision,* and the *Journal of Multicultural Counseling and Development.* She is also a licensed marriage and family therapist in North Carolina.

Christine Sacco-Bene, PhD, is a clinical associate professor in the rehabilitation counseling program in the School of Medicine at the University of South Carolina. Her research interests focus on student professional identity development, teaching and mentoring, and working with individuals and families with disabilities. Her leadership roles include serving the American Rehabilitation Counseling Association as the public relations and awareness director (2019–2020; 2020–2022) and as a board member for Lift Disability Network in Florida. Foremost are her roles as wife and mother.

Jodi L. Tangen, PhD, NCC, ACS, is an assistant professor and the counselor education program coordinator at North Dakota State University. She focuses her research on spirituality, relational depth, and social justice and diversity. She is also the proud mama of two delightful young children!

Andrew W. Wood, PhD, NCC, is an assistant professor of counseling and the mental health counseling track coordinator at the University of Cincinnati. His research interests primarily focus on psychosocial issues in cancer care and health as well as social justice and activism. His role as a counselor educator includes understanding the role of advocacy for students from an ecological perspective and integrating radical mental health theories and pedagogy into his teaching alongside traditional perspectives.

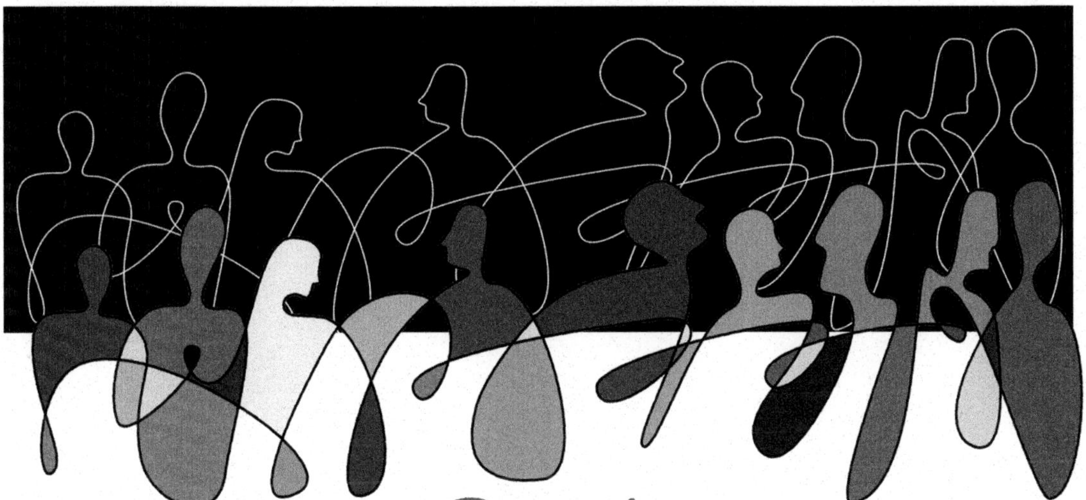

Part I

Perspectives on Leadership & Advocacy in Counseling

Chapter 1

Introduction

Cassandra A. Storlie and Barbara Herlihy

In this brief introductory chapter, we share how this book came into being and provide an overview of its organization. Part I focuses generally on culturally responsive counseling leadership and counselor leadership in the field. Part II profiles 13 leaders and advocates in the counseling profession. And Part III provides a synthesis and some concluding thoughts on how you might make the best use of what you have read.

Book Development and Organization

Our plan for creating this book began serendipitously with a series of informal conversations that we enjoyed during breaks at the meetings of a national counseling organization in which we both held leadership positions at the time. We found that we shared a keen interest in leadership and advocacy and were excited to see how the counseling profession's attention to these topics has grown in recent years. We talked about how much we had enjoyed *Leaders and Legacies: Contributions to the Profession of Counseling* (West et al., 2003), and as we talked, we realized that this was the most recent book that profiled leaders in our field—and nearly two decades had gone by since it was published. Some of the leaders profiled then are still active in the counseling profession and continue to make significant new contributions, others are no longer living, and some new leaders have emerged in recent times. With consultation and the inspiration of a decades' long counseling leader, we recognized the need for a text that holistically integrated leadership and advocacy insights from current counseling leaders. It was time for a new work!

As we discussed our ideas about how to organize this book, an outline emerged for a book with three parts. These parts would capture the phenomena of counseling leadership and advocacy in counseling, the stories of individuals who have advanced our profession as leaders and advocates, and the "common threads" that unify the contributions they have made. Furthermore, it was imperative for us to emphasize practical guidance for counselors, counselor educators, and counseling students who aspire to be leaders and advocates.

Part I: Perspectives on Leadership & Advocacy in Counseling

Part I highlights current perspectives on leadership and advocacy in our profession. In addition to this chapter, two chapters provide information critical to the growth and development of new counseling leaders. In selecting this framework, we wanted readers to better understand key historical aspects of the development of the counseling profession while also considering the current social climate, particularly the impact of racial and ethnic injustices that have been prevalent throughout U.S. history. Likewise, we wanted newer professionals to have a clearer sense of what leadership and advocacy looks like *on the job*, to supplement what they had learned in the classroom.

Chapter 2, *Culturally Responsive Counseling Leadership and Advocacy*, chronicles salient aspects of the history of the American Counseling Association (ACA), including "Operationalization of the Multicultural Counseling Competencies" (Arredondo et al., 1996), the "ACA Advocacy Competencies" (Lewis et al., 2003), and the "Multicultural and Social Justice Counseling Competencies" (ACA, 2015), highlighting how they have led our profession not only in gaining multicultural competence but also in taking it a step further to engage in culturally responsive counseling leadership and advocacy. The growth in the perspective of counselors, moving from being culturally *sensitive* to becoming culturally *responsive*, is described through the lens of an ecological systems framework. The chapter authors address the history of the counseling profession and its roots in advocating for individuals and groups who are most marginalized in our society. Through transparency and engagement, the authors provide insights into how one can become a culturally responsive counseling leader and advocate by providing specific action steps in relation to the Black Lives Matter (BLM) movement. Essential characteristics of culturally responsive counseling leaders are also emphasized in this chapter. The chapter concludes with practical applications and describes how counseling students and practitioners can develop into culturally responsive counseling leaders and advocates.

Chapter 3, *Leadership and Advocacy in the Field*, describes how counselors advocate for their clients within the complex communities in which they reside. The chapter authors present a historical perspective that demonstrates how client advocacy has been the prominent focus for practicing counselors from the inception of our profession. Professional advocacy, which developed over time as counselors gained a sense of professional identity separate from other mental health professions, is also highlighted as a way to both unify and strengthen the counseling profession. The authors discuss how leadership and advocacy are inherently related and how advocacy initiatives taken on by counseling leaders affect our world today. Information on how to engage in the types of ground-level leadership that takes place daily within K–25 educational settings, clinical mental health and community settings, and counseling programs and universities is provided. The authors conclude by describing how counseling students and counseling practitioners can develop into servant leaders.

Part II: Leaders & Advocates—Their Stories

Part II is the "heart of the book." It contains the personal and professional stories of 13 prominent leaders and advocates in the profession of counseling. Inspired by West et al. (2003), we established an Academy of Advisors to assist us in a systematic process to identify the leaders who are profiled in this book. The academy comprised five individuals who had held significant leadership positions in major counseling professional associations, had been widely acknowledged as leaders in the counseling profession, and remained actively engaged in the profession. As the editor spearheading this process, Cassie asked each advisor to independently generate a slate of 20 to 25 leaders/advocates they would nominate to be profiled in this book. Cassie then created a combined slate containing all names that appeared on at least two individually submitted lists. This slate was sent back to the advisors, who were then asked to narrow the list by selecting those whose "leadership and advocacy has had a long-term, broad impact on the counseling profession" and to consider "a representation of diverse leaders to be showcased." Cassie then asked the advisors to place these names in rank order. The 13 individuals profiled in this book were ranked highest and identified most frequently by our advisors.

We are honored to present their stories, and we are painfully aware that many other exceptional leaders and advocates are equally deserving of recognition. Advancing our profession actually does "take a village," and the full community of highly influential leaders and advocates is much, much larger than the exceptional individuals we introduce here. Our hope is that these stories will inspire you and guide you on your own path toward leadership and advocacy.

Part III: Synthesis & Concluding Thoughts

Chapter 17, *Synthesis*, contains a thematic analysis based on the profiles of the selected leaders and advocates. We enlisted two coauthors, an assistant professor and a doctoral student, who both have a strong interest in leadership and advocacy, to assist us in this analysis. Their engagement helped ensure that our theme identification process would represent the perspective of our readership. We discuss how the themes they discovered relate to the current literature on leadership and advocacy, both reinforcing what we know and extending our understanding as we look toward the future. This analysis reflects how the 13 leaders/advocates profiled related to and differed from one another in the spirit of strengthening the profession. A variety of reflective questions encourage you to deepen your connections to leadership and advocacy in the field of counseling.

In *Concluding Thoughts*, we offer our thoughts on the work as a whole and the wisdom shared by leaders as they look toward the future.

Considerations and Suggestions for Readers

We encourage you to spend intentional time reflecting on your own thoughts about counseling leadership and advocacy as you read this book. How do you understand these processes? Where are the gaps, and what remains to be done? You are the future generation of counseling leaders and advocates, and we invite you to pause and reflect on this question as you read: What motivates *you* in your aspirations to become a leader/advocate?

It is easier for us to answer that question as it relates to advocacy. Advocates are driven by a passion to make positive change in the lives of their clients, in the systems that contribute to marginalization and oppression of clients and client populations, and in the profession to increase our capacity to reach out and help those in need. What types of advocacy stand out for you as you read the profiles of our leaders?

What drives people toward leadership seems a bit more complex. As you will see, some leaders had a desire to lead from an early age, whereas others found themselves in leadership positions seemingly by happenstance. What kinds of leadership do we need to see more of to strengthen the profession of counseling? If you are a new counseling professional or a counseling student, this may feel like a daunting question. But those of you a little further along in your counseling career may have already established as interest in engaging leadership. Making space and time for leadership and advocacy initiatives can be a part of your regular practice, and we hope the practical suggestions in this book will assist you in reaching your goal.

Getting the Most Out of This Book

We believe you will get the most out of this book by having some brief, introductory knowledge about leadership theory and philosophy. Most notably in the counseling profession, you will come across the term *servant leadership*, which was first introduced by Robert Greenleaf in 1970. Greenleaf believes leadership begins with wanting to serve, and this service is followed by aspiring to lead. Servant leadership "shares power, puts the needs of others first and helps people develop and perform as highly as possible" (Center for Servant Leadership, 2020). Eva et al. (2019) described servant leadership as "a holistic leadership approach that engages followers in multiple dimensions (e.g., relational, ethical, emotional, spiritual), such that they are empowered to grow into what they are capable of becoming" (p. 111). Greenleaf (1970) emphasized how servant leaders help others grow and "become healthier, wiser, freer, [and] more autonomous" (p. 15). Servant leaders have a strong impact on the community and on their followers, and they inspire others to become servant leaders.

Servant leadership blends well with the underpinnings of the counseling profession—taking care of others and helping others to develop. Although servant leadership is often described as the core of counseling leadership practices, it is important to acknowledge that counselors embrace a variety of leadership theories. You will find a few of the following theories woven into the stories of our profiled leaders.

Authentic Leadership

Authentic leadership has been defined from intrapersonal, interpersonal, and developmental perspectives, all of which are characterized by their genuine, relational, and ethical qualities (Northouse, 2019). George (2003) identified authentic leaders as having the dimensions of purpose, values, relationships, self-discipline, and heart. George asserted that the characteristics of passion, connectedness, consistency, and compassion are required of authentic leaders. As you consider the qualities and personal traits that influence your understanding of leadership, what traits do you notice among our profiled leaders? What characteristics do you see within yourself as a future leader in our profession?

Transformational Leadership

Transformational leadership is "the process whereby a person engages with others and creates a connection that raises the level of motivation and morality in both the leader and the follower" (Northouse, 2016, p. 162). Transformational leadership encompasses four basic dimensions: inspirational motivation, intellectual stimulation, individualized consideration, and idealized influence (Piccolo & Colquitt, 2006). These dimensions appear to meaningfully overlap with dimensions of the therapeutic counselor–client relationship (e.g., inspiration/hope, contextual considerations). Transformational leadership has been notably visible in the school counseling profession (Gibson et al., 2020).

Adaptive Leadership

Adaptive leaders "prepare and encourage people to deal with change" (Northouse, 2016, p. 257). Adaptive leaders encourage effective changes over multiple levels, from those as finite as the self to those as infinite as our global society. Using a systems approach, adaptive leaders try to understand the complexities of problems and provide supportive environments for their constituents. In the face of the ongoing coronavirus pandemic and the social unrest that revolves around inequalities in the United States, it is important for each of us to have an understanding of adaptive leadership. Change continues to shape our behaviors as we navigate through the upheaval of these times. How can we be reflexive and encourage others to change and learn new ways of living together so that all of us will be successful and can grow?

• • •

This brief review of leadership theories provides a mere sliver of the depth that they encompass. Only a few of the profiled leaders specifically name a leadership theory that guided their work, but you will find traits, skills, procedures, and philosophies that are common to both leadership theories and counseling practice in these stories. They all, in one way or another, speak of leadership as a process of empowering others and as an opportunity to advocate. None of the leaders espouse a traditional view of leadership as a power-over position; rather, they speak of "leading from behind," working "behind the scenes," and "leading by doing," not for their own aggrandizement but to move our profession forward and improve services to our clients. One can deduce that leadership in counseling is ineffective when leadership practices move away from our core values as professional counselors.

Alignment With the 2016 CACREP Standards

Accredited counseling programs help to support a unified counseling profession (Council for Accreditation of Counseling and Related Educational Programs [CACREP], 2015). As we continue to strive for this unity, which strengthens the future of the counseling profession, it is critical to attend to the standards that guide our counseling programs and curriculum. The 2016 CACREP Standards focus on the foundation of a strong professional identity that includes advocacy on behalf of the profession and initiatives needed to address systemic barriers that impede client success. Chapters 2 and 3 discuss counselor professional identity and the advocacy interventions that can address institutional and social barriers that affect clients.

Section 6 of the 2016 CACREP Standards clearly delineates "Leadership and Advocacy" as one of the five core areas of doctoral-level counselor education and supervision, and features that address many of these standards can be found throughout the text. We list the 2016 CACREP Standards that have been addressed in the text at the conclusion of each part. (CACREP standards are currently under revision, and new standards are scheduled to be released in 2024.)

Onward!

The next generation of leaders and advocates must embrace the complex issues facing our clients, the profession as a whole, and our national and global societies if we are to advance and continue to distinguish excellence in professional counseling. We hope this book inspires you to engage in leadership and advocacy opportunities as counseling continues to evolve. Perhaps one or more of the profiled leaders' journeys will resonate with you and your story. Whether you are studying to become a counselor or counselor educator, beginning your career in counseling, or have been practicing for years, we hope this book will encourage you to examine the deeper meaning of your leadership and advocacy roles.

Chapter 2

Culturally Responsive Counseling Leadership

Cassandra A. Storlie, Christian D. Chan, and Michael Hannon

As is true with many works addressing multiculturalism and social justice in counseling, this chapter may take time to fully digest and understand in a way that empowers you to acknowledge yourself as a cultural being and reflect on ways you can incorporate culturally responsive counseling leadership in your practice. To become a culturally responsive leader, it is essential to have a historical understanding of the role of race, culture, and "otherness" within society and in our profession. We will not know where we are going if we don't know where we have been. By striving for culturally responsive counseling leadership, you will embark on a journey in which you voluntarily accept both the privilege and the responsibility of intervening. Your leadership will help our profession become stronger and more inclusive, representing more diverse voices and combating systemic injustices. By becoming a culturally responsive leader, you will examine how intersectionality (Crenshaw, 1989) affects each of us and others, focus on challenging your worldview for unconscious bias, and move forward reflectively to ameliorate barriers to inclusion.

Racism. Prejudice. Sexism. Discrimination. Oppression. Microaggressions. Heterosexism. Poverty. These words represent concepts that have perpetuated inequities in the United States that affect our clients, our students, and even ourselves as privileged members of the counseling profession. There has long been a call for cultural awareness (Sue et al., 2019), cultural sensitivity (Whaley, 2008; Wright & Reese, 2015), and cultural competence (Ratts et al., 2016; Sue et al., 1992) in the counseling profession. These three terms are not synonymous; each has a well-defined meaning (Whaley, 2008). Taken together, they provide a foundation for cultural *responsiveness* and enable counselors to provide leadership in guiding socially just practices in unity for current and future counselors. *Culturally responsive counseling leadership* is enacted when professional counselors move beyond mastery of cultural knowledge to action-oriented approaches, concurrently engage in reflective evaluation for effective practices, and develop community and solidarity with marginalized groups.

Culturally responsive counseling leaders encompass four core characteristics: cultural awareness, culturally sensitivity, cultural competence, and cultural responsiveness (see Figure 2.1). Each of these characteristics is salient in the growth and development of our profession, and integration of these four characteristics is necessary to effectively lead others toward culturally responsive counseling.

The ethnic and racial makeup of the United States reflects a diverse population, and the number of Black, Indigenous, and people of color (BIPOC) has been growing by historic proportions (Pew Research Center, 2019). Since 2010, the "U.S. population increased by 18.9 million, and Hispanics accounted for more than half of this growth" (Pew Research Center, 2020). As the population of BIPOC increases, the disparities between White individuals and BIPOC have also increased on measures of mental/physical health and poverty/socioeconomic status. According to McGuire and Miranda (2008), "racial and ethnic minorities have less access to mental health services than do Whites, are less likely to receive needed care and are more likely to receive poor quality care when treated" (p. 396).

Racial and ethnic minority health disparities have become more evident during the coronavirus pandemic. Communities of color (specifically Black and Hispanic/Latinx) are disproportionately diagnosed with coronavirus and suffer more serious effects from the virus than White individuals (Centers for Disease Control and Prevention, 2020). Communities of color remain incessantly burdened with limited health care coverage (Buchmueller et al., 2016) and are more likely to live in low-income areas that are also engulfed in the pandemic of racial injustice (Rogers et al., 2015). Internalized racism and colonialism affect attitudes toward seeking help (David et al., 2019; Tuazon et al., 2019), and ethnicity has been identified as a relevant variable in mental health stigma (Crowe & Kim, 2020). As a result, racial

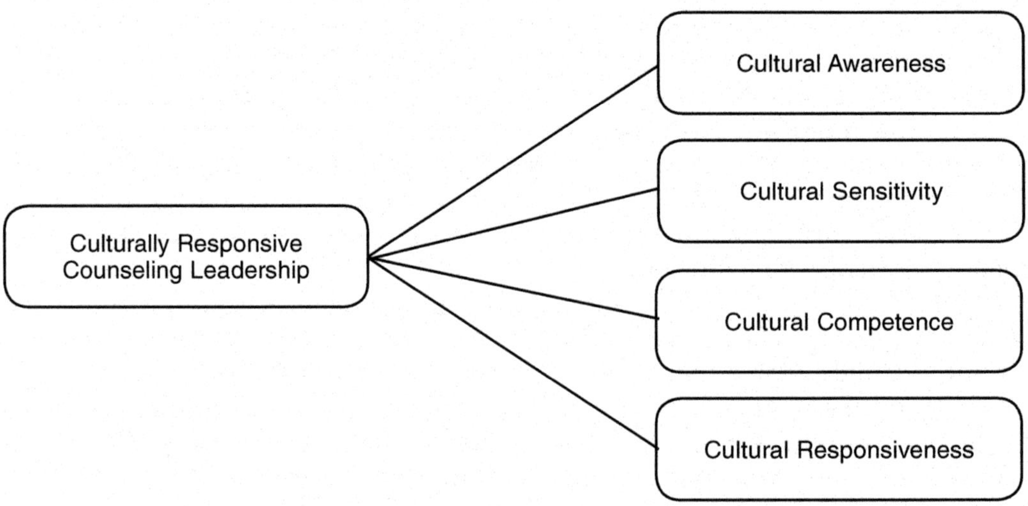

Figure 2.1
Culturally Responsive Counseling Leadership Characteristics

disparities in health care may prevent BIPOC from participating in counseling services critical to their wellness. This pattern is often an outcome of cultural mistrust toward providers within the health care/mental health care system combined with culturally insensitive practices (Flynn et al., 2020; Sue et al., 2019). Scholars have made multiple recommendations to revise the latest version of the *Diagnostic and Statistical Manual* (*DSM-5*) to enhance its cultural sensitivity and inclusion (Chang & Kwon, 2013; La Roche et al., 2015).

As the authors of this chapter and persons of color, we recognize that the terms *diversity* and *culture* expand beyond race and ethnicity. Historically, we have witnessed discriminatory practices in our society related to a variety of "isms" that represent "otherness" and affect oppressed populations including, but not limited to, women, the LGBTQ+ community, individuals with visible and invisible disabilities, immigrants without documentation, older adults, and Indigenous populations. As counselors, it is paramount that we believe and behave in ways that align with the *Code of Ethics* of the American Counseling Association (ACA; 2014):

> Counselors do not condone or engage in discrimination against prospective or current clients, students, employees, supervisees, or research participants based on age, culture, disability, ethnicity, race, religion/spirituality, gender, gender identity, sexual orientation, marital status/partnership, language preference, socioeconomic status, immigration status or any basis proscribed by law. (Standard C.5.)

We call upon professional counselors to move beyond simply understanding the current needs of diverse individuals and to *engage in action-oriented interventions* that address systemic injustices. Culturally responsive counseling leadership extends this approach across several counselor roles and functions, including professional counselor, advocate, supervisor, and leader (Peters et al., 2020; Ratts & Greenleaf, 2018).

We have much work to do in combating systemic racism (Lenes et al., 2020) and biased-based bullying (Toomey & Storlie, 2016) in our schools, in our agencies, within society, and in our own profession. We begin our exploration by providing some historical context for the inception of multiculturalism in counseling. We follow that with an overview of the development and endorsement of advocacy and social justice movements within our profession. We then present an ecological systems framework and discuss how counselors can become culturally responsive counseling leaders. As you read, we encourage you to reflect on the following questions:

- What does it mean to you to be a culturally responsive leader in counseling? What does a culturally responsive leader do that is different from other leaders?
- How can counseling leaders leverage their power and privilege to dismantle overlapping forces of oppression and extend opportunities for advocacy across contexts (e.g., professional associations, legislative bodies, universities, communities)?
- How can counseling leaders identify their proximity to Whiteness and actions that reinforce White supremacy? How do they work with colleagues, teach, and mentor students and supervisees about these mechanisms?

- How do we, as professional counselors, denounce the "deafening silence of dehumanizing and complicit inaction to address these systemic ills within our society?" (ACA, 2020b)
- And last, but perhaps most important, how do we evaluate whether our culturally responsive actions have been effective? What do we need to do to ensure their sustainability?

History of Multiculturalism in the Counseling Profession

The very roots of our counseling profession are multicultural in nature, beginning with Frank Parsons and his advocacy work in vocational guidance with the immigrant population (Zytowski, 2001). Culturally responsive practice has been woven into the fabric of the counseling profession throughout its development (Chung et al., 2011; Peters & Luke, 2021). However, active and intentional discrimination was also present during the inception of counseling as a profession.

In the civil rights era of the 1950s, systemic inequality and racism were common in the United States, and those prejudices permeated institutions and organizations (Morning & Sabbagh, 2005). People of color, particularly Black individuals, were twice blocked from developing a unique and separate division in the American Personnel and Guidance Association (APGA; AMCD, n.d.), which later became the American Association of Counseling and Development (AACD) and changed once again to become the American Counseling Association (ACA, n.d.). Discrimination was evident in counseling research as well, and BIPOC researchers had difficulty getting multicultural research published (Ratts & Pedersen, 2014). This prejudice in the counseling profession limited access to evidence-based, culturally sensitive, responsive counseling interventions for non-white populations. Instead, "clinical practices focused on assimilating culturally diverse clients into White culture" (p. 8).

As the 1960s began to unfold, societal turbulence in the United States led to changes in discriminatory policies such as those reflected in discrimination against BIPOC in counseling. It was during this time that counseling professionals began to push back against the monolithic approach to counseling and to recognize the various cultures that make up our society (Neukrug, 2016). Notably, a number of leaders and groups called attention to the problematic lack of representation of BIPOC among the ranks of leaders and the overall membership of the APGA (now ACA). Before 1972, the Association for Non-White Concerns in Personnel and Guidance, which would eventually become the Association for Multicultural Counseling and Development (AMCD), had limited representation in the APGA and had no voting rights on its board of directors or senate (AMCD, n.d.). This important group, in effect, demanded representation of BIPOC in the overall membership of APGA and throughout the counseling profession. As this multicultural paradigm shift gained traction and support in counseling, it was evident that culturally responsive and socially just values were cornerstones for the evolution and continued development of the profession (Ratts, 2009, 2011; Ratts & Pedersen, 2014). This multiculturalism movement set a precedent for attending to the needs of a variety of culturally and linguistically diverse clients, students, and communities. Simultaneously, this movement embedded humanistic thought, strengths-based practices, developmental approaches, and wellness models into counseling practice, education, and supervision (Vereen et al., 2014). Stemming from the growth and visibility of the AMCD in the counseling profession, the need for guiding documents to supplement codes of ethics included a drive to develop the first iteration of the Multicultural Counseling Competencies (MCC; Sue et al., 1992).

Multicultural Counseling Competencies

AMCD commissioned the first edition of the MCC (Sue et al., 1992) to illustrate the tasks, responsibilities, and functions of professional counselors to uphold the values and standards of multicultural practices. The integration of inclusive values helped meet the needs of diverse communities, and professional counselors took more active steps to help eradicate social conditions that persistently impeded client and student trajectories toward optimal wellness across the life span. Implementing the MCC (aspects developed from the tripartite model consisting of Knowledge, Attitudes and Beliefs, and Skills) fostered a sense of attending to client, student, community, and public welfare while supporting professional counselors in successfully bridging the gaps in their own multicultural practice. The MCC gave professional counselors a launching point to address issues related to race and culture in their work settings, to further examine their individual roles in cross-cultural counseling, and to consider strategies for advocating for clients from various marginalized groups (Sue et al., 1992).

The early stages of the MCC marked an innovative and courageous step in both counseling practice and counselor education (Sue et al., 1992). Numerous counseling researchers began to establish measurements to assess effective multicultural counseling practice. The MCC highlighted the importance and responsibility of counseling leaders to serve as multiculturally sensitive practitioners and to ethically integrate multiculturalism into their leadership and advocacy efforts. Counseling leadership began to magnify multiculturalism, which established a pathway to a professional counseling identity that was distinct from that of other helping professions (Lee, 2012). Thus, it is imperative for counseling leaders to recognize and integrate the history and core tenets of the MCC to broaden their knowledge and scope of culturally responsive practices.

Advocacy and Social Justice in Counseling

Advocacy in counseling customarily has been connected with empowerment and action that professional counselors take on behalf of clients (Newsome & Gladding, 2014). Between the inception of the MCC and the appearance of the Multicultural and Social Justice Counseling Competencies (MSJCC), a series of ACA presidents, particularly Jane Goodman, formed initiatives to substantiate the role of advocacy in the counseling profession. These initiatives centered on explicating that advocacy has a dual purpose of client advocacy and professional advocacy (Myers & Sweeney, 2004; Myers et al., 2002). Client and professional advocacy are not competing forces; rather, they are both critical components in the preparation of effective professional counselors (Farrell & Barrio Minton, 2019; Myers et al., 2002; Storlie et al., 2019).

Goodman created a task force with the specific purpose of formulating the ACA Advocacy Competencies (Lewis et al., 2003). Endorsed by the ACA Governing Council, the ACA Advocacy Competencies introduced professional counselors to an advocacy continuum (micro- to macrolevel) that included multiple domains in which counselors could act *with* or act *on behalf of* clients, students, schools, communities, and the greater public. The ACA Advocacy Competencies have been an exemplar in the promotion of systemic change (Toporek et al., 2009), advocacy with clients and students (Ratts & Hutchins, 2009), school counseling (Haskins & Singh, 2016; Ratts et al., 2007), and community collaboration (Lopez-Baez & Paylo, 2009). It is also well understood that "many situations call for multiple forms of advocacy concurrently" (Lewis et al., 2011, p. 9).

Critical to the expansion of advocacy initiatives, social justice was prioritized and became an elucidating force, enveloping the multiple levels where systemic marginalization existed. The act of advocating became the route to social justice (Fickling & Gonzalez, 2016) because advocacy was (and is) a means of pursuing equity and justice for clients and students. As social justice began to be described as the fifth force in the counseling profession (Lee, 2012; Ratts, 2009), additional systemic and contextual factors influencing client and student wellness were recognized, especially among historically marginalized clients and students (Ratts & Greenleaf, 2018; Ratts et al., 2016). Counseling leaders engaged in political, legislative, and community advocacy and acknowledged this advocacy as a key responsibility of professional counselors. These distinct responsibilities for professional counselors are documented in the *ACA Code of Ethics* (ACA, 2014) with explicit language that counselors do not condone discrimination or any of its forms (Standard 5.c.). It is important to note, however, that "not condone" does not mean the same as "advocate."

Counselors for Social Justice (CSJ) was formed in 1994 to reinforce the counseling profession's commitment to multiculturalism and advocacy (Anderson et al., 2015). In particular, CSJ's early developmental stages signified a movement to work in tandem with AMCD, the Association for Specialists in Group Work (ASGW), and the National Career Development Association (NCDA) to remove social conditions and barriers affecting clients' and students' life span development for optimal wellness. Professional associations, such as AMCD and CSJ, upheld overarching values attached to the distinct movements of multiculturalism and social justice. The scope of their organizations and their ensuing accomplishments serve as a call to action for all professional counselors to embody these values, roles, and functions as a lifelong career commitment (Ratts et al., 2016). As leaders and advocates fully immerse in the histories of professional associations, governance, and leadership, it is critical to remember that culturally responsive counseling leadership is not a one-time incident, a response to a crisis or urgent gap, or the sole responsibility of a single group. The development of cultural awareness and responsiveness is an ongoing process over a career and should be a priority for every counseling leader, advocate, and professional.

MSJCC

With the advent of the seventh iteration of the *ACA Code of Ethics* (ACA, 2014) and the 20/20 definition of professional counseling (Kaplan et al., 2014), AMCD leaders commissioned a task force to update the MCC. Given the history of the MCC, it was important to highlight the philosophical underpinnings of the original document and expand it to fit more current research and scholarship on multiculturalism and social justice (Ratts et al., 2016). Consistent with culturally responsive counseling practices, AMCD leaders and the commission task force noted the importance of drawing from lineage, ancestry, and generational wealth to reflect the values, expertise, and foundation instilled from past leaders (Singh, Nassar, et al., 2020). To fit more cohesively with the introduction of the fifth force of counseling as social justice (Ratts & Pedersen, 2014), the MCC transformed into the MSJCC to accurately reflect a more action-oriented set of values for practice and solidarity with historically marginalized communities. The MSJCC moved beyond a predominant focus on multicultural communication strategies, intercultural dialogue, and cross-cultural skills to a global enterprise predicated on action, systemic change, and advocacy (Fickling et al., 2019; Ratts et al., 2016).

The model of the MSJCC intentionally connected to the MCC (Sue et al., 1992) and the ACA Advocacy Competencies (Lewis et al., 2003; Toporek & Daniels, 2018), and the newly minted MSJCC added multiple aspects to broaden the application of social justice to reinforce its priority for training and practice within professional counseling. The MSJCC incorporated philosophical underpinnings of intersectionality theory to properly reflect the simultaneous coexistence of privilege and oppression and the multiplicity of dimensions beyond race and ethnicity, including sexual identity, affection, ability status, spirituality, social class, and gender identity (Chan et al., 2018; Ratts et al., 2016; Singh, Appling, & Trepal, 2020). Annexing intersectionality theory to the MSJCC served as a response to critics claiming that multiculturalism was predicated solely on race and ethnicity. The underlying characteristics that define intersectionality are power and social context (Collins, 2015; Collins & Bilge, 2020), and counselors need to consider each context and relationship (e.g., counselor and client) as a reflection of power relations. The MSJCC also explicitly infused action as a domain within the previous tripartite model of attitudes and beliefs, knowledge, and skills. Hence, the MSJCC reinforced the development of multicultural competence, social justice in counseling, and culturally responsive practices as a lifelong commitment rather than a status to achieve or a checklist to complete (Ratts et al., 2016).

Moving Toward Culturally Responsive Counseling Leadership and Advocacy

Consistent with a proliferation of scholarship about leadership and advocacy, multiculturalism, advocacy, and social justice have become intertwined as the counseling profession has evolved (Lee, 2012; Ratts, 2011). Incorporating multiculturalism and social justice can occur at multiple systemic levels of leadership (Cashwell & Barrio Minton, 2012; Chan et al., 2018, 2019; Storlie, 2016; Storlie & Jach, 2012). As an explicit example, Cashwell and Barrio Minton (2012) identified myriad ways for administrators and leaders to meet their responsibility for institutionalizing multiculturalism and social justice into the culture and operations of academic units (e.g., departments). Other counseling leaders (Chan et al., 2018; Day-Vines et al., 2018; Remley & Herlihy, 2020; Singh, Appling, & Trepal, 2020; Singh, Nassar, et al., 2020) highlighted the importance of establishing multiculturalism, advocacy, and social justice as intuitive priorities across the counselor education curriculum, which would ultimately become a cultural norm rather than an isolated specialty. The Council for Accreditation of Counseling and Related Educational Programs

(CACREP) 2016 Standards (CACREP, 2015) address social and cultural foundations as a core area, and the *ACA Code of Ethics* (ACA, 2014) further outlines multicultural competence as an ethical obligation for counseling practitioners, supervisors, and counselor educators.

Culturally responsive leadership has been evident in school and educational research for some time (Johnson, 2006; Madhlangobe & Gordon, 2012). We have seen that "school counselors must understand how their skills and ethical responsibilities interface within the context of their one school system and the idiosyncrasies and interactions that exist within and across various systems" (Beck et al., 2018, p. 45). We acknowledge, however, that little has been written about culturally responsive leadership for the remaining specialty areas within the counseling profession (e.g., clinical mental health, clinical rehabilitation, counselor education and supervision), and much more work is needed (Peters & Luke, 2021). It is essential to explore how we can best engage in cultural responsiveness through the lens of counselor leadership and advocacy in the current times of social unrest and systemic injustice against communities of color.

Applying Ecological Systems Theory to Enhance Culturally Responsive Counseling Leadership

Ecological frameworks, and frameworks that embed the context of the culture to our overarching society, can help us better understand a larger social ecology (Schriver, 2011) while also considering the environmental context of various subsystems, both close and farther away from the individual. We introduce a framework to better understand the systemic influences on culturally responsive counseling leadership that we conceptualized by applying Bronfenbrenner's ecological and sociocultural model (Bronfenbrenner & Morris, 1998). Bronfenbrenner's ecological systems theory incorporates various levels of ecosystems situated within a complex system of relationships influenced by the surrounding environment (Tissington, 2008). When considering culturally responsive counseling leadership, ecological systems theory highlights five nested structures—microsystem, mesosystem, exosystem, macrosystem, and chronosystem—that have been applied to counseling in the past to construct an understanding of how environmental influences can affect development (Bronfenbrenner, 1979). Using this model, we suggest advocacy steps in support of the Black Lives Matter (BLM) movement that highlight how counseling leaders can take direct action to combat systemic injustices.

BLM

BLM (https://blacklivesmatter.com) was founded in July 2013 in response to the acquittal of George Zimmerman for the murder of Trayvon Martin (Black Lives Matter, n.d.). Trayvon Martin, a 17-year-old Black teenage boy visiting family in the community, was killed on February 26, 2012, by 28-year-old George Zimmerman. Zimmerman, of White and Hispanic ancestry, was the neighborhood watch coordinator for his gated community. He racially profiled Martin, assumed he was there without reason, and called authorities to report Martin as suspicious. Zimmerman was armed, and he pursued and initiated a physical altercation with Martin despite repeatedly being advised by a dispatcher to cease his pursuit. Zimmerman fatally shot Martin and claimed self-defense. He was acquitted of second-degree murder in July 2013. The highly publicized and polarizing case functioned as a catalyst for organizers and activists fighting against anti-Black racist violence.

Alicia Garza, Patrisse Cullors, and Opal Tometi founded the BLM movement and organization following Zimmerman's acquittal. BLM gained national and international attention in the aftermath of two more deaths of Black men at the hands of police: Michael Brown in Ferguson, Missouri, and Eric Garner in New York. In each case, the accuser was found not guilty of murder. The BLM website describes itself, in part, as "a global organization in the U.S., UK, and Canada, whose mission is to eradicate white supremacy and build local power to intervene in violence inflicted on Black communities by the state and vigilantes" (Black Lives Matter, n.d.). Black Lives Matter is a decentralized network comprising 15 to 30 chapters within and beyond the United States. It has become an influential force in the fight against anti-Black racism in several contexts, including schools and government, while unapologetically affirming the humanity of all Black lives.

BLM and Counseling Leadership

As the counseling profession endorses and advocates for culturally responsive leaders, we must be ready and willing to situate ourselves within the context of the sociopolitical landscape in the United States and globally. The BLM movement explicitly aligns with the profession's espoused value and ongoing work against anti-Black racism in all of its forms. Washington and Henfield (2019) address this issue and describe how the MSJCC can function as an ethical framework for counselor educators in their work with preservice counselors to increase their awareness, knowledge, and skills about how state-sanctioned violence against Black people is routinely experienced and impedes their wellness. They make clear connections between the BLM ethos and the counseling profession and recommend specific action steps. Specifically, they suggest that counselor educators enhance their pedagogical practices and curricula by inviting members of the BLM movement into their classes and "creating an awareness-raising assignment that inverts the immersion activities/assignments commonplace" in our programs (p.156). They also recommend enhancing our counseling scholarship by initiating research projects that document student, faculty, and alumni perceptions of and experiences with the BLM movement as a baseline for more expansive and in-depth research projects.

As an extension of the work by Washington and Henfield, we offer suggestions for how counseling leaders can further engage in advocacy in support of the BLM movement. Drawing on Bronfenbrenner's (1979) ecological systems theory to contextualize that work, we operationalize each of the five levels of the ecological systems framework and provide ways to evaluate the effectiveness of advocacy work within each level (Figure 2.2).

Microsystem

The microsystem is the immediate environment that influences the culturally responsive counseling leader. This could include an already diverse environment of individuals closest to the counseling leader or may include individuals who share identities with the leader. It encompasses the counseling leader's worldview in relation to age, culture, disability, ethnicity, race, religion/spirituality, gender, gender identity, sexual orientation, marital status/partnership, language preference,

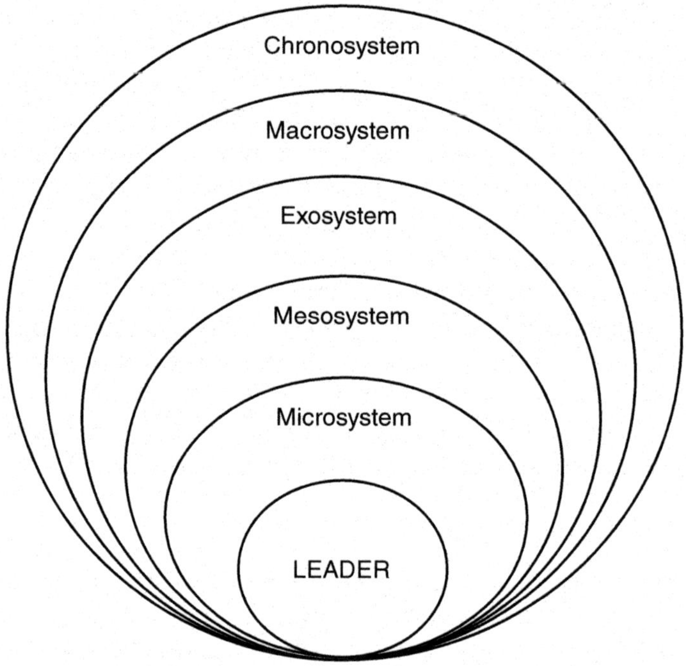

Figure 2.2
The Culturally Responsive Counseling Leader and the Black Lives Matter Movement

socioeconomic status, immigration status (ACA, 2014, Standard 5.c.), and all other dimensions of identity. It is important to note that culturally responsive leaders intentionally include individuals who are different from them (and safe for them) to be a part of their microsystem. This inclusion enables safety for diversity of thought and background. Furthermore, this broader understanding can challenge leaders' thinking while maintaining a consistent focus on inclusive practices in their personal and professional lives. Culturally responsive counseling leaders are reflexive and reflective and are open to growth and to expanding their perspective.

BLM advocacy step. Culturally responsive counseling leaders can advocate for and with the BLM movement by taking two steps within this microsystem. First, leaders can actively familiarize themselves with the foundation and ongoing activities of the BLM movement. This can take the form of reading and watching information sources supportive of the movement and taking time to critically think about ways the movement can be constructively criticized for its benefit and success. Second, leaders can invite and engage members of the movement into their microsystem for meaningful relationships. This step has the potential to further humanize and affirm the critical importance of the fight against and resistance to all forms of white supremacy.

Evaluating the effectiveness of this advocacy step. Culturally responsive counseling leaders can evaluate their effectiveness in this advocacy step by simply assessing their microsystem. Leaders can ask themselves, "With whom do I most frequently and intimately engage? How do those forms of engagement support or impede my ideas and sensibilities about the BLM movement?"

Mesosystem

Throughout the mesosystem of the culturally responsive counseling leader, the focus is on connections. According to Bronfenbrenner (1979), the mesosystem focuses on the interactions between individuals' microsystems. For example, how do counseling leaders' students (i.e., classroom as one microsystem) interact with other counseling faculty at programs or events (i.e., faculty colleagues as microsystem). Counseling leaders work hard to be present and accessible in a variety of contexts (e.g., department-wide programs, student events, information sessions) that provide opportunities for deeper and more meaningful connections, helping to ensure that their connections are diverse and meaningful.

BLM advocacy step. Culturally responsive counseling leaders can advocate for the BLM movement in the context of their mesosystems by connecting the various members of their microsystems to provide opportunities for shared learning about the movement. For example, leaders can invite speakers or presenters to their campuses for professional development and continuing education activities that support the BLM movement. A variety of counseling and allied mental health educators can provide professional development for preservice counselors, practicing counselors, and counselor educators.

Evaluation of the effectiveness of this advocacy step. Culturally responsive leaders can evaluate the effectiveness of this step by having the courage to evaluate the scope, sequence, frequency, and diversity of how their microsystems interact. Counseling leaders must be brave enough to closely examine who they engage with to provide professional development for their learning community and reflect honestly on their motivations for those choices. This stronger and more structured approach enables leaders to closely examine the choices they make.

Exosystem

Bronfenbrenner (1979) described the exosystem as our indirect environment, or the policies that influence our microsystems and mesosystems. Counseling leaders may have direct or indirect roles in their indirect environment. Examples of counseling leaders' exosystems are university guidelines that influence how they use instructional technology in the classroom, or actions taken by ACA on certain issues that the membership may or may not have had a direct influence in deciding. For example, members who did not and do not agree with ACA's statement endorsing BLM are still influenced by ACA's statement denouncing all forms of racism.

BLM advocacy step. Supporting the BLM movement at the exosystem level requires culturally responsive counseling leaders to willingly step out and openly endorse ACA's position on the BLM movement, even in the midst of potential discomfort or disagreement. Doing so is an acknowledgment of the courage, reflection, and reflexivity required of culturally responsive counseling leaders to support collective action that humanizes, legitimizes, and supports diverse ways of supporting Black lives.

Evaluation of the effectiveness of this advocacy step. Culturally responsive leaders can evaluate their effectiveness in this advocacy step by assessing their visible, vocal, and written support of ACA's public statements, as well as statements of other counseling organizations, in support of the BLM movement.

Macrosystem

The macrosystem encompasses the overall influence of the broader social and cultural values of the larger community. In this application, counseling leaders recognize the historical and systemic racism that has been enacted in the United States since its inception and has been acknowledged by the counseling profession and use this knowledge as an impetus to systematically fight against racism through social justice advocacy.

BLM advocacy step. Culturally responsive counseling leaders can advocate for the BLM movement within the macrosystem by taking individual and collective action to actively recruit and support Black counselor educators, help enable their success as faculty, and encourage their pursuit of leadership opportunities within the profession. The faculty in counseling programs and in counseling leadership remains overwhelmingly White, reflecting the historic lack of effective recruitment, retention, and engagement of Black counseling faculty.

Evaluation of the effectiveness of this advocacy step. Culturally responsive counseling leaders can advocate for the BLM movement by actively acknowledging and resisting the ways Black counselor educators have been marginalized in the profession. By examining issues ranging from grossly underrepresented Black counseling faculty to poor recruitment of Black students in counseling programs, counseling leaders can assess their role in resisting and disrupting these problems.

Chronosystem

The chronosystem represents the environmental and sociohistorical influences that prompt changes over time. In the counseling profession, leaders can acknowledge this and recognize that things will change over time, and we hope they will change for the better. In our current sociopolitical climate, some government leaders are endorsing and actively taking action against long-standing issues of racism and discrimination by endorsing the removal of some historic statues from communities and military bases or by supporting reparations for Black citizens.

BLM advocacy step. Culturally responsive counseling leaders can openly acknowledge the BLM movement and model the reflexive behavior associated with cultural responsiveness in the context of their leadership role, which directly supports and aligns with the BLM movement. This action requires an ongoing assessment and consideration of what and how they can learn in this moment and requires the transition from reflection to action by finding ways to acknowledge and support the changing tide in their respective communities and overall counseling profession.

Evaluation of the effectiveness of this advocacy step. Evaluating culturally responsive counseling leaders' effectiveness in implementing this advocacy step requires leaders to publicly acknowledge the environmental and sociopolitical influences responsible for shifting the paradigm. It also requires leaders to align themselves with others in support of BLM and the ACA divisions supporting those shifts. This evaluation requires a personal and professional assessment of how and why counseling leaders take such action.

• • •

As you further explore and understand your role as a current/future culturally responsive counseling leader, we encourage you to explore the *Journal of Counseling & Development* July 2020 special issue titled "Integrating the Multicultural and Social Justice Competencies Into Practice, Research, and Advocacy," wherein multiple authors examine the "transformative opportunities that the MSJCC have to influence counseling"(Singh & Nassar, 2020, p. 235). Singh et al.'s (2020) call to use the MSJCC to decolonize counseling practice has an important bearing on how professional counseling leaders (e.g., national, regional, elected, appointed) can make clear connections with the BLM movement and the MSJCC. The authors suggest four key multicultural and social justice theories as a mechanism to disrupt White supremacist hegemony and implement their use of MSJCC in practice: relational-cultural theory (Miller, 1976), critical race theory (Bell, 1995), intersectionality theory (Crenshaw, 1989), and liberation psychology (Martín-Baró, 1994). Finally, Na and Fietzer (2020), in the same issue, report on the relationship of a sample of more than 150 counselors' social justice engagement and demographic, personality, and contextual factors. They suggest that counselor training and, by proxy, counseling leaders' choices about social justice should be focused on quality over quantity and that awareness of individual personality and identity characteristics should be considered in supporting such engagement.

Culturally Responsive Counseling Leadership in Action

As you reflect on the content of this chapter, we hope you have had the opportunity to consider some of the practical steps you can take to integrate culturally responsive leadership in your practice. We can attest that culturally responsive leaders address issues of oppression, discrimination, and microaggressions in the classroom, while working with clients, and within their supervisory relationships. Culturally responsive counseling leaders are keenly aware of the systems of power and hierarchy that exist within their relationships and act in ways to mitigate those power differentials (Peters et al., 2020). We further recognize that culturally responsive leaders understand the role of culture when diagnosing and treating clients in the community. They utilize the cultural formulation interview (American Psychiatric Association, 2013) when working with clients who have differing identities and concurrently embrace the intersectionality of each unique client.

Cultural responsiveness is also being embraced on behalf of counseling students in hundreds of Chi Sigma Iota (CSI) chapters. As Storlie et al. (2016) confirm, counselor community engagement "may provide a means to respond to and advocate for the needs of marginalized groups in ways that traditional counseling practices have not" (p. 53). In their examination of counselor community engagement activities, the highest reported levels of outreach began with local programs and the most common areas addressed were issues of poverty and mental health. To become culturally responsive leaders, we must move beyond action or intervention itself and evaluate the effectiveness of our actions as seen by the recipients of our services.

Culturally responsive counseling leaders evaluate the outcomes of their actions to ensure that interventions are effective when working with students, clients, supervisees, and the greater community. Counseling leaders can draw feedback from multiple sources to inform their continued use of advocacy action steps and to provide context in their own self-evaluations. This reflexivity supports formal and informal evaluation as an indicator to move forward and does not necessarily need to be solely quantitative in nature. Guth et al. (2019) identified the importance of evaluation through qualitative and quantitative means as catalysts for action to undo hate and oppression. Although they contextualized evaluation specific to group work, they posited that evaluation demonstrates the effectiveness and success of specific interventions and informs reflections for future action, community organizing, and mobilization. Evaluation can institute reflection on the meaning and process of individual and collective change for justice.

Additional Considerations for Culturally Responsive Leadership Practices in Counseling

As we look to the future in strengthening our profession in leadership and advocacy, contemplate the following considerations as you move forward in your culturally responsive leadership journey:

- *Systems surround us in all aspects of our lives. Remember, it's not just the system, it's multiple systems, and you, as a culturally being, are a part of those systems.*

  As a culturally responsive counseling leader, you are responsible for taking deliberate action with and on behalf of those who do not have a seat at the table. How can you get involved in state, regional, national, and international professional associations to continue to combat systemic injustices that permeate our society? Where does your voice need to be heard?
- *How can we best create a pipeline for diversely represented counseling leadership?*

  As a profession, we know that many of our ACA counseling divisions have focused on improving diversity among their leadership (e.g., Association for Counselor Education and Supervision, AMCD, CSJ, and the Society for Sexual, Affectional, Intersex and Gender Expansive Identities). We further recognize the push for diversity and inclusion in other counseling organizations such as CACREP and CSI. We need to continue to strive for and increase the diversity in our counseling leadership at every level and consider how executive boards engage and address diversity concerns in their practice. It is essential to increase the representation of voices that are often not acknowledged while simultaneously avoiding tokenism.
- *How can we improve our selection of speakers, resources, and content within our schools, agencies, and work environments to include diverse individuals and to have the crucial conversations necessary for growth and development?*

  It is not enough to have one (or maybe two) multicultural classes in your counseling program curriculum. As professionals in training and in the field, we need to think strategically about how to improve our selection of guest speakers who can offer perspectives and worldviews that differ from our own. In addition, we need to be purposeful and intentional with the resources and content we explore with our students, supervisees, and colleagues and be prepared to have challenging conversations that move beyond cultural competence to action and evaluation.

• • •

We hope this chapter spoke to you. Part II of this book highlights some exceptional culturally responsive counseling leaders and advocates whose work is illuminated in these narratives. You will see the recognition of their privilege and how they used their privilege to support marginalized and oppressed people. Each of these profiles provides insights into how to become a culturally responsive counseling leader. As you read the next chapter and move toward Part II, remember this:

You are a light. You are the light.
Never let anyone—any person or any force—dampen, dim or diminish your light.
Study the path of others to make your way easier and more abundant.

—Rep. John Lewis

Chapter 3

Leadership and Advocacy in the Field

Michael D. Brubaker and Andrew W. Wood

*I do not see myself as a leader, though I have served in many leadership positions.
I see myself as an advocate, and leadership positions are
the avenue through which advocacy is implemented.*

—Jane Myers, former president ACA, AACE, CSI
(Nichols & Carney, 2013, p. 244)

*When there was a need for someone to work with persons with AIDS, I did that.
When there was a need to work with the homeless, I did that.
When there was a need to break down some of the prejudices here in Charlotte,
I did that.*

—Mary Thomas Burke, former president of CSI and chair of
the Counselor Education Program at UNC–Charlotte
(Nassar-McMillan, 2001, p. 498)

*In these challenging times, it is important to extend thinking
and action beyond national boundaries.
To be a professional counselor means being a true citizen of the world.*

—Courtland C. Lee, former president of ACA, AMCD, IAC, CSI
(Gladding, 2011, p. 498)

• • •

Counselor leadership and advocacy are inseparable practices (Sweeney, 2012), which is shown most fully in the lives of those in the field who have changed the counseling profession and, ultimately, the communities we serve. When you read the quotations from noted leaders in the profession, you can see that they were not driven by a personal pursuit of power or notoriety. Instead, these leaders understood the current needs in our communities and the world. They responded as advocates to better the lives of others, often mobilizing the resources within the counseling profession.

We begin this chapter with a look at the history of client advocacy and professional advocacy in counseling, noting their inseparable nature. We then describe strategies used in counselor leadership and advocacy that are consistent with servant leadership (Greenleaf, 1970), a philosophy that aligns well with the counseling profession and its leaders (Lewis, 2012). Each of us has the opportunity to advocate for change using these strategies and following the example of our predecessors. In the final section of this chapter, we provide examples of how you may lead and advocate across practice settings.

History of Leadership and Advocacy in the Field

When identifying current opportunities and strategies to lead and advocate, counselors can learn from the successes and struggles throughout the counseling profession's history. The efforts of early counseling professionals have shaped our present, providing momentum for new leaders to push our field forward and expand our reach into the community. Much has changed in the counseling profession in the past 100 years: Counselor licensure now exists in all 50 states, the focus on multicultural and social justice counseling continues to increase, and outreach has been made to countless clients previously unable to access counseling services. In this section, we focus on the efforts of a few key leaders, along with the tireless efforts of others, who created our current landscape. We invite you to consider not only how far the counseling field has come but also how far it still has to go to become your ideal profession. Even more, we hope you will reflect on how you can lead our field forward into the future.

Counseling Pioneers: Meeting Clients Where They Are

Advocacy and leadership in counseling are firmly rooted in our history (Kiselica & Robinson, 2001), established both by leaders from within the profession and by those from other professions who have inspired our humanistic, multicultural, social justice focus. To be sure, counselors have not always acted with social justice at the forefront of their efforts, and mental health professionals have, at times, perpetuated oppressive and harmful systems (Fox et al., 2009). As counselors, we must be careful not to idealize our profession or the leaders within it. Nonetheless, it is important to highlight those who have stepped forward with novel ideas and actions to meet the needs of the community and to advocate for social change.

The first of these leaders, Frank Parsons, is known as the founder of both the social justice movement in counseling and the counseling profession itself (Capuzzi & Gross, 2017; Zytowski, 2001). Parsons was a vocational guidance worker in Boston during the early 1900s who organized career preparation and support for immigrant youth while providing services free of charge. He, along with others working at the Vocation Bureau, helped disenfranchised youth find jobs that spoke to their interests and prepared them for work. Parsons aimed to meet the needs of these workers and the community, including local labor leaders, government officials, leaders in the arts, college presidents, and religious leaders (Zytowski, 2001).

Around this same time, Clifford Beers (1908) published his famous book, *A Mind That Found Itself: An Autobiography*. In this book, Beers describes his experience of being detained in a psychiatric institution. Beers was not a clinician; he was a patient who suffered from chronic depression, and he observed the indignities suffered by those with mental health disorders who lived in psychiatric institutions (e.g., state psychiatric hospitals). These indignities included isolation and seclusion in straightjackets, little care from staff, forced oral and nasal medication, and many other treatments not known to the general public at the time. Subsequently, Beers started the mental hygiene movement, which advocated for reform of psychiatric institutions and urged that they become more humane in their care. Through this process, Beers addressed the stigma of mental health that existed in the public domain (Capuzzi & Gross, 2017; Parry, 2010). He, along with psychiatrists, physicians, and philanthropists inspired by his words, developed associations nationally and internationally to improve care for those with mental health disorders. One such association, the National Committee for Mental Hygiene, was at the forefront of lobbying efforts to petition the U.S. Congress for new laws to improve the conditions in psychiatric facilities (Neukrug, 2016). This association continues today under the name Mental Health America (n.d.). Through Beers's own experiences in mental health care, he became an advocate, leading and inspiring others to improve conditions in psychiatric institutions and, in a larger way, inspiring a humanistic perspective that was emerging within the counseling profession.

Carl Rogers wrote *Counseling and Psychotherapy* in 1942, inspiring counseling professionals to adopt a humanistic perspective and extend their practice beyond vocational guidance (Neukrug, 2016). His approach challenged earlier psychoanalytic and behavioral approaches by recognizing the power of empathy and human potential for health and healing. In addition to proposing a paradigm shift toward an egalitarian relationship with clients, Rogers was an advocate for social justice and argued against the social injustices of his time, such as McCarthyism and political oppression in Northern Ireland and Brazil (Barfield, 2019; Demanchick & Kirschenbaum, 2008). It should be noted that Rogers has been criticized for his involvement with the Central Intelligence Agency (Demanchick & Kirschenbaum, 2008), which funded research on personality that is now considered ethically questionable.

Overlapping interests have long existed between counseling and psychology, with leaders affiliating across professional associations and publishing in both American Counseling Association (ACA) and American Psychological Association (APA) journals. This was especially true throughout the emergence of the multicultural and social justice movements, which some consider the fourth and fifth theoretical forces of the profession (Pack-Brown et al., 2008). Counseling psychologists Derald Wing Sue and Patricia Arrendondo (a past president of ACA) took leading roles in calling psychologists and counselors to task for their training and practices, which were "monocultural" and often ineffective with racial and ethnic minorities (Sue et al., 1992). These and other leaders established the first multicultural counseling competencies adopted by the counseling profession (Arrendondo et al., 1996), which would evolve into the Multicultural and Social Justice Counseling Competencies (Ratts et al., 2015) that recognize the multifaceted and intersecting privileged and oppressed identities.

The social justice counseling movement was largely influenced by leaders in social psychology and education. One such individual, Ignacio Martín-Baró, was a social psychologist who practiced in El Salvador in the 1970s and 1980s. Martín-Baró, a Jesuit priest, advocated for individuals mistreated and subjected to oppression and violence at the hands of their own governments during political upheavals in Latin America (Lykes & Sibley, 2014). One key aspect to Martín-Baró's work was an approach that was not directed *to* the poor but was designed to be *of* the poor, a theme reflective of Beers's efforts on mental health reforms. This included understanding what the needs of those with mental health issues are, rather than what psychologists and counselors assume those needs should be. Martín-Baró's philosophy and practices aligned with Paulo Freire's (1970/2006) view of critical pedagogy, which is commonly reflected in the social justice literature. This focus calls on providers to understand the historical context of the people with whom they are working as well as their ecological context (Cook, 2015), understanding how oppressive forces influence individuals and communities.

Each of these leaders advocated for clients in the field and through reforms within the profession. Client advocacy includes work done to provide better treatment and conditions for potential clients as a whole, whether focusing on the community level or nationally or internationally. Counselors, as effective agents of change, remove barriers for clients as well as for the profession, particularly when the barriers inhibit serving those in need.

Professional Counselor Advocacy: Bringing Licensed Professional Counselors to the Masses

As counseling began to expand its reach to include more mental health services, many individuals sought and obtained licensure through psychology boards (Goodyear, 2000; Lawson, 2016). Over time, these boards became less amenable toward professional counselors, making it difficult for them to obtain licenses and attempting to shut down their community practices (Lawson, 2016). Although counselors were well trained and fully qualified, they were being told they could no longer serve their communities, which jeopardized client care nationwide.

Just as counselors must be careful not to idealize our leaders, we must also be careful not to villainize other professionals. Although state psychology boards were discrediting professional counselors, many individual psychologists did not agree with these actions and positions (Goodyear, 2000). For example, Joe Wittmer, the first executive director of the Council for Accreditation of Counseling and Related Educational Programs (CACREP), was one such counseling psychologist who gave up his license when he realized that his annual fees were used, in part, to stop counselors from being licensed (personal communication, February 10, 2007). Many others were also instrumental in the foundation and shaping of the counseling profession during these challenging years.

Sweeney (2012) detailed his experiences as the first chair of the ACA Committee on Licensure when state psychology boards ordered counselors to cease and desist their practices. One salient case was that of Culbreath Cook (*City of Cleveland, Ohio v. Cook, 1975*), an African American counselor who was arrested on a felony charge for practicing psychology without a license under a law that had been enacted only shortly before his arrest (Sweeney, 2012). The charges were dismissed after a rigorous defense, supported in part by the American Personnel and Guidance Association's (now ACA) Committee on Licensure. Attempts to limit the practice of competent counselors affected not only these well-established professionals but also their many clients.

As the *Cook* case illustrates, professional and client advocacy intertwine; advocating for the right to competently serve the public is a social justice issue that affects our communities. Sweeney (2012) defined professional advocacy as the "knowledge, skills, and competencies that advance the profession through deliberate, thoughtful actions that inform and influence others to support professional counselors because of the benefits their services bring to individuals, groups, and institutions" (pp. 81–82). Advocates aid our broader community by expanding the behavioral health workforce, expanding licensure opportunities for counselors, and increasing clients' ability to be reimbursed for our services.

Behavioral health providers are in high demand and low supply. As of December 31, 2019, there were 6,117 federally designated Health Professional Shortage Areas in Mental Health, affecting more than 116 million people living in the United States (U.S. Department of Health and Human Services [USDHHS], 2020). The nation lacks adequate numbers of school counselors to meet the academic and socioemotional needs of students in Pre-K through 12th grade settings. Despite a recommended ratio of 250 students to 1 counselor, the current ratio is 464 to 1 (Education Trust, 2019), with approximately 8 million students lacking access to a school counselor at all. The Education Trust noted that this shortfall is affecting ethnic minority students to a greater extent than others because school counselors who predominantly serve these groups have disproportionally higher caseloads of students. The influence of school counselors on a student's decision to seek postsecondary education is greater among Black youth (Cholewa et al., 2015), and this shortfall may have consequences for them that extend well into adulthood.

Throughout the past 50 years, professional counselors have advocated by informing legislators and the general public of the capabilities of counselors and by creating organizational structures and standards to guide competent training and practices. School counseling led the pathway to professionalization in the 1920s, when New York became the first state to adopt certification requirements (Wright, 2012). Professional advocacy efforts grew through collaboration of the Association for Counselor Education and Supervision (ACES) with the American School Counselor Association (ASCA) as they developed training standards for school counseling programs. By the 1960s, certification was required in all 50 states (Foxx et al., 2017).

For professional counselors specializing in clinical mental health care, nationwide licensure would take much longer. As the counseling profession continued to evolve, training standards became more important and would support advocacy efforts for state licensure. Stripling (1978), and later Lawson (2016), noted how licensure and certification depend on accreditation standards that establish the measures and evaluations of counselor preparation. Accrediting bodies carefully review the quality and consistency of training, whereas licensing boards often have limited resources and purview and commonly review academic preparation only through applicant transcripts.

Although the American Personnel and Guidance Association was founded in 1952 (ACA, n.d.), it was not until 1981 that the first accrediting body, CACREP, was created to uphold training standards in counselor education (CACREP, n.d.). After years of lobbying and grassroots advocacy, in 2009, California was the last state to establish professional counselor licensure (Lawson, 2016). At that time, professional recognition was finally complete, or so it seemed.

Despite the success of licensure, professional counselors still could not participate in federally supported programs, such as those operating in the Department of Defense, due to a lack of alignment between state licensure laws and national accreditation standards (Lawson et al., 2017). To circumvent this limitation, programs such as TRICARE, the Army Substance Abuse Program, and the U.S. Department of Veterans Affairs (VA) have adopted standards that require any licensed professional counselor working independently to have graduated from a CACREP-accredited program (TRICARE, 2014; Lawson et al. 2017). Clinical mental health counselors can now become TRICARE Certified Mental Health Counselors, allowing them to serve active military personnel and their families (Hyatt-Burkart & Lopez Levers, 2020). ACA continues to maintain advocacy efforts for employment within the VA, providing information about how to enter these settings because individual and systemic barriers may impede access (e.g., Pollack, 2019). Even with licensure in all 50 states, not all counselors have permission to serve those in need.

Private health care expansion through the Patient Protection and Affordable Care Act of 2010 has also increased opportunities for counselors to serve the public. This law was designed to expand access and quality care through improved coverage, integrated services, and reduced costs with provisions that prohibited health plans from discriminating against behavioral health care professionals by their type of licensure (Sweeney, 2012). Medicaid and Medicare expansion are the current focus of professional counselor advocates, and pending legislation is moving through both the House and Senate. These examples illuminate how professional and client advocacy remain a major concern for the counseling profession and its emerging leaders.

Counselor Leadership and Advocacy Today

Building on our profession's history of effective advocacy for clients and the right of professional counselors to serve students and clients in the community, counseling advocates continue to press for important changes across all levels (individual, community, systemwide) and settings. Many of these efforts occur daily on behalf of an individual student or client as counselors work with individuals to navigate the barriers that impede their growth and wellness. Other efforts may require more extensive leadership skills that address systemic concerns, which is evidenced through the lives of courageous and determined counselors who put service before individual rewards and conveniences.

Our hope is that you, like the leaders profiled in this book, will identify the needs of today and step forward with a servant leadership approach (Greenleaf, 1970; Lewis, 2012) that makes a difference in our profession and in the world. As an initial guide for your journey, we offer some practical strategies rooted in Trusty and Brown's (2005) advocacy model, and we identify ongoing challenges in schools and institutions of higher education, clinical mental health settings, and in counselor education.

Practical Strategies for Invoking Change

Having discussed the "why" of leadership and advocacy, we now turn to an understanding of the "how." That is, how do counselors engage in client and professional advocacy? And how does this differ across the various settings in which they serve? It can be daunting to consider the steps necessary to invoke change, particularly in school, community, and legislative arenas. This is often where leadership and advocacy intersect, where organization meets inspiration, and where many individuals feel ill-equipped to meet the challenge. We offer a model of counselor advocacy commonly used across specialty areas and settings, and we share some examples.

One of the earliest models of advocacy was proposed by Karen Eriksen (1997), who developed a seven-stage model to advocate for professional counselors through legislation, rulemaking, and the courts. Trusty and Brown (2005) adapted Eriksen's model for school counselors, applying it to student and professional advocacy required in K–12 settings. Subsequently, Lawson et al. (2017) identified how Trusty and Brown's model was the basis for counseling advocacy to change licensure laws in Ohio, North Carolina, and Virginia. Trusty and Brown's model is foundational as an advocacy model for school and mental health counseling leaders, useful for professional and student/client advocacy, and commonly cited in the counseling literature (Chang, 2012; Sweeney, 2012). We describe each stage of the model, keeping in mind counseling specialty areas (e.g., school, clinical mental health, clinical rehabilitation) and types of advocacy (i.e., professional and student/client).

1. *Develop advocacy dispositions.* To begin, counselors understand how they are motivated to advocate for their students/clients and the profession, attending to their professional identity while determining their roles with other professionals and with those whom they serve.
2. *Develop advocacy relationships and advocacy knowledge.* In this stage, counselors not only build their networks but also pursue understanding about the people and systems they are seeking to affect.
3. *Define the advocacy problem.* In the third step, counselors gather data through needs assessments and other sources, defining both the problem and its roots. This occurs after connecting with others, which suggests that decision-making is not accomplished by one person alone.
4. *Develop action plans.* Trusty and Brown (2005) suggest that these plans be clear, but flexible, unless "an important moral principle is at stake" (p. 264). Eriksen's (1997) model for legislative advocacy assumed that training others was an essential part of planning, but some forms of advocacy may not require such actions.
5. *Implement action plans.* Once leaders have implemented the plan, they need to collaborate with other stakeholders to monitor progress, address setbacks, and determine together when advocacy goals have been achieved.
6. *Make an evaluation.* To assess the impact, evaluation is critical. Evaluation criteria and planning must be considered earlier during the advocacy problem definition process (Stage 3) as well.
7. *Celebrate or regroup.* When successful, leaders call for celebration; when not, they call stakeholders to regroup and support one another, considering alternatives for new advocacy efforts.

Although other models are worthy of consideration, this model includes the essential elements of both one's professional disposition toward advocacy and the organizational, data-driven steps to help leaders prepare for action across multiple settings. As we continue to explore advocacy opportunities in the sections that follow, consider how you might use this model to affect larger organizational and systemwide changes, but also consider the individual, everyday advocacy you might use to serve others.

Leadership and Advocacy in the Schools and General Higher Education

As schools have increased their accountability for student academic performance, greater pressure has been placed on teachers and administrators to ensure that state testing scores and graduation rates are at optimum levels (Hines et al., 2020; Wright, 2012). Given this context, comprehensive school counseling programs are more important than ever, particularly as school counselors seek to close the achievement gap and when schools fall below performance standards. Turnaround schools, or those with consistently low academic performance (20% or more falling below state minimums), often require overhauls in leadership, staffing, practices, and school culture (Hines et al., 2020). School counselors with expertise in data analysis as well as programming in the social/personal, academic, and career needs of students play an essential transformative role in these schools, aiding students in removing systemic barriers that impede their success (Hines et al., 2020). School counselors, collaborating with teachers, administrators, students, parents, and other stakeholders, garner additional resources to support students as they identify policies and practices that can be changed to improve student outcomes.

When students were learning in school buildings (before the coronavirus pandemic), teachers and administrators may have noticed increased behavioral concerns that appeared to be "disruptive" and counterproductive to the academic aims of the school. What they may not have realized is that students could be presenting symptoms of adverse childhood experiences (ACEs), most notably, trauma. School counselors can use attendance, passing rates, and behavior data to better understand potential symptoms of trauma (Howell et al., 2019). Furthermore, they may lead training and policy changes to implement trauma-informed approaches that support student and teacher self-care and wellness practices that coincide with other healthy behaviors (Howell et al., 2019; Martin et al., 2017).

School counselors faced new challenges as a result of the coronavirus pandemic. Distance learning became a primary teaching modality when 50.8 million public school students were affected by K–12 school closures during the pandemic (Maxwell, 2020). As a result, school counselors needed to connect with students in a virtual environment—that is, if students had access to the internet and had a tablet or computer with which to communicate. School counselor roles also changed during the pandemic, and many found themselves being a primary support not only for students but also for parents and school personnel (Meyers, 2020b).

For school counselors to be effective in leadership and advocacy efforts, they often must advocate for themselves, clarifying their roles and skills. Administrators may lack awareness of the capabilities of school counselors and their full potential to implement effective programming that can affect academic outcomes

(Fye et al., 2018; Hines et al., 2020). This may be especially true in turnaround schools, where immediate crisis demands present an urgency that may pull school counselors out of the role they were trained to fulfill. Professional advocacy is paramount, and having a strong relationship with the school principal can be key (Beck & Lane, 2019). In fact, forging such a relationship was a top concern in the advocacy work of 2019 finalists for the ASCA School Counselor of the Year Award (Beck & Lane, 2019).

School counselors may review the ASCA Legislative Issues web page (https://www.schoolcounselor.org/About-School-Counseling/Legislative-Issues) for more information about advocacy issues that are of great concern to the profession. Two current issues are the need to reduce staffing ratios for school counselors and related personnel and promoting school safety. The Elementary and Secondary School Counseling Act, proposed in 2019 and pending approval as of this writing, provides grant funding of no less than $1 million per state to fund additional school counselors, particularly in high need areas. School safety has become a concern both in terms of gun violence and in the recent coronavirus pandemic. Many perspectives exist on how to address gun violence, but ASCA strongly opposes the diversion of funding allocated for academic achievement and student learning toward efforts to arm educators (ASCA, 2018). In 2020, the coronavirus pandemic raised new concerns about safety and health for students and teachers alike. Students are faced with new challenges to their academic performance due to remote learning and social isolation from their peers. All of these are concerns at the school and district levels, and public officials and administrators are making budget decisions to cut or fund specific personnel as well as setting policies related to school safety.

College counselors serving transitional-aged youth (18–25) may have similar concerns as universities and community colleges try to keep up with demand for mental health services. The Center for Collegiate Mental Health (2016) found that the 29.6% increase in students seeking counseling services nationwide far exceeded the 5.6% increase in student enrollment. They also noted that the demand appeared to result from higher levels of distress reported by these students, particularly anxiety and depression. Counselor advocacy can address these staffing shortfalls while also addressing the sources of student distress. Advocacy may be somewhat different based on the population and university structures, but the larger planning process could still apply (Trusty & Brown, 2005).

Clinical Mental Health Counseling Leadership and Advocacy

The role of the mental health counselor as an advocate for clients and the profession is long-standing but is increasing in importance in the current political landscape. As mentioned previously, the counseling profession has been making inroads working with the VA and has achieved reimbursement for services with TRICARE. Other areas of leadership and advocacy in which counselors can engage are working toward reimbursement for Medicare, licensure portability, and other social issues (e.g., eliminating conversion therapy and police violence). This work can be done in accordance with the previously listed advocacy models, including the ACA Advocacy Competencies (Toporek & Daniels, 2018).

Medicare is the public health plan for individuals over the age of 65 and for younger individuals with long-term disabilities. By the year 2030, this will include more than 80 million individuals as the "silver tsunami" of baby boomers (i.e., those born between 1946 and 1964) grows older and relies on Medicare for physical and mental health care coverage (Bartels & Naslund, 2013). Today licensed professional counselors are not reimbursed for their work by Medicare, and they will not be able to serve Medicare clients if the current situation remains. Today there is a shortage of behavioral health professionals (USDHHS, 2020), and this raises serious concerns for seniors and the counselors trying to serve them (Fullen et al., 2019). As mental health counselors, we have a duty to use client advocacy and counselor advocacy to push for reimbursement for Medicare services.

Counselors are in a difficult place with direct client advocacy when it comes to Medicare, whether they offer pro bono or sliding scale services or refer clients to other providers (Fullen et al., 2019). This issue has been targeted by the government affairs group in ACA as a national priority, which is focusing on legislative advocacy to help potential clients and our profession. Counselors are encouraged to write to their congressional representatives (in the U.S. House and Senate), focusing their legislative advocacy on three themes that address Medicare reimbursement: mental health parity, long-term program savings, and the wellness paradigm (Fullen, 2016). Collaborating with those reliant on Medicare and the agencies advocating with seniors and those with disabilities may broaden these efforts and better inform legislators of the unmet mental health and wellness needs of these individuals.

Cooperative advocacy may lead to in-person visits en masse, which can create a formidable presence and require the attention of elected officials. However, social distancing guidelines brought on by the coronavirus pandemic have made in-person advocacy more difficult, if not impossible. In response, counselors can utilize the increasingly common venues of social media, video conferencing (e.g., Zoom), and the tried-and-true methods of letter writing and call-in campaigns (e.g., phone zaps) to express their voice to those with legislative power (It's Going Down, 2018). Sustained efforts are necessary, including efforts on behalf of those approaching retirement who could lose their current providers as they switch to Medicare, as well as those living in professional health shortage areas (see Fullen et al., 2019, for additional counselors' experiences). While counselors wait for legislative changes, they can network with other providers offering sliding-scale and pro bono services through organizations such as the Open Path Psychotherapy Collective (https://openpathcollective.org/), although these alternatives are clearly limited and are not likely to address the large-scale needs of these populations.

Licensure portability is another important topic for clinical mental health counselors, and it affects every licensed and license-eligible clinician. Although counselor licensure now exists in every state in the nation, education and examination requirements as well as professional titles vary, preventing counselors from moving between states to practice (Bayne & Doyle, 2019). Unifying licensure under the CACREP Standards or the equivalent has been a major focus among many counseling leaders and professional advocates (Kaplan & Kraus, 2018), and a few states (Arkansas, Kentucky, North Carolina, Ohio, Utah, and Virginia) have adopted these standards (Lawson et al., 2017). For counselors moving to other states, differences in requirements may result in counselors having to take new examinations, complete new coursework, and engage in other lengthy tasks to pursue licensure, delaying their ability to produce income and putting their financial status in jeopardy.

Furthermore, telebehavioral health is becoming an integral part of our work, yet counselors can work only with those whose primary residence is in the same state as that of the counselor, limiting the reach that counselors can have in global crises.

As counselors consider advocating and providing servant leadership on these issues, we suggest developing advocacy knowledge and relationships through the extensive writing of Kaplan and others (Kaplan & Gladding, 2011; Kaplan & Kraus, 2018) and through professional organizations involved in the collaborative project titled "20/20: A Vision for the Future of Counseling" (Kaplan et al., 2014). ACA currently has many web pages dedicated to this topic that are useful for students, practitioners, and educators. In addition, Bohecker and Eissenstat (2020) suggest investigating the licensure language model as a way forward for license portability for professional counselors. Thinking ecologically, this process involves local and regional counseling communities and states and a national push for licensure, advocacy that any counselor may join.

Client advocacy concerns for clinical mental health counselors are discussed elsewhere in this text and are in continual development at the grassroots level. Some of these concerns include eliminating conversion therapy for the safety of LGBTQ+ clients and especially youth (Fore, 2014; Streed et al., 2019), eliminating police violence for the safety of Black, Indigenous, and people of color (Bryant-Davis et al., 2017; Hargons et al., 2017; Washington & Henfield, 2019), fighting climate change (Hilert, 2020), and fighting immigration enforcement and use of documentation to harm individuals who are undocumented (ACA, 2020a; Hacker et al., 2012), among others. We strongly suggest that counselors look toward their own communities to better understand the local needs for advocacy work. Working at the local level will have the most immediate impact on their clients and future clients, and this work has the potential to expand into advocacy for larger systemic concerns.

Counselor Educator and Supervisor Leadership and Advocacy

Chan et al. (2019) emphasize the role of counselor educators as they advocate for and with their students, conceptualizing this work ecologically. Faculty attend to student needs in the classroom, in their programs and departments, in field service activities, and across their universities. Furthermore, counselor educators influence the counseling profession through their scholarship and leadership roles, including serving in professional associations and on state boards. These leaders bring expert testimony to state and national legislatures and advocate for clients and the profession. One of the unique aspects of their work is that counselor educators and supervisors advocate for consumers of counseling services as well as for their students/supervisees. Servant leadership is particularly important in inspiring these up and coming leaders of the profession to be the next generation of advocates. Many counselor educators are also providing supervision, and some supervisors are working in the field directly for schools and agencies. We will focus on how counselor educators may lead and advocate, and then examine how field supervisors may do so in their respective positions.

In counselor education programs, educators can support students who face cultural, economic, and other social barriers that may impede their success (Chan et al., 2019). This may be in their role as teacher, advisor, or supervisor. International students who experience acculturative stress and social hardships may find it particularly difficult to continue their studies, manage stress, and navigate the bureaucratic requirements of being in another country while trying to handle the already difficult challenges of being a graduate student (Behl et al., 2017). Counselor educators, serving as academic advisors, play an important role in advocating with university international affairs offices, who serve as liaisons with the U.S. government, and with international consulates and other organizations that often require letters of support and status updates. Domestic students experiencing financial hardships, social oppression, and personal setbacks also may benefit from having faculty allies. It is important for programs to hire diverse faculty to broaden the perspectives of counseling programs and build bridges of cultural understanding (Baggerly et al., 2017). Once hired, those from historically marginalized groups may benefit from peer advocacy, particularly as they face institutional barriers and are unjustly challenged by students, colleagues, and administrators (Cartwright et al., 2018).

Moving outside of the ecosystem, counselor educators can also advocate at the macro level, engaging in legislative action (Chan et al., 2019). Farrell and Barrio Minton (2019) found that counseling leaders can engage in legislative professional advocacy (LPA) through a process of being catalyzed by internal personal and professional motivators, resourced by local communities and professional networks, and enacted through prioritizing various forms of engagement with legislators. Indirect engagement, or practical advocacy, may come in the form of writing letters, calling a legislator, signing petitions, or building LPA into a course syllabus.

Direct advocacy occurs when counselor educators meet with legislators in person. Some state counseling associations host legislative advocacy days, or "Days on the Hill" (Farrell & Barrio Minton, 2019, p. 153), and counselor educators may include such activities in their courses as one form of service learning. Organizers of legislative advocacy days may lead participants through at least four steps of Trusty and Brown's (2005) model: developing relationships and knowledge about key issues, defining the professional advocacy problem(s), preparing talking points and handwritten notes to address congressional representatives, and meeting with elected leaders. Chapters of Chi Sigma Iota, Counselors for Social Justice, and other groups may provide advocacy leadership by organizing transportation to these events or even coordinating them with their own legislative initiatives. Similarly, counselor educators may invite legislators to their classrooms to host constructive dialogue around local counseling concerns and legislative needs to support the mental health and overall wellness of their constituents.

Like counselor educators, supervisors in the field can support the leadership and advocacy development of student interns as well as early career professionals. Storlie, Baltrinic, et al. (2019) interviewed seven current or former site supervisors and discovered that they fostered leadership and advocacy through a process of modeling a strong professional counselor identity, appropriate clinical practices, and health self-care. These supervisors also served as leaders and advocates by involving their supervisees in learning experiences, advocating for them to have time and resources, and empowering them to think on their own and be self-advocates. In summary, supervisors and counselor educators alike have important roles to play in guiding the next generation of professional counselors to be effective advocates for the profession, for their clients, and for themselves.

How Can Students and Counselors Become Servant Leaders?

Greenleaf (1970), in his early essay on servant leadership, claimed the powerful truth that it takes courage to change the paradigms of leadership. There is a tendency for individuals to perpetuate the status quo to maintain their positions of power, often at the expense of others. Referring to the early works of Albert Camus, Greenleaf called on us to "create dangerously," to be willing to get out of our comfort zones and fulfill our potential to solve the problems counselors encounter in new and powerful ways. Furthermore, he evoked courage not only for natural servants to become leaders but also for followers to identify servant leaders and join their efforts. This may be the first step for any of us on our journey to become advocacy leaders.

Samuel Templeman Gladding (2017), counseling author, leader, and advocate, described early career decisions that were most influential to his development. The most fundamental step was simply to identify himself as a counselor, which then inspired him to get involved in professional associations. Remley and Herlihy (2020) affirm that "having a sense of pride in one's chosen profession" is an essential step toward becoming a professional (p. 55). As you begin your journey, counseling associations may be a place not only to learn from servant leaders but also a place where students and new professionals shape those divisions and priorities (Brubaker, 2020). It is also where critical networking may occur to share common concerns (Remley & Herlihy, 2020) and to organize advocacy efforts (Brubaker, 2020).

All great leaders in the counseling profession had the same beginnings; that is, they were once master's students considering how they could help others. But they also learned the importance of connecting with others in the profession to gain knowledge, secure resources, and mobilize advocacy efforts. As you reflect on the needs and opportunities that lie before you, we encourage you to create dangerously as you listen to your communities, collaborate with other professionals, and leverage your training as a counselor, leader, and advocate to make a difference.

PART I: 2016 CACREP Standards Alignment

Chapter 1: Introduction

SECTION 2: PROFESSIONAL COUNSELING IDENTITY: COUNSELING CURRICULUM
1. PROFESSIONAL COUNSELING ORIENTATION AND ETHICAL PRACTICE
    d. the role and process of the professional counselor advocating on behalf of the profession

SECTION 6: DOCTORAL STANDARDS: COUNSELOR EDUCATION AND SUPERVISION
B. DOCTORAL PROFESSIONAL IDENTITY
5. LEADERSHIP AND ADVOCACY
    a. theory and skills of leadership
    b. leadership and leadership development in professional organizations

Chapter 2: Culturally Responsive Counseling Leadership

SECTION 2: PROFESSIONAL COUNSELING IDENTITY: COUNSELING CURRICULUM
1. PROFESSIONAL COUNSELING ORIENTATION AND ETHICAL PRACTICE
    a. history and philosophy of the counseling profession and its specialty areas
    d. the role and process of the professional counselor advocating on behalf of the profession
    e. advocacy processes needed to address institutional and social barriers that impede access, equity, and success for clients
2. SOCIAL AND CULTURAL DIVERSITY
    c. multicultural counseling competencies
    h. strategies for identifying and eliminating barriers, prejudices, and processes of intentional and unintentional oppression and discrimination

SECTION 6: DOCTORAL STANDARDS: COUNSELOR EDUCATION AND SUPERVISION
B. DOCTORAL PROFESSIONAL IDENTITY
5. LEADERSHIP AND ADVOCACY
    h. current topical and political issues in counseling and how those issues affect the daily work of counselors and the counseling profession
    i. role of counselors and counselor educators advocating on behalf of the profession and professional identity
    j. models and competencies for advocating for clients at the individual, system, and policy levels
    k. strategies of leadership in relation to current multicultural and social justice issues
    l. ethical and culturally relevant leadership and advocacy practices

Chapter 3: Leadership and Advocacy in the Field

SECTION 2: PROFESSIONAL COUNSELING IDENTITY: COUNSELING CURRICULUM
1. PROFESSIONAL COUNSELING ORIENTATION AND ETHICAL PRACTICE
    d. the role and process of the professional counselor advocating on behalf of the profession
    e. advocacy processes needed to address institutional and social barriers that impede access, equity, and success for clients

SECTION 6: DOCTORAL STANDARDS: COUNSELOR EDUCATION AND SUPERVISION
B. DOCTORAL PROFESSIONAL IDENTITY
5. LEADERSHIP AND ADVOCACY
    b. leadership and leadership development in professional organizations
    c. leadership in counselor education programs
    d. knowledge of accreditation standards and processes
    e. leadership, management, and administration in counseling organizations and other institutions
    h. current topical and political issues in counseling and how those issues affect the daily work of counselors and the counseling profession
    i. role of counselors and counselor educators advocating on behalf of the profession and professional identity
    j. models and competencies for advocating for clients at the individual, system, and policy levels
    k. strategies of leadership in relation to current multicultural and social justice issues
    l. ethical and culturally relevant leadership and advocacy practices

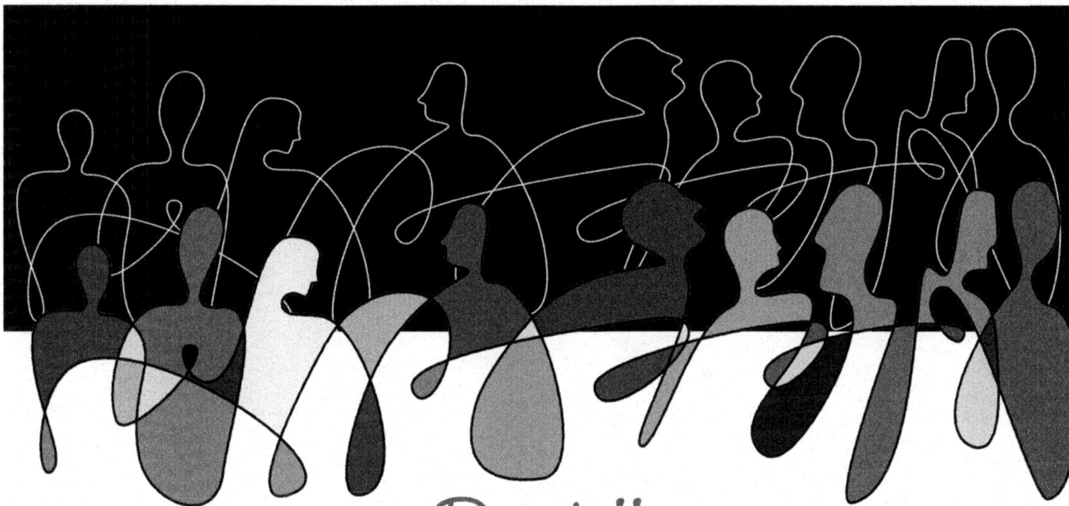

Part II

Leaders & Advocates—Their Stories

In Part II, we present 13 leader/advocate profiles selected by our Academy of Advisors (see Chapter 1 to review the selection process). The leaders/advocates emerge through their stories as distinct individuals, but we have asked the mentees to use the same structure in each chapter to help you grasp the depth and breadth of their stories. Each chapter begins with an introduction written by the mentee who interviewed the leader/advocate and wrote the story. Leaders/advocates reviewed this text before submission to the book editors. The journeys of the leaders/advocates are described beginning with their early years and tracing their career path. In most of the profiles, the leaders/advocates reveal pivotal moments in their career and discuss points of pride. This is followed by a description of their leadership and advocacy philosophies and practices, including how they developed over time. Finally, the leaders/advocates offer their views on the future of counseling and provide words of wisdom gleaned from their personal and professional experiences. Mentees present their final reflections at the end of the chapter, sharing what they learned from the process of collaborating with their mentor through their interviews and writing about their mentor's journey.

Each individual's story is unique, and you will discover that there are many diverse paths to leadership and advocacy in the counseling profession. We hope you find these profiles engaging and inspiring and that you see yourself in elements of their stories.

Chapter 4

Patricia Arredondo

Daniel C. Rosen

Mentee's Introduction

I am Daniel C. Rosen, and Patricia Arredondo has been my mentor for two decades. She provided invaluable support while I was a graduate student at Arizona State University (ASU), making sure she introduced me to a network of leaders in the field. She also included me as her coauthor on publications and as a copresenter at national conferences (where she is treated like a rock star, barely able to make her way across a convention hallway). As important as each of these CV-building experiences was for my career, they are not what has mattered most.

Patricia encouraged and supported me at a more foundational level, helping me find my own voice and passion. I recall sitting in her office on the fourth floor of Payne Hall and feeling affirmed when pursuing my own path, whether by exploring my identity and beginning a new line of research on American Jews, organizing for community healing after 9/11, applying for an internship, or deciding where to accept my first position as an academic. In each case (and many more), she listened deeply, not from her own frame or self-interest but attempting to understand what mattered to me, and she's had my back as I've pursued it.

Patricia redefined for me what it means to be a professor. When I entered my doctoral program, I had no intention of staying in academia, which I had regarded as the proverbial ivory tower disconnected from community needs and challenges. Patricia demonstrated what it looks like to use one's professional expertise in service of meaningful change. She taught me that working toward social justice is not a pursuit separate from being a counseling psychologist but is integral to it. Twenty years later, this systemic and values-directed frame inspires everything I do professionally.

Patricia Arredondo's Journey

Early Years and Career Path

Patricia's maternal grandmother (Doña María) immigrated to the United States from the village of Santa Ana in Oaxaca, Mexico, fleeing her hometown in search of greater opportunities when she was only 13 years old. She eventually settled in Lorain, Ohio, and gave birth to Patricia's mother, Evarista (Eva) Zaldívar. Patricia's father, Apolinar (Paul) Arredondo Orozco, came to the United States from Salamanca in Guanajuato, Mexico, and arrived in Lorain just before the Great Depression. Some 15 years later, Patricia was born, the second in a family of seven children.

Patricia was influenced in her leadership development by both of her parents, although in markedly different ways. Her mother survived a difficult childhood, living with an alcoholic father at home and experiencing racism at school before financial need forced her to quit school and go to work. Patricia commented that, for her mother, "there were some unrealized dreams for her, obviously, regarding not finishing school." This resulted in demanding high standards for her own children. Eva worked to make sure that Patricia and her siblings had access to the opportunities she didn't have, enrolling them in a Catholic school despite limited family funds. "I know she desired better things, and she brought that into our lives as a family: how we dressed, protocol, etiquette, all of those things."

In her father, Patricia observed a natural leader. "He was president of the bowling league. He worked with Mexican immigrants who were trying to get their papers prepared for citizenship. Then he was the treasurer of the Mexican Mutual Society, probably for 50 years. He modeled civic engagement and activity that was, I would say, culture-based, but also social." Beyond observing her father's engagement and commitment to the community, Patricia felt his love and support in her development. "Growing up, my father was probably my best mentor. He appreciated me for who I was. He didn't say that girls couldn't learn how to play baseball or that we couldn't go bowling. He clearly empowered all of us in ways that opened doors and, of course, in a loving way. I would say he was a feminist and a mentor."

Leadership began to develop early for Patricia and was influenced by a sense of being different; she noticed who was being left out or mistreated. "It was a motivating theme because [of] that sense of being different, being a Mexican American in Lorain, Ohio, where people were not in professional roles. Every now and again, you heard so-and-so was an attorney or a police officer, but that whole sense of being different based on ethnicity and color is something that was salient to me growing up." She also observed people perceived as "different" being mistreated around her. Patricia recounted stories of seeing, as a young girl, a Puerto Rican boy and a Hungarian immigrant bullied at school by both her teachers and the children around her. She responded to this challenging school environment by taking on leadership roles. "It meant at times maybe just feeling like I had to work twice as hard. . . . I was the editor of the yearbook. I was the business manager for the newspaper. I was president of future teachers. I can go down the list." Service and caring were fundamental to Patricia and were modeled by her parents and *abuela*.

Her intellect, achievement, and leadership did not go unnoticed. The nuns in her early schooling experiences saw her strengths. "As a kid in school, if you have the kind of affirmation and encouragement from your teachers, that made a big difference. . . . The nuns thought I was smart, so much so that they wanted me to join the convent. . . . Clearly, that wasn't in my program!" This support, combined with her internal capacity, the emphasis her family placed on the importance of education, and her motivation to prove herself resulted in being recognized with honors, including winning the prestigious Service Award in her graduating class. Patricia, however, did not regard this as an individual honor. "It was intentional not so much to be a leader but to demonstrate that people of Mexican heritage could perform, could distinguish themselves. . . . I got satisfaction, but I know that I was consciously doing that to prove a point about people of Mexican heritage, and I was getting leadership skills along the way."

Patricia noted a few experiences during these years that especially inspired her interest in counseling. As an adolescent, she helped out at a Catholic church that welcomed Puerto Rican newcomers and witnessed how the nuns cared for this community. "I remember doing intakes with the family members and also looking at the kind of work the nuns were doing on their behalf. These were missionary nuns, different from the ones I had in school. How caring they were. I played a role there in helping, in listening." From this experience, she learned about the challenges of immigrants, especially the young people she met. "I couldn't imagine how it would be to leave your home and go somewhere else thousands of miles away." Along with these service experiences, Patricia was invited to serve as the aide to her high school guidance counselor, Mrs. Mehlow. "She was a very commanding and an impressive looking woman. That was also something that was very cool to me. . . . She had a very clear way of speaking, clear and caring." Patricia had the chance to observe Mrs. Mehlow as she worked with her students and took note of the encouragement and support she provided. This was Patricia's first direct experience with a counselor, and she was impressed by both her style and her substance.

After high school, Patricia became the first in her family to attend college. This was unfamiliar territory for her family, and it was her father who advocated most strongly that she pursue this path. Awarded multiple scholarships, she began her studies at Kent State University, a 2-hour drive from Lorain, where she studied journalism and Spanish. Spanish studies allowed her to stay connected to her culture as she launched her career as a teacher. After graduation, she accepted a position in Randolph, and later, Brookline, Massachusetts. The choice to move outside her home state and away from her family for the first time was not easy, but she was ready for new opportunities and adventures as she began her professional career.

Among Patricia's many notable contributions to the fields of counseling and psychology is a theoretical model that understands an individual's identity from a contextual and holistic view, the dimensions of the personal identity model (Arredondo & Glauner, 1992). To frame the factors of identity that shaped her lifetime of leadership and advocacy, it seems fitting to pause and consider her journey within the model's three primary dimensions.

The *A dimension* of the model contains those innate elements of identity that are commonly regarded as consistent across the life span, each representing a characteristic of identity assigned to an individual at birth. Patricia's identities as a female, Mexican American, and Latina were all central to her narrative, as was her family's working-class background (her father was a steelworker; her mother, a homemaker) and her bilingual (English and Spanish) upbringing.

The *C dimension* represents the contextual forces that influence one's identity, including the historical, political, sociocultural, and economic realities into which one is born that are critical to early developmental periods. Lorain, Ohio, an industrial city on the shores of Lake Erie, was home to multiple immigrant groups (e.g., Polish, Slavic, Hungarian), including her own family, and it remained her home until she began college. "Growing up in an immigrant community, a multiethnic immigrant community, low SES (socioeconomic status), and everyone striving to become higher SES was a very big lens that I've taken with me, and I don't underestimate how important that's been to me." Another salient aspect of this context were explicit and implicit messages of racism and belonging: "A city of immigrants is a city of people who are striving to be included and accepted as American. . . . Clearly if you're not White, there's a disadvantage, and I could see that right away in the schools. I recognized that my ethnic identity was not the most valued." Her model holds that the C dimension (contextual factors) accounts for the role our environment plays in shaping the way we make sense of and respond to our environment.

The *B dimension* of identity emerges from the relationship between our innate characteristics (A dimension) and the environment that surrounds us (C dimension). In her narrative, this included elements such as educational background (e.g., first-generation college graduate, completion of her doctorate) and work experience (e.g., professor, consultant, university president). The B dimension is often regarded as more fluid and is chosen by the individual to the extent that freedom exists to make such choices. In this profile, I focus on this dimension and explore Patricia's work as a leader and an advocate within and beyond the fields of counseling and psychology, always centering her work within the values of multiculturalism and social justice.

Pivotal Moments

Doing justice to Patricia's four decades of experience is a task worthy of hundreds of pages. In an effort to relay the richness of her work, I will focus on the central themes that emerged in our interviews. Patricia's professional journey has involved navigating multiple pathways, sometimes intersecting, that opened new opportunities for knowledge-building and leadership. At every step, her work has centered on multiculturalism, expanding worldviews, and mentorship.

The first theme, evident from early in Patricia's life, is her ability to remain open to pursuing new and emergent possibilities. Rather than following a conventional path, throughout her career she has attended to the ways she may best actualize her deeply held values of "inclusion, diversity, respect, and fairness." As a new professional in Boston, Patricia began working as a teacher at Brookline High School. She started to notice a specific need connected to her role that she was able to fill. "I found students, particularly girls, would seek me out to talk with me about social issues or issues with their parents." Motivated by wanting to help and encourage her students, she began pursuit of a master's degree in counseling at Boston College, setting herself on a new trajectory.

Working at Brookline High School also afforded Patricia the opportunity to work with immigrant students, something she has done throughout her career.

She recalled a constant influx of immigrants into the school, with students arriving from "Vietnam, the Soviet Union, Romania, Hong Kong, Taiwan, Haiti, and Jamaica." She began to notice that the school "was not working in favor of the immigrant students who had arrived." They were dispersed throughout the school's several houses and given little support, and this lack would become Patricia's first organizational intervention. "It occurred to me that we might better serve them if we created systems that would allow them to be more connected to certain teachers who wanted to help them, and to one counselor (me) who would work with all of them." This structural change resulted in the students having a designated space to congregate and receive specialized support and a system where staff could work effectively with one another to respond to challenges as they arose. To address obstacles standing in the way of immigrant student success, Patricia's colleagues offered to create a new course section on U.S. history to meet the students' learning needs, improve record keeping from the student's prior schools, and secure scholarships to support the students' college studies. This work also illustrates another theme in Patricia's professional life: her commitment to "opening doors" for others and ensuring that everyone has access to the resources necessary to fulfill their potential.

Moreover, this experience served both as a foundation for her future work with numerous corporations, universities, and nonprofits as well as a direct application of the skills she was learning as a graduate student in counseling. "I'm using the same skill sets that I use in counseling, which is assessing the environment, the situation, getting data, talking to people. In counseling, you work with clients to look at some goals and where they want to go. . . . I see the counseling competencies as applying to organizations but [through] a bigger lens and not just dealing with a person or a couple of people. I'm dealing with the whole system." From this early professional experience, she learned skills that would become relevant to her work as a clinician and consultant and as a senior administrator and president of multiple organizations. Her attention to her students' context (C dimension) and to the failures in the existing system was, no doubt, supported by her own identities, observations, and early experiences in Lorain. "It's the way a person was dismissed that is producing this result," she said, "not any flaw or deficit."

She continued her work at Brookline High School and continued her graduate studies, pursuing a doctorate in counseling psychology at Boston University. "Earning my doctorate was pivotal. It was a platform from which I could spring and actually be seen in a way that had a lot of credibility. That was in 1978, and it did open the doors to what has become a career in higher education with many opportunities and significant moments within that journey of the last 40 years."

Patricia accepted her first academic position at the University of New Hampshire, although she returned after a year to Boston University where she worked as an assistant professor and primary investigator for a Bilingual-Bicultural Counselor Training grant from the Department of Education. Despite a productive 6 years in the position, publishing numerous articles and chairing 23 dissertation committees, she was told that she "was not tenurable," a major disappointment given her hard work, dedication, and career goals. She later learned that none of her junior colleagues within the department were promoted during this time. Nevertheless, Patricia responded to this setback by once again staying open to new possibilities and considering where she could make an impact. "I had a year on my contract, so I began to explore what I wanted to do and how my skills as a psychologist and counselor could be leveraged in other sectors. I did my homework on how to start a small business (in this case a consulting business) and launched Empowerment Workshops. As they say, the rest is history."

For the next 14 years, Patricia developed her consulting business, focusing on translating her professional skills as a counseling psychologist into workplace programs (e.g., improving communication, increasing psychological well-being, delivering feedback) and into diversity-management initiatives with local and national businesses. She assembled a team of professionals with diverse areas of specialization (e.g., body image, career planning) and some attorneys (whose work addressed sexual harassment), regularly met with CEOs, published her first book (on diversity consulting), and eventually moved her office to Newbury Street, in the heart of Boston. In that period of time, she experienced "renewed confidence about following my own intuition."

Another theme of Patricia's career that emerged during this time was her focus on relational leadership and community engagement. She spoke of how meaningful it was to serve alongside respected colleagues on the Board of Registration of Psychologists of Massachusetts, where she began to expand her professional network as an early career psychologist, to serve on six nonprofit boards (as president of two), and to start a diversity-focused conference in Boston. She also stayed active in her professional associations with the American Counseling Association (ACA) and the American Psychological Association (APA), and Patricia continued to publish "outside of the university walls," both affirming her academic identity and building relationships with colleagues who would become trusted friends.

These relationships also opened important doors for her professional contributions. In particular, she recounted Thomas Parham, incoming president of the Association for Multicultural Counseling and Development (AMCD), inviting her to join his cabinet and to help draft what became the landmark 1992 article on multicultural counseling competencies. "I found that working with Thomas, who was really about inclusion, opened the door for me into AMCD leadership. . . . I'm so grateful, because it really legitimized my multicultural collaborative interests and my work as an academic. I worked to build multicultural trust."

Twenty years after her doctoral hooding, Patricia received an honorary doctorate from the University of San Diego. Her mother was able to travel to attend the ceremony, making it especially meaningful. It was a celebration of all Patricia had accomplished in her first two decades of professional life. She reflected that these years were a significant time of "creativity, innovation, and integration," in demonstrating her ability to contribute as a scholar and professional leader outside the conventional norms of academia, and all while growing a thriving business.

Colleagues across the country took note, and a few years later, a good friend, Miguel Arciniega, made a call to Patricia that would again change her career trajectory. "'Patricia, we have a position here at ASU. Might you be interested?' I always laugh and I say to him, 'Miguel, I didn't hang up on you when you called me.' That was significant, that I entertained the call." Once again, rather than follow the conventional path of continuing with her successful consulting firm and familiar home in Boston, she considered this new possibility. "I knew that I was opening some new doors for myself and didn't know what they were going to be, but by taking the risk to leave what was safe and familiar after that many years; it was just a life-changing moment."

For the first time in her life, Patricia lived in a place that reflected her cultural heritage, on land that once was part of Mexico. She expressed a dissonance that emerged during these years between the tremendous pride she felt being a member of the Latinx community in Arizona and the pain of recognizing the impact of colonization: "People of Mexican heritage were (and are) too often marginalized and made invisible in businesses and at the university, and this was especially hard to see in a land that had been our home for so long." Patricia was motivated by these feelings, becoming a leader in the Chicano/a Faculty and Staff Association at ASU, developing a graduate-level course with Arciniega on counseling Latinas/Latinos, and publishing a book similarly focused with Azara Santiago-Rivera and Maritza Gallardo-Cooper. "The social-cultural context of being in the Southwest influenced my attention to Latinx mental health, looking at it from a strengths-based perspective, and being back in the academic world allowed me to prioritize these needed contributions."

Patricia described her stay at ASU as "7 dynamic years," and it is easy to understand why. During this time, she resumed her work in traditional academic roles within the classroom, mentored numerous students (myself included), and was incredibly productive in her scholarship, coauthoring the APA Multicultural Guidelines as well as numerous journal articles and three books. She also engaged in her relational style of building community within the organization: "I did what I would have done in Boston—I worked my way around the campus meeting people, then having people say, 'Well, go meet so and so.' So, they would open the door for me. I found that to be very easy to do, but also [it was] part of my own style of engaging, which is to find out what's going on, what opportunities exist here." These years also included larger roles in professional leadership: Patricia was elected president of Division 45 of APA, the Society for the Psychological Study of Culture, Ethnicity, and Race; founded and served as the first president of the National Latina/Latino (now Latinx) Psychological Association (NLPA); and was elected to lead ACA in 2005–2006. "It's a matter of knowing what needs to be done. There are opportunities, and stepping into the opportunity can be life changing, not only for me, but for the cause."

A leader in her professional associations, Patricia was now being sought to directly apply these skills within the university setting. "I was so happy to become a full professor, and yet being in an academic department was not enough. I think having been in the world of business entrepreneurship, I needed a bigger space to actualize some of my leadership talents and values." With this realization, Patricia launched into her work as a senior administrator, first within her home university (ASU, as deputy vice president/university dean of student affairs, among other roles) and then at subsequent positions at the University of Milwaukee–Wisconsin (including her role as associate vice chancellor for academic affairs) and as president of the Chicago School of Professional Psychology, Chicago campus. "Those roles gave me opportunities to be a leader among leaders."

A final pivotal career moment came when Patricia left Chicago to create a new consulting business. "I find that having this kind of independence and flexibility allows me to be more creative and include more people than I could within the constraints of another institution." Beyond organizational consulting, this flexibility includes her work in academic scholarship, nonprofit leadership, and coaching women of color. Her latest venture also reflects the multidimensionality she has brought to her entire career. "My life has been this kind of crossing over all the time, always being on the borderlands, but intentionally. It's got many meanings—living on the borderlands—but I feel like I had many borderlands I've lived in and continue to live in as a woman of color. . . . I can make that enjoyable because I'm not feeling at all restricted. . . . I have multiple identities and so I'll enact them."

Leadership and Advocacy

Patricia has served in many leadership positions throughout her career and, with this experience, gained clarity about what it means to lead. "Putting my privilege to work—this is what leadership means to me. Awareness and knowledge of unmet needs and opportunities to advance others' collective benefits have always moved me to enact leadership, or to take charge." She continued, "Leadership is about initiating and bringing others along to join in the achievement of shared goals. It is not about followership but empowerment of others to colead and, in turn, put their privilege to work and lead."

As her model would predict, Patricia's leadership philosophy emerged contextually, related to themes that developed early in her life. Central among them is the focus she has given to the values of inclusion and social justice. Throughout her career, she has focused on "identifying the gaps . . . giving voice to people who couldn't speak up for themselves . . . because my awareness was piqued about some injustice." Beyond recognition of inequities, Patricia described how her deeply held values have motivated her to create new possibilities and opportunities for both herself and others. "I think my work is symbolic of creating access, of opening doors, of bringing people along, of all my values for inclusion, and diversity, and respect, and fairness. I've crossed many thresholds. Those thresholds . . . barriers, yes, they probably were barriers, especially because I didn't have the social capital to cross them, but I would say I never turned away from them."

Patricia identifies as a servant leader, a commitment demonstrated by her attention to the needs of others, empathic and compassionate listening, and natural ability to work within communities to promote health and well-being. Her leadership has often focused on serving girls and women to address the impact of sexism and devaluation. "I found that the work I wanted to do was to empower women to not denigrate themselves, to not accept the blame, whether they were hearing it from their parents or in the workplace. . . . Helping them to own their power and own their achievements and question the criticism."

Patricia's servant leadership has also been demonstrated in her involvement with numerous community organizations throughout her career. "In each city I've lived, I've found organizations that allow me to express my values and have my cultural identity affirmed." Her civic engagement has focused on Latinx community groups, where she has often been the sole academic among businesspeople. "Growing up in Lorain and not seeing visible leaders who looked like me, I've felt motivated to be a visible Latina Servant Leader. I put myself to work advancing the health of the Latinx community, and I've brought who I am to each of those conversations."

She also describes herself as a cultural-relational leader, which extends to the way she mentors and teaches. This relational style is especially evident in her work with the NLPA, the organization she founded. "The fact is that there's a set of values within NLPA that creates cohesion. We always think of ourselves as a *familia*. Mentorship occurs across lines, no matter who the person is. Students will write to me and ask if they can talk to me. . . . I have developed so many rich friendships and colleague-ships through NLPA." Consistent with descriptions of her own family, where each child was seen as important and the collective provided a sense of safety, Patricia has brought these values into her work as her natural, authentic style of leadership and mentorship.

Among the aspects of leadership she believes others do not readily see, Patricia identified the preparation and coalition building required to advance organizational change. She described her process, beginning with identifying a gap or need, and then digging into the data. "There's that behind-the-scenes data gathering to make sure that whatever I was passionate about, that needed to be addressed, in fact that there were data to support that." Once confirmed, she described a collaborative process to engage others in "coalition building," a process of creating a shared understanding of the need and a plan to address it.

As an example, Patricia recounted a time in the Association for Counselor Education and Supervision (ACES) when women were largely unrecognized in leadership and for annual awards. Indignant, she made multiple calls to women members across the country, creating the Women's Interest and Mentoring Network. Before launching this effort, however, she engaged the male leadership, so they could see this opportunity and buy in rather than being reactive. She explained, "What I've done is found people who would be open-minded and listen, and they generally were. I give them the benefit of the doubt that their ideas for making change or advocating, in this case for the women's network, was really in the best interests of the women members . . . and men's too. That's how I calculated it in my mind."

Patricia also described some of the less visible challenges of leadership as a woman of color, and the necessary resilience she has developed when she has been unwelcome or dismissed based on ethnicity, gender, or their intersection. She described having often been the only woman, Latina, or person of color at the table and finding her voice to lead no matter how others perceive her. "I'm outspoken, and if there's a matter, I do give it a voice. Or somebody just thinks I shouldn't be there. For me, that's old. I show up, regardless, to situations, and I give my voice." She explained that she has done this by staying connected to her goal: "I have had to keep in front of me the purpose of what I was intending to do or asked to do, that I was the person with the skills to do it or lead it. I couldn't apologize for who I was because that was just who I was."

She noted that her ability to "take her seat at the table" developed over time, aided in part by early professional experiences consulting for business leaders in the private sector. In a volunteer role chairing a scholarship committee at the Sankaty Head Golf Club, Nantucket Island, she recalled leading a group that included Jack Welch (of General Electric) among other CEOs in the Boston area. These moments gave her the direct experience of "being able to thrive in different types of contexts," and this knowledge continues to support her in advocating for herself and others.

Patricia has also found meaning in opening doors of leadership to other women of color. "As a woman of color, I would say to you that it is important for me to assume leadership roles so that other women will see that they too can be president of AMCD, or president of ACA, or on this or that board, president of NLPA." Mentorship is intrinsic to her definition of leadership, and she has mentored numerous students and early career professionals, inspiring a new generation of leaders to carry on this work.

The Future of Counseling

In reflecting on counseling and its future, Patricia emphasized the need to engage the public in more direct and impactful ways. She referenced "the two pandemics" of 2020 that have affected people nationally and globally: the coronavirus and the racial unrest and reckoning after the murder of George Floyd. "These pandemics are a call to action to the counseling profession to practice cultural competency and social justice advocacy on a national and global scale. We have to confront institutional and personal racism." She described each as having profound mental health consequences that demand to be addressed by ACA and the counseling profession. "The profession has to be more public. . . . Counselors must step into the public spaces to demonstrate the benefits of attending to mental health . . . using our skills to communicate, and create awareness, promote knowledge, and help individuals and families develop coping skills." She believes this will require a shift of focus for the ACA from an "inward facing" organization to one serving the public as well as a shift in the prioritization and teaching of leadership skills within counseling programs. "I think that the profession can benefit from servant leadership being part of our identity." This would reflect a marked shift and require counselors to expand their sense of professional identity. "Intervening in your office is one thing, but we have to intervene on a larger scale—at an organizational level, at a societal level. . . . It's about intervening so that, collectively, we see that there's power in healing as a result of what we've gone through, so that we'll come out stronger. This societal crisis is our opportunity."

Patricia also believes in the importance of collaborative efforts between the professions of counseling and counseling psychology. Rather than continuing to engage in territorial or divisive efforts to prevent each other from educating and training students or obtaining licensure to deliver care, she suggested that the two disciplines align in their "aspirations" and "motivations" to help people. To this end, she believes that a focus on cultural competency development and social justice is essential because "both professions espouse these themes and practices." A shift in focus is necessary for both ACA and APA for either organization to remain relevant and effective in serving the public.

To ensure the sustainability and growth of the counseling profession, Patricia advised that future leaders begin by taking a comprehensive view of their constituents. "You have the societal inputs, the professional, the community. You have to recognize all the stakeholders . . . so you're not going to overlook or exclude someone." Leaders need to "anticipate and plan so that what you would like to accomplish will be in fact doable." She noted that a common pitfall in this effort is taking a limited 1- or 2-year view, often corresponding to a leadership term within an organization, rather than attending to the more important legacy of the work, thinking about "how the organization will continue to evolve after you're in the role." To this end, she returned again to the necessity for leaders to work within their community and as part of a collective. "Whatever I do as a leader has to have some way that it can be maintained. That's why bringing other people into the development of a new idea or influencing a new idea or new initiative means I don't do it alone. I'm initiating it, but I'm not doing it alone—that just doesn't work. Leadership is much more collectivistic." On a more personal level, she continued, "I think that's why leaders shouldn't be lonely. If you're enacting leadership, you should not be a lonely person. You should feel your life is abundant."

Words of Wisdom

Patricia's central message to aspiring leaders is that working toward change means staying connected to their hope and passion as they take action. "It's believing in possibilities; that an idea can become fulfilled. I've remained hopeful that there are changes in our society, in our profession, that would be beneficial to humankind. It's where I think the counseling profession can assert more of our preparation to help and to heal and to encourage well-being." She continued, "I'm hopeful and I'm optimistic, but I don't stop there. . . . It may take time. I learned this many years ago growing up, and later with my business, that it takes time to realize a dream or an idea. But if you do it well, and if you stay the course, the goal can be realized."

Reflecting on what she wished she would have known sooner, Patricia underscored the power of culturally responsive counseling skills to affect change across domains: "Your counseling skills, when informed by the importance of culture and context, have such a wide range of applicability in multiple contexts beyond the clinical, because we're trained as counselors to be clinicians. Well, guess what? Those are skill sets that transcend clinical work. I would have never thought of the universe possible for applying my counseling skills . . . the universe is available to us."

Daniel C. Rosen's Final Reflections

Throughout our interview process and my experience writing this profile, I was aware of the resounding consistency with which Patricia lives her life by "putting one's privilege to work" in the service of collective benefit. As someone attuned to addressing injustice where she sees it, she spoke often of ensuring that "doors are open" for people to live purposeful and healthy lives, not as an act of charity but as an access point to leadership and agency for all. In fact, she has spent the past four decades opening as many doors as possible—doors to her own new perspectives and experiences, and many more for the people around her to pursue their own paths. In this process, it is clear that Patricia has found both meaning and vitality.

Another remarkable aspect of Patricia's career and leadership is the sheer fluidity and grace with which she's moved across multiple and diverse professional contexts, all while staying centered on advancing multiculturalism and social justice. Being able to transition from classroom to boardroom to community center—sometimes all in the span of 24 hours—is extraordinary, as is her level of effectiveness in doing so. The image of her running a meeting staffed by infamous CEOs on Nantucket brings a smile to my face. She relayed this story with her usual groundedness and humility—"The point is, Dan, first of all, I'm from Lorain, Ohio"— but also with a recognition of her own worth and deservedness of her place as a leader among leaders.

One of my most cherished memories is celebrating earning my doctorate with a festive family dinner in Arizona. My parents, brother, grandmother, aunts, uncles, and cousins had made the trip to join my wife and me for graduation. And Patricia was there too, understanding the significance of this togetherness, and what it means to pay forward the gifts you have been given, while recognizing and celebrating her own beginnings.

Notable Accomplishments

1978	EdD, counseling psychology, Boston University
1985–2000	Founder and president, Empowerment Workshops, Inc.
1992	Coauthor, "Multicultural Competencies and Standards: A Call to the Profession"
2002–2004	President and founder, National Latina/o Psychological Association
2003	Promotion to full professor, Arizona State University
2005–2006	President, American Counseling Association
2013–2016	President, The Chicago School of Professional Psychology
2016–present	President, Arredondo Advisory Group

Chapter 5

Casey A. Barrio Minton

Isabel C. Farrell

Mentee's Introduction

Casey A. Barrio Minton truly is prized by many in our profession. She is a down-to-earth and active mentor who gives to people, expecting nothing in return. I am Isabel C. Farrell, and Casey has been my mentor. She has fulfilled many roles in my professional and personal life. She has been my instructor, supervisor, coteacher, dissertation chair, Chi Sigma Iota (CSI) faculty advisor, professional mentor, and friend. She is my role model as a counselor educator, researcher, mentor, and academic mother. For this profile, I had the opportunity to interview Casey A. Barrio Minton and asked her to reflect on her experience and insights about leadership and advocacy.

Casey A. Barrio Minton's Journey

Early Years and Career Path

Casey A. Barrio Minton completed her undergraduate degree at St. Norbert College with double majors in sociology and communication. She completed her master of science in counseling (community counseling emphasis), graduate certificate in women's and gender studies, and PhD in counseling and counselor education at the University of North Carolina at Greensboro (UNCG). Since completing her studies, she has accumulated 15 years of experience teaching, supervising, and mentoring students. Currently, she is a professor of counselor education, counselor education unit coordinator, and clinical mental health counseling program coordinator at the University of Tennessee, Knoxville.

Casey identifies as a cisgender woman who has Latinx roots but was raised to be assimilated to White dominant culture. She is a first-generation college student. She was raised in a rural area outside of Buffalo, New York, where most people worked at manual, semiskilled labor and very much stayed close to home. Her decision to go off to college and beyond was counter to the way her working-class family had operated for many generations. She grew up learning to be a practical person. Her family stressed productivity and responsibility, and they valued working with their hands, whether that was working on projects in the land around her home, cooking, or providing direct service to others. She shared memories of standing by her grandfather as he fixed something and working on chores alongside her grandmother so that she could earn enough money to shop from the tote of gifts her grandmother kept to distribute when family members needed birthday or special-occasion gifts. As a result, Casey developed a strong desire to know why something was being done and what the projected outcomes would be. She attributes this practicality to shaping her early leadership engagements, and it remains with her today. Casey recalls being quite resistant to larger-scale initiatives that seemed fuzzy or impractical. Although this resistance persists at times, she now can see a bit more of the strategy and long-term evolution of larger-scale engagements within professional organizations.

Her high school and undergraduate years marked a pivotal period in her leadership development. In high school, she belonged to a faith-based youth group that had a strong focus on social justice and community service. Casey got involved in service and immersion projects that helped her understand systems and poverty in a new way. These often involved concrete, practical projects such as tutoring, preparing meals, or building homes. Eventually, she became a member of the youth leadership team. A relationship that she formed there led her to St. Norbert College to pursue her undergraduate studies. Looking back at that time, Casey said she decided to attend college because "somebody looked out for me and opened a door for me, and I didn't even know that door was there."

Casey entered college with no idea of what major she wanted to choose during her undergraduate years. During her exploration phase, a series of work experiences led her toward wanting to help people through relationship. While she was a resident assistant, three female students were sexually assaulted. Casey supported them through this process and realized the impact the trauma had in their lives. She got involved in the campus Women's Center (which she came to direct during her senior year) and started volunteering at a local sexual assault center. Both experiences fueled her interest in understanding longer-term services and programs that helped people to regain health after experiencing adversity. Although these were not the only experiences that led her to counseling as a profession, she highlighted the importance of these events and relationships as being central to helping her realize she wanted to be a counselor.

At St. Norbert College, she learned to think critically, even if it went against doctrine. Her resident assistant role included leadership development and training. She had opportunities to experience cultural immersion during alternative spring breaks, plan a conference, and direct a campus Women's Center under the direction of a licensed professional counselor whose focus was on outreach and engagement. Mentorship during her undergraduate years was instrumental and opened the opportunity for graduate school.

Pivotal Moments

A pivotal event that occurred for Casey while she was in graduate school was her involvement with CSI, an international professional honor society. Casey has been engaged over the past 19 years with CSI International and local chapters, including 4 years as a student and 15 years as chapter faculty advisor (CFA). She chaired her first committee with her local CSI chapter and served as its president. During this engagement, she had a mentor who helped her understand the importance of procedures, mission and vision, and strategy. These lessons have permeated throughout all the levels of her leadership within CSI and beyond and have helped her remember the importance of on-the-ground leadership and engagement and healthy ways to navigate an organization.

Leadership with CSI, both locally and nationally, taught her to recognize when professional organizations lack clarity around their mission or vision and when gaps exist between the mission and the organization's initiatives. This recognition can help an organization reconnect with its mission and build initiatives that are congruent. In addition, the structure of CSI has helped her apply these parallel structures (when appropriate) to other organizations, increasing their effectiveness. For example, Casey noted her appreciation for how CSI committees received charges and how the leadership team used reporting structures and ongoing check-ins with the executive board to ensure that these charges were addressed and committees and task forces were staying on track for the good of the organization as a whole.

Outside of CSI, Casey also believes she has learned every time she has a new engagement with a professional association. She explained, "One of the things I couldn't have envisioned was all of the interconnections that we have in our field, across our organizations and across their programs." Her work with CSI, and then building to the Association for Assessment and Research in Counseling (AARC), the Southern Association for Counselor Education and Supervision (SACES), and the Association for Counselor Education and Supervision (ACES), has shown her this connectedness.

Points of Pride

When Casey was asked about the professional accomplishments in which she takes the most pride, she highlighted her leadership with CSI. The *Journal for Leadership and Advocacy* (*JCLA*) was developed during her time on the CSI executive board. The idea for the *JCLA* started with conversations among the CSI executive board members, who realized that it was getting more difficult to publish or find a venue for scholarly articles that addressed the professionalization of counseling and "out of the room" counseling issues (topics that align with CSI's vision and mission.) A task force, which included Casey, was assigned to research the possibility of launching a journal in 2010, Casey's CSI president-elect year. The idea was endorsed by the CSI executive board, who decided to transition the newsletter, *The Exemplar*, to an online format to cover the cost for the *JCLA*. Originally, it was not Casey's intention to be the founding editor. In fact, Casey drafted the editor's job description and had a couple of candidates in mind for this position. As it turned out, she was nominated by the CSI executive board to serve as the founding editor, and she was glad she had this opportunity.

As founding editor, Casey took the lead in building the journal from scratch, including determining review formats and selecting an editorial board. It was her goal to ensure "scholarly rigor and yet stay open to provide leadership development for newer professionals." When a call was made for initial articles, Casey feared that they would not get any submissions. To her surprise, more than 80 articles were submitted for the first issue. This proved to Casey that there was a space and a need for the *JCLA*. The first edition of the *JCLA* went to press in 2013, the same year Casey became a mother. Casey joked that she gave "birth" to two babies that year.

Casey's term as *JCLA* editor was initially for 3 years. Unexpectedly, during her initial term, Jane Myers became ill and CSI had "some really important transitions to handle." Thus, Casey accepted a 2-year extension to support CSI through this transition and served for 5 years. During the term extension, the *JCLA* brought on Melissa Luke as associate editor, and she became the editor after Casey.

Casey stressed that she does not want to own the *JCLA* as *her* journal because it was a team effort, and CSI was uniquely positioned to create the journal at the time. She guided the *JCLA* from idea to development to implementation. She believes the *JCLA* has a unique impact in the field because it provides a place for "the things that we don't always have space to talk about in other journals," and it is an important platform for the counseling profession.

Leadership and Advocacy

During her early leadership years, Casey had a drive to do "concrete things that mattered." She felt a sense of social responsibility to be connected and engaged in our profession, which stemmed from the mentorship she received during her master's and doctoral programs. For example, Casey was eager to accept requests to plan and implement workshops or to coordinate a specific program.

These acts of service spoke to her drive to engage in projects that had clear, measurable outcomes. Early in her development, these included spearheading local professional development programming, serving on CSI grants committees, orienting new faculty members through the ACES New Faculty Interest Network, and matching CSI leadership fellows with mentors who helped them navigate projects and leadership assignments. Each contribution was a clear project that had a beginning, a purpose, and an end.

Although Casey has had many mentors during her career, the most salient for her was Jane Myers, a faculty member at UNCG and the faculty advisor for the Upsilon Nu Chi chapter of CSI. Initially, their relationship was strictly hierarchical, but it evolved into a deeper mentor-mentee relationship across the years. Casey recalls that Myers required their CSI chapter to read the bylaws, mission, and vision during each planning meeting so that the leadership team could target their efforts to match them (Casey says she may have rolled her eyes at this practice more than once). In addition, Myers was incredibly direct with Casey about the opportunities to gain experience, develop relationships in the field, and serve the profession. For example, on one occasion Myers purchased a meal ticket for an event at the ACA conference, stuck it in Casey's name badge, and told her who to sit with when she arrived. Casey expressed that Myers "had a way of knowing what her mentees needed and, in particular, her first-gen mentees. I think she looked out for me, as she did with them, pretty consistently."

At the beginning, Casey's leadership and service were not particularly intentional; her philosophy was that "you need to do what you're asked." Myers mentored her in specific ways to develop her leadership skills. For example, Casey found the once tedious bylaws reading practice to be essential for ensuring that professional organizations stayed focused on developing programs consistent with their unique mission, vision, roles, and responsibilities. She also described learning from Myers's deep commitment to service leadership, leading with integrity and long-term investment in the leaders themselves. As she grew as a leader, Casey worked to anticipate new professionals' needs, understand leaders' unique strengths, affirm leaders' contributions, and ensure a strong match between the task at hand and the leaders assigned to it.

Eventually, Casey's perspective shifted. As she got more involved in the field and gained experience with professional organizations, she became more aware of longer-term strategy, longer-term relationships, and connections among people and organizations in the counseling profession. During this period of transition, Casey realized that strong organizations are founded by strong leaders who are able to see that greater system and help put concrete strategies into place within it.

True to Casey's philosophy as a servant leader, a lot of her work happens behind the scenes. Her advocacy work is dedicated to building strong organizations and supporting strong leaders, counselors, and counselor educators. She noted that it is easy to overlook the importance of systems and long-term relationships in a particular context. Strong leaders and advocates understand, build upon, and align their initiatives to that context and systemic perspective. The roles and responsibilities of leaders might provide a glimpse of the work leaders do, but they do not give the full picture. They do not explain *why* the work leaders do is important and *how* it connects to outside systems. Casey added, "I would encourage people to be aware of and stay attuned to that."

Casey believes that most of her advocacy work is through community engagement and student mentorship and support. Her community engagement involves helping organizations serve our clients and communities more effectively. In Texas for 7 years, she worked pro bono with a sexual assault advocacy center to train their crisis line personnel in suicide intervention and help the organization obtain grants by assisting with program evaluation. Similarly, in Tennessee, she connected with a local National Suicide Prevention Lifeline affiliate and helped "revamp" their volunteer training, increasing its effectiveness and helping them meet accreditation standards. She currently serves on their board of directors. Through her student mentorship, Casey advocates for individual students to address "less-than-optimal" experiences and policies within programs and universities. In addition, she sees her job as CFA (serving for 15 consecutive years now) as one of advocacy with students. She supports students by helping them find a passion for advocacy and develop the skills they need to be excellent leaders. Casey is intentional about connecting and advocating for students to be part of development programs (e.g., CSI leadership fellows and interns) and uplifting them by nominating them for awards.

In terms of leadership outside of CSI, Casey has been president of AARC and SACES, and she will serve as president of ACES in 2021–2022. She has a way of coming into associations at important moments or turning points, and she said they do not always have a "flashy product" at the end. CSI had the *JCLA* at the end, but CSI also had a transition in the executive director when Tom Sweeney retired and Myers came on during Casey's 3-year term. Later on, CSI experienced another transition as Myers became ill and passed away. So, as Casey recalls, "a lot of the work was around stabilizing." During her presidency at AARC, the board was navigating a change in the mission and vision of the organization and realigning initiatives to reflect assessment and research. During her SACES leadership, SACES merged with ACES as part of a fiduciary restructuring, and the organization doubled their membership. Casey noted that, as a result, they had increased financial resources but had less control of them. Therefore, the leadership team had to restructure their operations. This restructuring was the focus of her entire presidency, and she believes it resulted in some meaningful outcomes for SACES, including a more clearly articulated mission, vision, and objectives; annual board meetings; webinars; a revised emerging leaders program focused on diversity and inclusion; and a new journal, *Teaching and Supervision in Counseling*. These achievements involved a multiyear, multipresident process, not Casey alone, and she said she was in the mix with "some really great people who all had a similar commitment to [the SACES] mission and vision."

All of these accomplishments were special because the servant leader philosophy very much calls out to Casey. It resonates with some of her core values in terms of connection and contribution to the greater good of the membership and organization over an individual's agenda, ego, or status. Casey thinks there is also an embedded component related to empowerment, fostering, and valuing of others. She believes that all of those elements wrap into how she leads, even if she sometimes makes unpopular decisions or voices something others might not quite like. Despite potential conflict, Casey is willing to put herself on the line to push an organization forward and honor their vision and mission.

In all pivotal moments, lessons can be learned. For Casey, a lesson learned was the importance of relationship beyond networking relationships. She spoke to the importance of relational connection for realizing potential and for helping people take steps that might not be comfortable or familiar to them. Her goal as a leader is to encourage others to stay open to those types of relationships.

She is also a true believer in happenstance. Although intentionality is important, Casey argues that it is OK to not always have a direct line or vision. Instead, start where you can and seize opportunities while you can, as long as what you are doing is consistent with your values and priorities. She added, "don't underestimate the importance of a small thing well done." If an opportunity arises to engage in an initiative that seems meaningful and important, Casey recommends that you "work on it, do it well, and see where it goes."

The Future of Counseling

Casey believes the counseling profession is standing at an important crossroads. There can be threats if leaders do not respond well to critical choices. The counseling profession is on the way to establishing itself as a recognized player and an essential mental health provider. Leaders in the profession have work to do, however, with parity, recognition, and Medicare access. What the profession needs now has been predicted for decades. In 1998, CSI hosted leaders from around the country to identify advocacy priorities to move the profession forward. Leaders identified initiatives that continue to be key in professional development today. "We need to continue these efforts. In addition, thanks to growing standardization of licenses across the United States, the profession is in a good position to begin attending to license reciprocity."

Casey believes that the counseling profession needs to make sure providers are well versed in evidence-based treatments and accountability for service delivery. At the same time, the profession needs to stay true to the foundations and services that make us unique. These include a unique synthesis of foundations of development, wellness, and holistic orientation and evidence-based practices. The combination of the foundations and evidence-based practices is essentially the integrated care movement. "If the profession can do both of those things, I think we've really carved out our place."

Casey noted that the counseling profession's service delivery system is changing rapidly, with providers counseling through online telebehavioral health services. Leaders will need to advocate for changes to engage in that system in a way that keeps counselors relevant and does not lose those values and priorities the profession prides itself in holding.

Casey believes leaders need to be engaged and proactive in conversations and initiatives. She advises new leaders to "invest in things that align with the values, mission, and vision of the leader and organization. Invest in initiatives that promote education, outreach, and advocacy. Additionally, increase research that is targeted to improving service delivery to real people." Casey called for leaders to "reduce research for the sake of research," adding that research should "further practice or education that leads to practice." More funding for outcome-focused research is necessary. In addition, as a profession, we need to increase awareness of what counselors uniquely bring to service delivery instead of researching methods developed almost exclusively by other professions.

Words of Wisdom

Casey stresses the importance of relationships in offering her words of wisdom. She spoke most personally about her relationship with Jane Myers, but she has learned from a number of other relationships throughout her professional journey that have "challenged me to be a stronger leader and stronger advocate, and I think a better person." In addition, she urges aspiring leaders to seize opportunities as they come, even if the opportunity might not be perfect or exactly what one wants. Those opportunities might open the door to relationships, organizations, or associations and help future leaders learn about the process (how decisions get made and things get done).

When seeking opportunities, it is important to consider that "good initiatives don't happen overnight." Very often, good initiatives take years and require sustained work. The *JCLA* is one example: moving from the original idea to the first issue took 3 years, and another 5 years were needed to have a solid product. In addition, leadership roles often involve administrative skills not found in counseling training, such as accounting or marketing. Leaders must balance willingness to learn skills required to serve and recognizing their own limits and bringing in outside help as needed. CSI could have placed the *JCLA* on their web page, but to honor the initial goal of a journal to serve the profession, the executive board hired experts to assist with publishing and indexing.

Future leaders should cue into what is important to them and what they value. Casey acknowledged that it can be hard to be invested in something that does not add personal value. Future leaders might find a home in any of the many different associations at state and national levels. "Just find this group where you feel like you're professionally connected, personally invested, and I think that makes a big difference." Casey also stressed the need to avoid overcommitting. Instead, she suggests doing fewer things but following through on them to make sure they happen. Finally, it is imperative to read and become familiar with the mission, vision, and bylaws of the organization; if they do not "fit" current demands or needs, one might advocate to change them.

The last words of wisdom Casey shared were to stay true to the mission and vision of the association or organization. If the mission, vision, and values do not fit, it could be because the association is not a great fit; or the organization may need a new, up-to-date perspective. If this is the case, it becomes the focus of the leader to help the organization move forward.

As the interview came to a close, Casey offered this reflection: "I think one of the most important messages I heard was that I was valued, and I had something to offer this profession. I did hear that, and I want others to hear that."

Isabel C. Farrell's Final Reflections

As a leader, Casey A. Barrio Minton is both my mentor and my role model. She truly embodies servant leadership. She gives her all without expecting any recognition. She builds up everyone around her. She's humble and caring, and her main goal is to serve our profession and those who are touched by it. Casey is not an idle mentor; she is there every step of the way. She has mentored me in all five of my roles as a counselor educator: counselor, leader, researcher, instructor, and advocate.

When I asked her how she saw herself as my mentor, she said that she wanted me to believe in myself and not get in my way. She saw how I built relationships, saw opportunities, and was not afraid of a challenge (even if I doubted myself at times). That description of her mentorship was spot on. As a mentor, Casey has always thought about fit. She has opened many opportunities for me with careful consideration of whether it would match my goals and focus. She has encouraged me to follow my passion, and with her mentorship, kindness, support, feedback, and resources, she has helped me find my voice as a counselor educator and own who I am.

As a new mother, Casey is also my role model and mentor as an academic mother. She has spent countless hours sharing her wisdom about how to balance family and work. She took the time to send books for me to read and selected Spanish books for my daughter, so I could integrate my culture and my language into my daughter's life.

Although my story may be uniquely based on my experiences, my story is not the only one. Dozens of people in our profession have been transformed by Casey's mentorship. She has influenced countless personal and professional lives. She is humble, caring, supportive, and overall a wonderful mentor. Casey's own mentor, Jane Myers, touched hundreds of lives, and Casey's mentorship is highly influenced by that example. Casey wishes to be as present as her mentor was, seeing individuals' potential and communicate that to mentees. When Casey asked Myers to be her chair, Myers responded, "This is a relationship for life." This is the same sentence Casey said to me when I chose her as my chair. I am honored to be on this journey with her. Casey has many years of service left in her career. So, in sense, her chapter is just beginning.

Notable Accomplishments

	Fellow, American Counseling Association
2003–2004	Leadership fellow, Chi Sigma Iota International
2005–present	Chapter faculty advisor, Rho Kappa and Upsilon Theta chapters
2011–2012	President, Chi Sigma Iota International
2012–2017	Founding editor, *Journal of Counselor Leadership and Advocacy*
2013–2014	President, Association for Assessment and Research in Counseling
2017–2018	President, Southern Association for Counselor Education and Supervision
2021–2022	President, Association for Counselor Education and Supervision

Chapter 6

Carol Bobby

Emily Goodman-Scott

Mentee's Introduction

Carol Bobby is best known for her work as the president and chief executive officer of the Council for Accreditation of Counseling and Related Educational Programs (CACREP) from 1987 to 2017. In her position with CACREP, Carol worked hands-on with counselor education programs and faculty across the United States, and she became active in higher-education accreditation policy and training issues through her leadership roles with other organizations.

I, Emily Goodman-Scott, am a newly tenured associate professor of counselor education at Old Dominion University. I fondly remember meeting Carol for the first time around 2007. I was a master's student, and our campus had started a new chapter of Chi Sigma Iota (CSI). Carol was the guest speaker at our first initiation, and I was the first president-elect of our chapter. I remember talking to Carol at length, directly after her speech, about the importance of a unified counseling profession. I continued to see her at professional gatherings, such as American Counseling Association conferences, and she attended the CSI awards ceremony when I was recognized as a 2008–2009 National CSI Leadership Fellow. About 3 years later, CACREP began a program that selected doctoral students to complete research studies for their organization. Tyler Kimbel and I, both doctoral students at the time, were the first CACREP doctoral researchers. Tyler and I reported directly to Carol for about a year as we investigated patterns in state-level school counseling leadership, licensure, and procedures.

Over the years since then, I've kept in contact with Carol through conversations at annual conferences and visits to the CACREP offices to say hello. I even stopped by while on maternity leave after the birth of my first child to introduce my little one to my friends at CACREP. I've appreciated Carol's role modeling, support, and mentoring, both professionally and personally, which has spanned more than a decade. And I was touched to be invited to write this profile honoring her legacy of leadership, especially because her legacy has been meaningful in shaping my identity professionally as well as personally.

Carol Bobby's Journey

Early Years and Career Path

Carol grew up in a loving, close family in the Midwest. She was the second of two daughters with a large extended family. She believes she was shaped considerably by her family of origin and by her experiences with loss at a young age. Her mom died unexpectedly when she was in second grade, and Carol reflected on that loss:

> It proved to be one of those before-and-after moments that you have in your life. It was a big deal in my life. I remember more than anything wanting life to go back to normal and wanting to go back to school. And when we did go back to school, everybody acted weird. I got to go first at jump rope, at playing marbles. The teachers treated me with kid gloves. Mother's Day would come around and I'd be taken in the hallway.

Carol's grandmother, who had also been a strong presence in her life, died shortly thereafter. In the span of 3 months, Carol lost the two female role models with whom she had lived since birth. Her father was a man in his 60s, brokenhearted at the loss of his wife, and he did his best to raise two young daughters. The heaviness of grief and loss hung in their home for the rest of Carol's childhood. She remembers that this grief was not addressed directly, and they did not seek guidance from counselors or through other outlets.

During Carol's sophomore year of college, her dad died of cancer. Feeling alone, without her parents, and having just turned 20, Carol faced another difficult period. In reflecting on these losses, Carol noted that a critical metamorphosis took place that shaped her both personally and professionally. After losing her dad, she said, "I was pretty much on my own. It's funny 'cause I think it [grief] changes you in ways that can be very good. I am who I am today because of those events . . . they drove me to the counseling profession." During her sophomore year, she was referred to Dr. Pullen, the head of the university counseling unit. Through her counseling sessions with him, she came to recognize the depth of her grief: "I came to acknowledge that I never once cried when my mother died, or when my grandmother died. And I didn't cry when my dad died. That's not a healthy way to live."

As a result of her counseling experience and insight, "realizing what people went through" in grief and loss, Carol pursued training and work in crisis counseling after she graduated with her bachelor's degree. Three years later, the next natural step seemed to be to pursue a master's degree in counseling.

> Like many people in the profession, I entered [counseling] because I saw the power of the profession and I had experienced the power of the profession. . . . There are many, many things that happen in people's lives, but I think those experiences of loss, and the power of somebody reaching out, hearing, and developing a relationship where you feel safe and where you can admit that things aren't going very well—that's what drew me into the profession. . . . I had a real draw to the profession as a result of actually experiencing the profession. Understanding the power.

Carol completed her counseling master's degree at the University of Florida and immediately started her doctorate there. She had the opportunity to study with Joe Wittmer, CACREP's first executive director, and with Robert Stripling, who is often credited as the father of accreditation. She and her spouse moved to Alexandria, Virginia, and she completed her doctorate at a distance as she learned a new role as a parent. She also worked for the American Guidance and Personnel Association (now ACA) and for the National Academy of Certified Mental Health Counselors, serving as their chief administrative officer. This experience prepared her for her future role with CACREP.

Carol earned her doctorate in May 1986; she defended her dissertation immediately after the birth of her second child. She joked, "I gave birth to two children and a dissertation." Immediately after completing her doctorate, she applied for CACREP's CEO position, fully believing she would not get the job. She saw the ad for the position and thought, "I'll never get the job because I know they're looking for a somebody and I'm a nobody. I just knew I wouldn't get hired. . . . I figured, 'Well they're looking for somebody with a name. I've got no name.'" She was surprised to be called for an interview and went to it thinking, "Well, this will be good practice."

> I went for the interview. I wasn't the least bit nervous during the interview because I knew they weren't going to hire me. I was just approaching it as a learning experience. And that night, doggone it, they called me and offered me the job. So I had to say yes, and I had no idea what I was getting into. . . . I went into the job with CACREP pretty naively. I didn't figure I'd get hired for the job. I was fresh out of graduate school, 32 years old!

Carol went on to serve as CEO of CACREP for 30 years. Her service to the counseling profession has been recognized in a plethora of ways. She was presented with the ACA's Arthur A. Hitchcock Distinguished Professional Service Award (2006), ACA's Thomas J. Sweeney Award for Visionary Leadership & Advocacy (2015), the Association for Counselor Education and Supervision (ACES) Robert O. Stripling Award for Excellence in Standards (2009), the ACES President's Outstanding Service Award (2013), the ACES Legacy Award (2019), and the American Association of State Counseling Boards President's Award (2018), all honoring her leadership and commitment to the profession. In addition, she received the Office for National Education Standards and Quality Assessment Plaque of Honour for Contributions to the Development of External Quality Assessment (2014), an award presented by Thailand's national accrediting organization, and she received the Association of Specialized and Professional Accreditors Cynthia A. Davenport Award (2015) for exceptional contributions in support of specialized and professional accreditation. In 2017, she was selected to be an ACA Fellow.

In 2017, after 30 years as CACREP CEO, Carol enjoyed her first day of retirement. Since retiring, she has remained active, pursuing both old and new interests through her volunteer service as a member on two international higher-education advisory panels and as a university trustee. In her free time, she enjoys spending time with family, going to the gym, reading fiction, playing games, and taking art classes.

Points of Pride

When Carol was asked about the aspects of her long, well-accomplished career that brought her the most pride, she reflected on a few key moments. A significant event was when CACREP became financially independent. "We went from having about a $50,000 budget, which was about 99.9% subsidized [by ACA] when I started, to being completely financially independent with a budget of $1.5 million."

She also highlighted the merger between CACREP and the Council on Rehabilitation Education (CORE) in 2017. CORE had accredited rehabilitation counseling programs since 1971. According to Carol, "When CACREP was created [in 1981], there was always this idea that there would be one accrediting agency that would help to unify the profession, strengthen the identity of counseling as a profession. Just like medicine, it would be a profession where people would specialize in different areas." Despite this vision for a unifying accrediting agency for the counseling profession, conversations about the prospect of merging CACREP and CORE had been unsuccessful for decades. Beginning in 2013, Carol collaborated with the leadership of CORE for several years, and a merger was finally approved.

Leadership and Advocacy

When discussing her leadership experiences, Carol expressed appreciation for the counseling skills and values she learned in her graduate program and reports that she regularly used these counseling skills, values, and dispositions—listening, valuing relationships, and respecting and remaining open to differing viewpoints—throughout her career. "There were a lot of things I did at CACREP that I wasn't prepared for at all. None of my education prepared me for budgeting or hiring good staff or whatever. But, in the long run, the communication skills that I learned in my counseling program, the listening skills, the relationship skills, they carried me through."

Carol emphasized the importance of listening. She reflected on her later years with CACREP when "there were always just a thousand things coming my way and sometimes I felt really pressed for time." In those moments, she made time to listen to people: "I mean really listen. Not let your mind go off in a thousand different directions or have your mind made up already." She made it a practice in her decision-making as a leader to "seek out the ideas of other people."

> While at CACREP, I often knew that I had to be the one to make the ultimate decision because I was going to have to bear responsibility for it as the CEO. I always did enjoy listening to how others might approach something or how someone in the field might approach something, because it gave me a different way of looking at things that I needed to consider.

Carol credits her listening skills with helping her get elected to the International Association of Quality Assurance Agencies in Higher Education (INQAAHE) board and then being elected president. "I don't think anyone ever expected for INQAAHE to elect an American as its president because it was an international organization. And they didn't necessarily want an American for president because America did everything else. I was sort of surprised when I was asked to run and when I was elected. I think it was because people realized along the way that I was going to listen."

Carol also learned about the skill of listening by watching the leadership skills of CACREP board chairs over the years. She served with every board chair until her retirement, and said she gained

> a lot of take-aways from watching board leadership skills across a lot of different people: watching how they interacted with people, watching when sometimes deliberate silence works best . . . there are those people who sit back and they're very, very quiet and they don't say anything for a long time, but when they speak, they have really thought through all of the issues and they're able to say all of the things they've heard around the table. And I know that I carry that with me into some of my leadership style with other organizations. Don't speak too soon.

Another value Carol gleaned from her training was prioritizing relationships. "Leaders can't work alone; leaders have to work in relationship with others. And so, relationship is probably the most important aspect of the way I've always tried to work with people." As a result of valuing relationships, she believed in the importance of shared work and shared credit: "Just because you're a leader you aren't exempt from doing the work. You need to get down in the trenches with everybody. I think that really influenced the way I ran CACREP. Anything that anybody in the office did, I was willing to do. I think that was an important way that I worked with the CACREP staff members." She stressed the importance of remembering that "it is a group effort, and everybody who has contributed needs to be recognized." She added, "It's not about the 'I' solving it, it's about the 'we' solving it."

Carol's listening skills and relational approach also guided her when she was approached with criticism:

> One of the things I remember learning very early in my role at CACREP was that if someone doesn't like the way something is being done and they are very critical of it, I would get them involved. I remember when I first took the job and CACREP was offering team chair training sessions . . . there were a couple of people that were pretty critical . . . so I invited [one of the most vocal] to be the lead trainer for the next team chair training, and I asked 'How would you like to do the training? Sounds like you've got some good ideas.' And so not taking the criticism personally. If people don't like how things are being done, bring them into the fold and let them help. I always felt that that paid off. When you invite them to be part of [the process] . . . then they know that you've heard them. And not only that, but [acknowledging] they have something to contribute. People are very invested in this profession . . . when we go into the counseling profession, you want to help. It's a very service-oriented profession. Part of being a good leader is helping to encourage that excellence in service. So, if people are critical, they're critical because they have high standards, and they want excellence.

Carol believes that effective leadership involves maintaining a larger perspective and staying aware of the context in which events are occurring. It has been important to "keep my finger on the pulse of what was happening in the profession."

> I had a unique perspective that the board could benefit from, as to what was happening not just necessarily with CACREP but with credentialing and licensure issues, what was happening in other accrediting agencies, the pressures coming from higher education at a very high level that might be coming down the pipe to affect our programs. And so, I began to understand the interplay between all of these different pressures and aspects of the profession, including the associations and what was going on at ACA and its divisions, which we know is a very political situation most of the time. I would try to share those perspectives with the board.

Carol noted that, in her position at CACREP, she was working at a high level in the profession, with many moving pieces. "I was constantly scanning. 'What is going on? Where are the tensions? Where are things that are working?' And it wasn't necessarily just in the counseling profession because I had to keep my eye on what was going on in higher education, in other professions, because a lot of things that happen in one profession happen in another."

She related her own use of this multidisciplinary perspective by learning what the pharmacy profession had done when confronted with members who refused to provide services. Some pharmacists didn't believe in birth control, and they didn't want to dispense birth control medicine. When the counseling profession began to address right-to-practice issues, such as school counselors who didn't want to deal with students coming in with diverse sexual identities, Carol talked to pharmacy professionals. She asked how their accreditation board handled this. What were the discussions that took place in the association world? What kind of policies did they pass to deal with this as an entire profession?

> So those are the kinds of things, scanning the environment, using resources, that I felt were really important. . . . I had great resources, because all the professions, all of my colleagues in the quality assurance world from [different] professions: psychology, social work, pharmacy, architecture, medicine, aviation, science, computer science, engineering. We found that we have more commonalities than differences, even though we were distinct and separate professions. Scanning the environment is important for a leader to do and to keep other people informed.

Carol observed that many people think that information is power. "But I always felt that in my position in the profession, sharing the information was one of the most valuable things I could do."

In leading CACREP, Carol valued honesty, integrity, and trust. She valued "working with honesty and integrity and keeping the big picture in mind. I've always tried to work toward excellence. I take a great deal of pride in whatever I do." In valuing excellence, she stated, "you can help people to see the best in themselves." In addition, trust is important to Carol, both personally and professionally. "It's good to have people you can trust to bounce ideas off of. People who will serve as your reflection. They can reflect back so that you can hear the idea a different way."

She observed that when a leader has invested a lot of time in something, it can be difficult to leave it to someone else or to the next person. Yet she watched board members do that with integrity: leave the board and trust that it would carry itself on.

> And I learned a big lesson about being able to trust that process and to let go. Because after 30 years as CEO, it was important for me to let go. It was important for CACREP for me to do that. And it was important for the successor to be able to come in and to have the authority and to not feel like what I did had to somehow be followed or that it was the magic formula.

She added that organizations have their own lives and offered the example of her relationship with M. Sylvia Fernandez, who followed her as CEO of CACREP. She noted that Sylvia "lives, like, six houses away from me, and we socialize with one another, but we don't talk about CACREP. That's not my role, and I have total respect for wherever she takes it. . . . My goal was always to leave [CACREP] in a good position, that it would have what it needed to carry itself on into the future.

And I wanted whoever came in to at least have an organization that they could start from a position of health and take it further."

Carol believes that effective leaders are able to balance their time and priorities at work and be purposefully efficient. It is important to focus on the big picture and not get weighed down by the details: "Sometimes you have to forget the weeds a little bit. You can't pick every weed. You have to really consider 'Which weeds are going to take over the lawn at that moment? And how can I spend some time where it's needed?' That's not easy. . . . I had to remind myself that more hours did not necessarily make me better in my role, nor was it a better use of my time."

In a similar vein, Carol described using a relational strategy for efficiency. "There's a lot of ways that you can [address work], but sometimes picking up the phone was a much more efficient way of handling something than emails. Emails take a lot of time . . . sometimes if you pick up the phone, you've shared that workload rather than bounce it back and forth through several emails . . . picking up the phone could save you a lot of headache and misunderstanding. People feel like you've reached out in a more personal way."

Carol acknowledges that the counseling profession is steeped in politics. Politics abound in many organizations, such as religions and churches, and Carol wondered whether organizational politics are human nature. She said, "Oh, the politics in [our counseling] profession. Professions are very political and not a whole lot different in terms of the kinds of competition you get sitting in a faculty meeting." Carol "didn't take the criticism personally, that people had about CACREP." She recalled a particular situation early in her career, at her first conference as CACREP's executive director. The CACREP board had made a change in policies, and when she announced this change, outrage erupted in the room. Carol described how she dealt with the situation:

> And I said, "Wow, well clearly there's a lot of emotion around this. I can't change the policy because that's not my role, only the board can do that. But I will make sure that I write down all of the things I've heard in here today, and I will make sure that the board hears your concern." And I remember I walked out of there, and receiving feedback after that meeting [from a] big tall man [who] put his hand on my shoulder, and he said, "You know what, Carol, you're going to do just fine in this job. You roll very well with the punches." I'll never forget that. Because I thought, "Wow, there's a lesson here and just the fact that he took the time, he recognized it was a pretty emotional session for people and I didn't take the bait. I didn't get upset." I just said, "Here's what I can do for you. I hear what you're saying."

Carol remains in touch with that "big tall man" who complimented her response in that meeting. "I still share Christmas cards with him. . . . Gosh, he's got to be in his 80s. But I thought, 'Wow, how great. How great that he took the time to do that [talk to me].'"

Mentoring was a crucial aspect of Carol's leadership and professional journey. Examples of being mentored peppered the stories she told to me: "I had a lot of mentors, and I still hold all of them in my heart. They were great to me."

The Future of Counseling

Reflecting on the future of the profession, Carol expressed concern about splintering and the need for greater professional unity. Two of ACA's former divisions—the American Mental Health Counselors Association (AMHCA) and the American

School Counselor Association (ASCA)—formally separated from ACA, and the ASCA is developing a recognition program for school counseling graduate programs. "The splintering is still going on, and the profession really needs to buckle down. They need to determine that they can be one profession and that it doesn't mean that everything across specializations is the same. It never has been." Carol pointed out that CACREP always had separate standards for different areas because counselors need to specialize in different ways, in "much the same ways as my OB/GYN isn't the person that I'd want to do my hip replacement surgery, and isn't the person I'd want to operate on my thyroid if I had a thyroid problem. But if the counseling profession doesn't get a grip on this, then they might as well continue to shoot themselves in the foot."

At the same time, Carol lauded developments in the counseling profession, stating that "the counseling profession made some strides. They had the 20/20 Vision for the Future of Counseling. Do I think that that was completely successful? Personally, no, I don't. But I think they at least saw that there were some elephants in the room, and they did try to come up with a definition [of counseling]. But it's not just about defining the profession, it's about owning it. It's about really saying that counseling can be a unified profession with lots of specializations and then moving it from there, working with that as your premise."

Carol also highlighted the leadership of the three organizations that work well together. "[The National Board for Certified Counselors] NBCC, Chi Sigma Iota, and CACREP really were the organizations that led the way on professional identity. The future of the profession could be very strong, but there is a need to deal with the current issues. . . . I think that the pieces are in place, they need to be built more, and somebody needs to have the passion to do it. It's a big job."

Carol concluded with her hope "that the leaders of the organizations can get together and recognize the threats [to the profession]. The counseling profession needs to think about the things that could happen if we don't get our act together [developing a unified professional identity]. I do understand some of ASCA's and AMHCA's complaints for leaving ACA. ACES has talked about it in the past. None of these discussions are new." She urged leaders "to take a look and say, 'Why have people been so disgruntled with being part of ACA that they don't want to stay?' If the organizations—ACA, its divisions, and the other supporting organizations—get together, they could really look at the problems and try to ask 'What steps do we need to take to rectify this continued splintering? Because it's not good for our constituents.'"

Words of Wisdom

One of the first lessons Carol learned influenced her entire career. She began her career by taking a chance and stepping outside her comfort zone. As a young woman with a newly minted doctorate, she went out on a limb and applied for a job she thought she'd never get. Carol retired from that job after a rich and dynamic career as CEO of CACREP for 30 years.

In fact, all of Carol's words about her leadership style and strategies can be taken as words of wisdom for those who wish to become leaders. Her thoughts about life-work balance are equally important for those who hold such aspirations. She recalled, "When I was in graduate school, I remember my first quarter, one of the other students introduced herself to me, and she said 'Oh, you're married. Most people that were married when they came into the program end up getting divorced.' Which was true. Yeah, most people did."

As Carol reflected on her work-life balance over the years, including her role as a mother, she said, "I did make sure that my kids always came first." In addition, she noted that when she had young children at home, she "had a much better work-life balance. It was very clear to me where my priorities were, where I had to draw the lines." If her kids needed her or she needed or wanted to be at an event with them, she didn't have any problem finding the time. "But as they got older and they went off, it was harder for me to separate those [work] boundaries and so 'at-work' things became muddled. I had to be more diligent about not letting work take over more of my life. Still make time for people the way I used to make time for my kids. . . . I think it's good to recognize when you're getting too involved [in work] and maybe sit back a little bit." She also detailed prioritizing her marriage throughout her career, and spending time together, "I've been married for 45 years this year. I love the theater. We have been subscribers to the Shakespeare Theatre Company here in D.C. for at least 30 years."

> When the news [of my retirement] came out, just about everybody said, "Oh, I can't believe you're going to be retiring. You're going to miss this so much. What are you going to do? Your whole life is CACREP." And I thought to myself, "They don't know me very well!" After all these years working in the profession, I did have a professional life and I did have a personal life. They don't know that I love to read, but not necessarily professional stuff. I love to read fiction. I have been in a book club for 30 years. We meet once a month. I have this whole network of friends. They don't know the only reason I haven't taken an art class is because I travel too much, and I don't have time, and I would miss class all the time. And guess what, I have this whole other life going on [in retirement], and I do not miss working.

Carol concluded, "It's probably good to have your *other* life [outside of the profession] and guess what, that *other* life is your *actual* life. You don't have to share it with everybody. I do think that's important and those are my words of wisdom." She added, "Make sure you nurture yourself in the ways you want to be nurtured. Take care of yourself."

Emily Goodman-Scott's Final Reflections

Although I have seen and admired Carol's impact on the field firsthand for almost 15 years, writing this profile has deepened my appreciation and expanded my awareness. First, it has been incredible to understand Carol's career in the context of the counseling profession's development. Early in her career, Carol witnessed the inception of several key organizations that are now strongholds in our profession: CACREP, NBCC, and AMHCA. Not only did she see these developments, but she also was meaningful in shaping aspects of our profession over decades, contributing to significant changes in accreditation, licensure, and professional identity. Carol's leadership occurred during a particularly crucial time; it was a time when the counseling profession needed strong leaders to provide vision, work hard, and build momentum. Carol's suggestions for the future of the counseling profession are rooted in decades of experience. She has identified factors that helped our profession flourish and now points to some challenges we still need to address.

Second, I also greatly appreciate Carol personally. She is funny, humble, grounded, and truly values her family, loved ones, and having a meaningful life outside of work. I remember running into her at the airport several years ago. We were on the same flight and headed to a conference. While waiting for our flight, we sat together in the terminal for a good while, discussing books we were currently reading (and these were not academic books). I also greatly admire Carol as a woman and a mother. She's been a mentor to me during a pivotal time in my life. I am a mother with three darling young children, ages 2, 4, and 6 years old. I gave birth to three children in just over 4 years when I was a pretenured faculty member in my first faculty position at a research-intensive university. It was a lot! However, Carol's role modeling assisted me in this transition. I have two distinct memories of this. I remember a stressful time at the end of my doctoral program when I was searching for academic positions, completing my dissertation, and in the midst of a tenuous high-risk pregnancy. I had lunch with Carol at a conference, and I told her about these stressors. I remember her saying, "Work is not everything." Her words meant a lot. To hear Carol Bobby, a groundbreaking leader in our field, suggest to me that *work isn't everything* helped give me permission and insight to make decisions that aligned with my values and to make decisions for myself as a whole person, not just as a professional. Furthermore, her words gave me insight into her values as well: her significant commitment to prioritizing her own family and life outside of work. That conversation helped me crystalize the idea that women can have meaningful careers and also be loving mothers who prioritize their children and spouse.

A couple of years later, I was asked to name a person I respected and admired as a woman, a mother, a professional, and one who had achieved a commendable work-life balance. It was a tall order! In that moment, I reflected on conversations and impressions I've had throughout the years, and I was reminded of a woman who was committed to her family and interests independent of the field but who was also a pillar of excellence and leadership in the counseling profession over many, many years. And, thus, my answer was—Carol Bobby.

Notable Accomplishments

1987–2017	President and CEO, Council for Accreditation of Counseling and Related Educational Programs
1992–1993	President, Chi Sigma Iota
1996–1998	Board chair, Association of Specialized and Professional Accreditors
1998–2013	Board chair, Center for Quality Assurance in International Education
2000–2001	Fellow, Middle States Association Commission on Higher Education
2013–2015	President, International Network of Quality Assurance Agencies in Higher Education
2017–present	Fellow, American Counseling Association
2018–present	Trustee, Palo Alto University

Chapter 7

Craig S. Cashwell

Jodi L. Tangen

If anyone is searching for the best within our profession,
I recommend they start with Craig Cashwell.

—Spencer G. "Skip" Niles, colleague, professor, and
former dean at William & Mary

Mentee's Introduction

I, Jodi L. Tangen, have known Craig S. Cashwell for approximately 8 years. I first met him when I was a student at the University of North Carolina at Greensboro (UNCG) and later came to know him as a colleague in the counseling profession and as a treasured friend. I have spent countless hours with Craig discussing research ideas, collaborating on projects, developing presentations, coteaching classes, serving together on research teams, and consulting on professional and personal issues. He has served as my research apprenticeship guide, teaching instructor and cooperating teacher, advisor, and dissertation chair. Most important, though, he has been an enduring mentor and friend.

In one of our first meetings together in 2012, Craig sat down with me (a brand new doctoral student plagued with a heavy dose of imposter syndrome) and asked, "What do you need from me?" He not only engaged with me about what it meant to be a doctoral student and a burgeoning researcher but also encouraged me to reflect on what it meant to become my deepest self. This experience with Craig served as an early touchstone of connection, and it has developed further over time. In my experience, Craig's humility, deep compassion, and earnest desire to serve others truly distinguish him as an exemplary leader in our field.

Craig S. Cashwell's Journey

Early Years and Career Path

Craig was born and raised in Winston-Salem, North Carolina, the youngest of four children. He was so much younger than his siblings that he felt like he grew up as an only child. His mother worked primarily as a homemaker, and his father worked as a truck driver. Some dysfunctional family dynamics and psychological struggles characterized his upbringing, and these experiences led to his dream of becoming a counselor, originally for a lot of unconscious reasons. He quoted the Christian mystic Richard Rohr, who said, "If we do not transform our pain, we will most assuredly transmit it." "For good and bad," Craig said, "I have done both."

After graduating from college (a first-generation college student), Craig began working in a grant-funded program for adjudicated adolescents. He really enjoyed his work with the adolescents and thought he might become a school counselor. After a short time in a master's program at UNCG, however, Craig became fascinated with what was then called "community counseling." Craig wanted to work one-on-one with individuals, and he believed that mental health counseling would better allow him this opportunity. It was not long into his master's program that young Craig secured a research assistantship with L. DiAnne Borders, and together, they worked on a review of supervision regulations within licensure laws. DiAnne noticed something special in Craig and encouraged him to apply to the counseling and counselor education doctoral program at UNCG. As a first-generation college student, Craig said he was humbled by her belief in his potential, so he mustered the courage to apply. When speaking about this experience, Craig's voice softened; he is clearly grateful for DiAnne's tremendous influence on his early career decisions.

Once Craig earned his doctorate from UNCG, he embarked on a career as an assistant professor in counselor education at Mississippi State University. In his 6 years there, Craig worked hard, published widely, and earned tenure. It was not long, though, before his former professors at UNCG (Nicholas Vacc and DiAnne Borders) encouraged him to apply for a faculty position at his alma mater, just a few miles from his hometown. He secured the position and built his career, honing his research interests in spirituality and process addictions. During his time at UNCG, Craig also slowly and steadily built his reputation as an authentic and humble leader. Craig and his partner, Tammy, settled into a home, established themselves within the surrounding community, and raised their son, Jack.

Pivotal Moments

Comments from Craig's former students that appear throughout this profile amply demonstrate that he was a key figure in their most pivotal personal and professional moments. When I asked about the moments that were most pivotal in his own professional journey, Craig softened his gaze and traveled back to times in his life when others had done the same for him. He recounted the times when DiAnne invited him to apply to the UNCG doctoral program; when a mentor at Mississippi State, Warren Housley, invited him to be treasurer of the Association for Spiritual, Ethical, and Religious Values in Counseling (ASERVIC); when Jack Culbreth and Bryce Hagedorn encouraged him to run for chair of the Council for Accreditation of Counseling and Related Educational Programs (CACREP); when Kelly Wester encouraged him to run as the Association for Counselor Education and Supervision (ACES) representative to the American Counseling Association (ACA) governing council; and when Jane Myers invited him to run for president of Chi Sigma Iota (CSI) International.

He also recounted the story of how he became interested in religion and spirituality. A close friend and former colleague, J. Scott Young, had wanted to conduct a dissertation on integrating religion and spirituality in counseling, but he found there was not sufficient literature on the subject at the time to support a dissertation. When they worked together as colleagues at Mississippi State University, they committed to conducting one study a year on that topic. Clearly, this endeavor has been fruitful; they have published numerous articles on the topic and penned a well-regarded book, *Integrating Religion and Spirituality Into Counseling: A Guide to Competent Practice* (Cashwell & Young, 2020), now in its third edition. In fact, throughout this interview, Craig wove in stories of encouragement from both his friend Scott and his partner, Tammy. He said that Scott's encouragement to step into the arenas that scared him and Tammy's enduring support were critical in these pivotal moments.

The core underpinning of these pivotal moments illuminates so much of who Craig has become as a leader. He openly shared, "Growing up, my core scripts were that I wasn't good enough and I wasn't wanted/needed." In these precious moments, then, when someone saw potential in him, he felt emboldened to step into the fear and trepidation of leadership. On a fundamental and personal level, he truly understands "imposter syndrome" and works tirelessly to help students step into their own potential. Allison Pow describes how this process worked for her:

> Craig has a knack for seeing the very best parts of people—the parts that they too often miss in themselves. He is keenly aware that the process of developing as a counselor is inherently tied to personal development . . . he saw me in places I never saw myself at first— researching at a top tier university, teaching in a doctoral program. And throughout the process, this gentle message emanated through all he did: "If you could see yourself the way I see you, you would know how far you can fly."

Points of Pride

With all Craig's accomplishments and accolades as a leader, one might assume that he has a big ego, but nothing could be further from the truth. In fact, when asked what accomplishment he is most proud of, he pulled away from the word "pride" and spoke more of gratitude. He highlighted the work that he had done with the CACREP board and CSI International as meaningful for him because it had a tangible impact on the counseling profession. As president of the CACREP board, he facilitated the process of adopting the 2009 standards. With an adept balance between task and relational foci, Craig maintained an eye on the group's vision and motivated and emboldened others to work together, making steady progress. As president of CSI International, Craig used a very different, yet nonetheless equally important, skill set as a leader. During his time as president, Jane Myers, then-executive director of CSI International, was diagnosed with terminal cancer and passed away a few months later. The organization was rudderless and grief-stricken. Craig found himself holding space, being present, and serving as a steady source of support during this trying time, all while guiding the organization through a temporary and long-term transition plan. Throughout all of our discussions about his impact as a leader, Craig repeatedly spoke of the gratitude he felt for these opportunities to serve. In his humble, soft-spoken manner, he reiterated the power of paying things forward.

This commitment to paying it forward is echoed by Janeé Avent Harris, a former student who is now an assistant professor at East Carolina University: "When I graduated from my doctoral program, I told him 'thank you.' He told me, 'If you want to thank me, then pay it forward.' I have never forgotten that, and it has shaped who I am as a counselor educator. I'm so thankful for the leadership and advocacy of Craig Cashwell, and I will continue to pay it forward." Another former student, Amanda Lee Giordano, an associate professor at the University of Georgia, added that Craig "set the standard of what I believe an ideal mentor looks like—and as a way of recognizing and honoring this mentorship, I try to be that type of mentor for my own students. I am exceedingly grateful for his influence in my own life and for his impact on the counseling profession." Yet another former student, Whitney Akers, an assistant professor at University of North Carolina at Pembroke, remembers when she was a master's student and Craig approached her and asked that she consider applying to UNCG's doctoral program. "It was in this moment that I felt he saw my potential to teach—to incite that beautiful riot of knowledge deconstruction, reconstruction, rich regeneration, and revolution—and I, for the first time, felt it in myself. As a counselor educator now, I could not imagine this adventure without his grace, humor, and guidance, and I continue to work to embody his radiance in all I do."

Leadership and Advocacy

During our interview, I asked Craig multiple times to describe how he perceived his influence as a leader on the counseling profession. This was clearly a challenge for him, and he recoiled from every suggestion I offered based on what others have said about him (humble, kind, authentic, inspiring). Eventually, he told me a story that he found deeply moving. One of his mentors, Dean Smith, the late and great North Carolina Tarheel college basketball coach, was lauded for bringing his African American players to restaurants and helping desegregate the South. When his actions were made public, Smith responded, "You should never be proud of doing what's right. You should just do what's right."

When asked about the ways that his leadership theory and philosophy have influenced his professional journey over time, Craig hesitated a little. He admitted that he felt as though he developed his early leadership style by watching other leaders whom he admired (here, he named Nicholas Vacc, L. DiAnne Borders, and James Benshoff). He carefully observed the subtle ways they facilitated groups, conducted meetings, and pulled people together. From there, Craig tiptoed into the leadership venue by volunteering for roles within ASERVIC. He started as treasurer, then became secretary, and eventually was elected president.

Craig continued to volunteer for various positions within organizations, and he said that it was not until his role as chair of CACREP that he realized he did not have foundational, textbook knowledge of leadership theory. He took it upon himself to research and reflect on leadership theories and contextualize them into his work.

Although Craig's upbringing sheds some light on his early journey as a leader, it doesn't quite capture *who* Craig is in the way that he leads. Anyone who knows Craig knows he is a soft-spoken, highly attuned, humble man with a quirky sense of humor. Cheryl Fulton, a former student and now an assistant professor at Texas State University, described him as having "a way of engendering a sense of trust in him because he is humble, willing to examine his own actions, open, mature, and genuine. He also has a subtle, but very present sense of humor. These qualities make him wonderful to work with in any professional capacity; they also make him wonderful to know as a friend."

Being the ultimate counselor, when Craig is leading a meeting, he first checks the temperature of the room. How are people feeling? What do they need to feel engaged and inspired to do this work? How can he facilitate this process? How can he step up when things are amiss and step back when the team is building its own momentum? His attunement to these matters is unprecedented and underscores his exemplary leadership. Furthermore, Craig emphasizes the importance of setting expectations and encouraging team members to stay focused on the work. He keeps an eye on the group's vision and maintains his arms around his followers.

Craig operates from authentic leadership and servant leadership theories. According to Ilies (2005), authentic leadership is composed of self-awareness, unbiased processing, authentic behavior/actions, and relational authenticity. Authentic leaders are true to themselves, confident, hopeful, optimistic, resilient, moral/ethical, and future-oriented, and they give priority to developing others to be leaders. Speaking of authenticity, this profile would not be complete without noting Craig's sharp and quirky sense of humor. It is a surprising twist on his more widely known spiritual presence, but anyone who knows him knows that leading from an authentic space, for him, means infusing the atmosphere with a little light-hearted relational humor. Allison Pow, a former student now in private practice, gives this description:

> Craig adeptly balances the relational depth of his mentoring relationships with a smart and sometimes goofy sense of humor and a love of laughter and fun. . . . The décor of his office is a perfect reflection. On one wall hangs a large photo of a young boy kneeling in front of a bowing elephant (an image that beautifully captures Craig's humility and reverence for life and wisdom). On the opposite wall stands a tall filing cabinet with a magnet bearing Jeff Bridges's likeness that reads "The Dude Abides"—a reference to *The Big Lebowski* (and perhaps Craig's alter ego).

In addition to authentic leadership, Craig embodies the ideals of servant leadership. According to Spencer G. (Skip) Niles, colleague, professor, and former dean at William & Mary, "Craig operates as part of the solution rather than the problem. This shouldn't be surprising, given that he is one of the leading scholars in spirituality and counseling. His reflective, centered, and compassionate approach elevates others in ways that strengthen our community. I rely upon his insight, guidance, and benefit from his empathy and compassion."

Although Craig highlighted authentic and servant leadership as foundational theories, he deemed his mindfulness practice as the most important aspect of his leadership style. Early in his career, he felt the imposter syndrome so keenly that he thought he was somewhat reactive in his leadership style. Driven by anxiety, he tried to manage everything and therefore made some impulsive decisions as a leader. Over the years, Craig believes he has become more thoughtful and patient in his work, although he also sees remnants of the old pattern emerge at times.

Craig's humble, gentle, thoughtful approach to leadership is evident; one could even argue that he was born to be a leader. Craig denies this, though, stating that he grew into leadership: "I always thought leadership was for other people. If you would have read my biography today to me 30 years ago, I would have either laughed hysterically or crawled in a hole with a panic attack. I would never have thought it was possible." Perhaps it is this perfect combination—the humble son of a truck driver, first-generation college student woven in with an authentic, mindful, service-oriented persona—that resonates so deeply with all of us as counselors. Craig is our leader precisely because he reflects the authenticity and messiness of the human condition . . . and the very essence from which potential is born and nurtured.

In his work today, Craig creates safe and nurturing environments where students can grow into their own potential. Zobaida Laota, a former student now in private practice, shares this poignant story:

> The earliest memory I have of Craig Cashwell is one that he likely wouldn't remember. . . . It was in my first semester of the doctoral program, shortly after the 2016 elections. He pulled me into his office one day to ask me if I felt safe on campus. I believe he was aware of Islamophobic rhetoric that was especially amplified at the time and wanted to offer even the smallest sense of security for me as someone who was new to the area and who wore a visible marker of my religion. He offered examples of some of the little ways he had thought about to help me feel safe and offered to construct a schedule and system for faculty and students to make sure that I always had someone to walk me to and from my car while on campus, for as long as I needed it. What he didn't know, and what I didn't share with him or anyone else at the time, was that my safety had been directly compromised the night before as I was walking to my car at the end of a long day, and the impact of hateful rhetoric was impacting my ability to show up and engage in my work that day on campus. I don't know what compelled him on that particular day to approach me, but nothing in my soul will let me believe that was a coincidence, and no words I share could capture what that exchange meant for me moving forward. I offer this anecdote as an example of his attention to the impact of the personal and spiritual on the professional, and his willingness to go out of his way to support students on all of these levels. On a personal level, he encouraged me to embrace the chaos and messiness of my journey and lean into the spiritual process of "breaking open."

Cheryl Fulton, another former student, highlights Craig's sustained commitment to mentoring. "As a mentor, Craig makes me feel like he is always looking out for my best interest. He unfailingly shows me respect and freely shares his knowledge and, more important, his wisdom."

The Future of Counseling

As Craig shared some of his ideas about the future of the counseling profession, he underscored the movements around increased licensure portability and innovative research on neuroscience and neurobiology. He became visibly excited when he described some of the ways research is beginning to explicate the neurobiology of attachment, and the ways coregulation can facilitate healing from traumatic experiences. He believes these are important efforts that will help the counseling profession circle back to a deeper understanding of Rogers's core conditions.

When asked what future leaders could do to sustain and cultivate the counseling profession, Craig—unsurprisingly—focused on self-awareness and dispositional leadership skills. In his words, "Focus on serving the profession rather than on serving the self. In my own experience, when I let my ego get in the way, I've been less effective. When I focused on the organization and the cause, I was a much more effective leader."

Words of Wisdom

When asked for words of wisdom, Craig stated simply, "Be yourself—you can watch others, but in the end, you have to do it the way that's you." He followed this by admitting that, early in his career, he worried too much about how he was coming across, trying so hard to be better than he felt like he was. He said he wishes someone had told him, in a way that he could have deeply heard, not to take things too personally, not to sweat the small stuff, and to be himself. He highlighted authenticity as his key struggle throughout his life. As he has gained experience in the field, he has let himself be known, faults and all, essentially giving permission for others to do the same.

Two of his former students underscore this commitment to being authentic and encouraging others to do the same. Amber Pope, graduate clinic coordinator at Old Dominion University, observed that Craig's "relational style of mentorship reminds me of secure attachment—Craig used his comforting presence; engagement in my learning process; encouragement to work on my own; and demonstrations of trust, respect, and confidence in me to create a secure mentoring bond in which I felt understood, supported, and safe to explore and take risks that aided my development as a counselor educator, and to grow on my own as a person and professional. Thus, one of the main things I learned from Craig through his mentorship is how to trust and be confident in myself and my capabilities."

Bryce Hagedorn, now a professor at University of Central Florida, summed up Craig's impact on others: "Craig brings a commitment to excellence into everything he does, yet his humility and quiet passion for people are what you notice first and foremost. Sit down with this man, share a cup or two of coffee, and really get to know how he sees God, his loved ones, his work, and his past times . . . you will find yourself influenced by his words and drawn toward wanting to be a better person."

Jodi L. Tangen's Final Reflections

Craig S. Cashwell is a quietly humble man, led by a heart for service. He actively encourages his students to state what they need, and he works in ways that support *their* professional development. One of his practices that stands out for me is that he highlights students' names in his curriculum vita. Such a small—but poignant—act underscores his humble leadership and mentorship spirit. Furthermore, he recognizes and acknowledges his vulnerabilities, giving students permission to be real and make mistakes along the way. At one point, I remember him telling me, "Remember from the *Velveteen Rabbit*, once you are real, you can never be ugly . . . except to those who do not understand." He acknowledges that the professional journey is characterized by periods of confusion and self-doubt, and he humbly shares his experiences, normalizing the process along the way.

Even more than his humility, Craig's deep compassion epitomizes the spirit of his leadership. One specific incident, for me, truly exemplifies the extent of his compassion. After the spring of my second year in the doctoral program, I found myself struggling, both personally and professionally. Having completed both my written and oral comprehensives that semester and enduring a number of stressful personal challenges, I began to question everything—the profession, the direction of my life, and myself most of all. It was in the midst of this existential crisis that I walked into Craig's office for our weekly dissertation meeting. His response to me that day can best be illustrated by Maya Angelou's famous quote, "People will forget what you said, people will forget what you did, but people will never forget how you made them feel." I will never forget the soft, inquiring compassion in his eyes that day . . . the feeling that he truly understood . . . and the way he patiently listened and gently guided me toward greater self-care. I will never forget the way he followed up with me, encouraged me to find my own internal compass, and helped me use my experiences as a professional launching pad. And perhaps most of all, I will never forget the way he seemed to believe in my potential after such an experience of raw personal vulnerability. Sometimes, if we are lucky, we are graced with the presence of someone who truly changes the course of our lives and teaches us lessons from a place we never even could have imagined. Craig has done that for me, and for that, I am eternally grateful.

Craig S. Cashwell simply does what's right—he creates safety for increased authenticity, offers compassion for those who are downtrodden, and inspires us all to become better people. In this regard, Craig is, as Spencer G. Niles called him, "the best in our profession." He leads from a compelling desire to serve, works tirelessly behind the scenes to embolden others, and shuns the spotlight. When praised for his work, he casts his eyes downward and speaks simply of his gratitude for others. He is, in the truest sense of the phrase, a man of quiet integrity.

Notable Accomplishments

2014–2015	President of CSI International
2008–2010	CACREP board chair
2007–2008	CACREP vice chair
2010–2013	ACES representative to the ACA Governing Council
2003–2004	President of ASERVIC
2016	ACA David K. Brooks Distinguished Mentor Award
2016–2019	Journal editor of ASERVIC journal *Counseling and Values*
2018	ACA Thomas J. Sweeney Award for Visionary Leadership and Advocacy
2018–2020	Chair of the Counseling and Educational Development Department at UNCG

Chapter 8

M. Sylvia Fernandez

Christine Sacco-Bene

Mentee's Introduction

I, Christine Sacco-Bene, met M. Sylvia Fernandez when I was a "newly minted PhD" starting my first position as a faculty member. Sylvia, also then a mother of two young children, let me know that it was perfectly acceptable to put my family above my career trajectory, that there is room for both, and that they grow at different rates throughout the career journey. This was a stark difference from the experience of my peers at other institutions who were being thrust into the "publish or perish" of academia. Almost 15 years later, I am so thankful for having that time with my family, because it is time I can never replace, and now I am having fun entering leadership roles with a fresh perspective. Learning from her journey, who she is, and what she brings to relationships, I am thankful for Sylvia's guidance in helping me find the first stepping stones of my own journey as a leader and advocate.

M. Sylvia Fernandez's Journey

Early Years and Career Path

M. Sylvia Fernandez was shaped by a number of institutions—family, school, and church, and the characteristic of being a member of multiple minority groups. Sylvia, the first of eight children and third of 28 grandchildren, was born in Trivandrum, India, but raised in Kuala Lumpur, Malaysia. From her first institution, her family, the message she received about being a woman was that women were meant to be wives and mothers; if they worked, it was only to supplement their husband's income. Her mother was a homemaker and her aunts who worked did so only to provide a very small second income. Her father, aligning to Malaysian social norms that abided by the patriarchal perspective at the time, did not expect much more from his four daughters. As the eldest female, Sylvia was tasked with the role of caregiver for her younger siblings and cousins. In this role, she was expected to be a role model and to set an example. She was supposed to be the one to give in; take a one-down position; and, most important, make the sacrifice for those in her care. These internalized expectations are evident in her style of leading from behind.

In her early schooling in Malaysia, Sylvia learned to work hard without looking at the boundaries set by her world, including gender-specific primary and secondary schools and being in the shadow of her well-known father, a respected school principal. The gender-specific schools reinforced the notions of relying on support within gender and being groomed for specific roles while perpetuating gender inequality and differentiated expectations. In addition, Sylvia and her siblings were always mindful of their actions because their father, being a school principal, would ultimately hear about it if they got into any mischief. These boundaries contributed to Sylvia being shy and living her life under the radar, but they did not stop her from doing her best academically and having fun with friends.

The expectations placed on her by her family blended into her life at school, the second institution of influence. Sylvia was often a "volunteer" in the jobs that no one wanted, or the one to "keep the ball rolling," and soon became known as the go-to person. When she was in secondary school, which was patterned after the British system, students were elected to be prefects (peers who maintained "law and order" in the school). To her surprise, being rather shy, Sylvia found herself not only on the slate of teacher-nominated students but also elected by her peers to be a prefect. This was the first time that others saw her leadership potential, even though she did not see it at the time. This became a running theme for Sylvia throughout her early journey; it took an overt statement from one of her supervisors years later for her to realize that not all leaders have to be seen front and center. Rather, they can inspire and work with others.

Sylvia was raised in a Catholic home, and it was from this third institution of church that she began to understand and live the constructs of service to and for others, working for the greater good, standing up for the underdog, and speaking for the voiceless. Humility and non-attention-seeking were instilled. She started serving as a lector when she was in high school, and when she went off to college on the other side of the world (United States), church kept her grounded in her new environment. She served in different capacities in numerous ministries, which she continues to do to this day. Being an international student, Sylvia used this as an opportunity to infuse her Malaysian culture into church celebrations.

Being a member of multiple minority groups further influenced Sylvia and shaped the woman she is today. As an Asian Indian growing up in Malaysia, she was considered an ethnic minority. The parameters of growing up in a paternalistic society in which being female was "strike one" and being an Indian was "strike two" did not hold her back; rather, they guided, motivated, and pushed her to go as high as she could academically and professionally. Sylvia and her sisters, breaking through the barriers and limitations set for them as young girls, excelled academically and, among them, hold one doctorate, two master's degrees, and five bachelor's degrees (Sylvia has two bachelor's degrees, one in English education to honor her father and one in psychology so she could follow her passion).

When Sylvia was in college, her minority status was not always at the forefront because the institution she attended was multiethnic and multinational. It was not until she began her career in academia that she recognized her status as a minority group member more clearly and resonantly. She began her career at a time when the social construct of multiculturalism was gaining a foothold in the profession. She wondered if she was now the token faculty member, as both an Indian and a woman, and she struggled with that for the first 10 years of her career. Nonetheless, those struggles didn't prevent her from educating others about diversity in a nonthreatening way. Sylvia succeeded in doing this as a faculty member in the rural South because she did not share the same historical baggage with her students; she brought them new understanding.

Early in her academic career, Sylvia found herself on the frontline of advocacy when she was pregnant with her first child and asserted her right to take 6 weeks of maternity leave. Even though two male faculty had recently welcomed the birth of a child to their own families, her department, for the first time, was faced with accommodating a parental leave of absence. Sylvia's self-advocacy challenged the unspoken expectation, in the male-dominated academic environment, that faculty should focus on their career and scholarship, not family. These experiences strengthened her resolve to bring about social justice and tear down barriers experienced by minorities and women. Throughout her career as a counselor educator, she unwittingly served as a role model for the female students she taught and those she encountered at conferences, demonstrating what they could aspire to be as a woman: a wife, a mother, an educator, and a leader. Although women can be all those things simultaneously, she conveyed a message to them that there are trade-offs and there is a need to find a balance within which they can live and thrive.

Sylvia became "hooked" on counseling while she was in her master's degree program at Southern Illinois University at Carbondale (SIU-C) in the mid-1980s. She was offered a graduate assistantship working with at-risk undergraduate students, and after completing her master's degree, she moved directly into her doctoral program in counselor education in the same department. She came under the mentorship of M. Harry Daniels, who was her major professor and who piqued her interest in teaching at the college level. What started as a required teaching internship became an additional year of teaching master's students. Later, at the gentle insistence of Mike Altekruse, an icon in the Association for Counselor Education and Supervision (ACES), Sylvia became a regular guest presenter in his multicultural counseling class and then a presenter at the first national ACES conference in St. Louis. Karen Prichard, who had been one of Sylvia's first instructors in her master's program, encouraged her to convert her master's thesis into an article, which was published in the *Journal of Multicultural Counseling and Development* in 1988. Now moving closer to her role within counselor education, Sylvia was introduced to leadership by Beverly Brown (Association for Specialists in Group Work [ASGW] president, 1996–1997). Sylvia served as cochair of the newly created ASGW International Relations Committee for 3 years. Her master's and doctoral program faculty were her role models for professional service and leadership.

Pivotal Moments

Sylvia's professional journey in counseling and into leadership, by action and position, has been punctuated by a series of significant events, experiences, and accomplishments. Her caregiving roles in her family, her peer support roles during primary and secondary school, her faith, and her positions (tutor, peer support provider, mentor) in the international student community during her college years all required her to understand people, to help them and herself navigate life, to empower and be empowered, and to find a voice that served to further strengthen her disposition. Her success with one-on-one relationships made her want to widen that reach, which is what led her to academia with the goal of preparing frontline professionals in the community.

Sylvia attended SIU-C at a time when the university had made a strategic decision to increase its international student population. Being among the early international student cohorts and working at the library on campus, she befriended many international students when they first arrived. In her volunteer role as an ambassador for the Office of International Services, she assisted students in navigating the new cultures of the university and the rural United States. The caregiver in her provided the support these students needed when they were homesick or felt displaced, but she also provided encouragement in times of celebration. International students from all over the world seemed to gravitate to her.

In 1989, Sylvia began her teaching career in the Psychology, Education and Social Sciences Division at Arkansas College (now Lyon College); and in 1992, she accepted a position in the Department of Psychology and Counseling at Arkansas State University. It was during her 11 years in Arkansas that she grew into her professional service in organizations relevant to counselor preparation and quality assurance. Beyond the service to her university and teaching core courses for students in the school counseling and rehabilitation counseling programs, Sylvia became involved in the Northeast Arkansas School Counseling Association, most notably as the newsletter coeditor. In 1995, she was appointed to colead the Strategic Planning Committee for the Arkansas Association for Counselor Education and Supervision, which naturally evolved into service in Arkansas ACES, first as its treasurer and then as president (1996–1998). Her service to Arkansas ACES was the beginning of her leadership in the counseling profession.

Her service and outreach went into action within the community in which she lived, when, on March 24, 1998, at Westside Middle School in Craighead County, Arkansas, a school shooting occurred, killing four female students and one teacher and wounding 10 others. Sylvia became immersed in the mental health response with the families and the teachers at the school, school counselors within the school district, students enrolled in the counseling program where she was on faculty, and the first responders. This response occurred both immediately after the event and during the long-term healing of the community. It was this tragic experience and the need for policy and perspective changes in the field of counseling in Arkansas that prompted Sylvia to move beyond her professional service in the state to the national arena. She became engaged in professional associations and credentialing and accreditation boards. Sylvia did not see herself as a leader; rather, she saw herself as a doer.

Sylvia was recognized for her work with Arkansas ACES, and she was appointed by the then-governor to a 3-year term on the Arkansas Board of Examiners in Counseling, serving as its chair for two of those years (1997 and 1998). Her attention to detail and order led Sylvia to serve with the Arkansas Counseling Association, first as the By-Laws Committee chair where she spearheaded the organization's major revisions of their bylaws. She subsequently served 2 years of the president rotation (president-elect, president) from 1998 to 2000. Her involvement in volunteer leadership afforded her an appreciation for and experience with many stakeholders in counseling-related professional organizations. In 2000, she and her family moved to Florida, where she solidified her role as a counselor educator and as an academic leader within the university setting and ventured into the national counseling service arena.

While at Barry University in Miami Shores, Florida, Sylvia served on numerous university committees at the program, departmental, and university levels. She was devoted to her students, challenging them within a climate of support. To Sylvia, the role of a counselor educator is to motivate students to open themselves up to new ideas and practices and to nurture students' personal and professional growth. She used this same skill set to motivate faculty, to mentor and encourage the individuality of each faculty member to try new things by scaffolding them until they had the confidence to continue and flourish.

She was named department chair at a time of crisis for the counseling program. Successfully moving beyond the crisis, she grew the program in terms of enrollment, securing initial accreditation by the Council on Accreditation of Counseling and Related Programs (CACREP) for the PhD program; ensuring reaccreditation of the master's specializations; and, for multiple consecutive years, gaining national recognition for their Chi Sigma Iota chapter. Sylvia's personal belief in servant leadership and commitment to action is exemplified in her work and professional service. Her steadfast dedication to her students was also realized in her success in bridging academics and the mental health needs of the community by expanding the services of the counseling program's on-site clinic to include a full range of educational diagnostics, interventions, and mental health support services that addressed the needs of the diverse South Florida community. While fully engaged at the university as a counselor educator and an advocate for providing services to the underserved, she was serving the counseling profession at the national level.

Although these leadership positions were integral to her developing into the leader she is today, she never considered any of them as particularly noteworthy. As a servant leader, she considered each of them as a way to simply commit to being of service and making a difference. Yet, in retrospect, she realizes they were pivotal to her leadership development. The lessons she shares about leadership from her engagement are to live in the moment, be in service of others, utilize one's gifts and talents, and start something that will live beyond your role and involvement.

Points of Pride

Sylvia has left her mark on every organization and in every place that she has been, and her influence has led to permanent change. At the state level, during her tenure with Arkansas ACES, she facilitated the momentum toward legislation for licensure for marriage and family therapists. With subsequent support and advocacy by Arkansas ACES and the Arkansas Counseling Association, among others, this effort came to fruition, and Sylvia happened to be the chair of the Arkansas Board of Examiners in Counseling when the governor signed into law the licensure for marriage and family therapists.

Sylvia's engagement in national leadership has ranged from professional association committees to credentialing and accreditation boards. It was during her tenure with the National Board for Certified Counselors (NBCC) that her actions reached across multiple countries and influenced other leaders across the world.

From 2000 to 2006, she served on the NBCC board for two 3-year terms. She was an officer for 3 years, including being its chair at a time when the NBCC was entering the global arena. During her service as chair, the first NBCC international office opened in Mexico at the Universidad Iberoamericana in Santa Fe in January 2006; and, in collaboration with the World Health Organization, NBCC developed the mental health facilitator program. Sylvia then went on to lead the newly formed NBCC international board of directors for 3 years, a board that was constituted of members from all over the world. The highlight during these years was travel to 22 countries, meeting with leaders of governmental and nongovernmental organizations, advocating for the professionalization of counseling, and presenting at international conferences.

Then, in 2010, Sylvia became engaged in accreditation when she was elected to a 5-year term on the CACREP board of directors, serving for 3 years as its chair. She shares that the true highlight of these years was the affiliation of CACREP with the Council on Rehabilitation Education (CORE) and their subsequent merger, which was not easy to achieve but was important in unifying the counseling profession. In her role as CACREP board chair under then-CEO Carol Bobby, she participated in negotiating the merger agreement and then served on the CACREP-CORE Merger Implementation Task Force from 2015 to 2017. Attending to the issues, challenges, and opportunities this merger presented, she worked collaboratively with rehabilitation counseling professionals, the true experts in the rehabilitation field, to obtain their input and insights, hear their concerns, and build alliances. Although many have served on both boards, Sylvia is particularly proud of the fact that she is the only person who has served as board chair of both NBCC and CACREP.

Sylvia left academia in 2018 to begin service as the president and CEO of CACREP, which seemed to be a natural progression of her leadership. When asked, Sylvia explains that every move she made in professional service has afforded her a wider reach of influence in the counseling profession. She has come into her leadership role with CACREP at a time of major transition in the profession. Long-standing leaders are retiring, shifts in academia are occurring, and influencing factors outside the counseling profession are gaining traction.

Leadership and Advocacy

Leading by doing is the hallmark of Sylvia's leadership style. The various institutions that influenced her early development helped to position her as a servant leader, a collaborative leader, and a transformative leader. Without taking on airs, she is not afraid of rolling up her sleeves to do what needs to be done, whether it involves negotiating with administrators for commitments of financial support or cleaning up after her administrative assistant's retirement party. Sylvia's leadership style, shaped by her early experiences, influences her ongoing interactions with others. When asked about her leadership style, Sylvia recounts that, although she may not see immediate results of her work, she takes pleasure in promoting long-term change by creating building blocks and scaffolding while promoting others' work. On her desk, as a constant reminder, is a gift given for her years of service as president of the Arkansas Counseling Association. Engraved on this figurine of a soaring eagle is "Leadership is Action. Not Position."

Her kindness, friendship, mentoring, and devotion to the counseling profession have left an impression on her students and colleagues. Sylvia celebrates the achievements of others and does not boast about her own accomplishments. For example, at an ACES conference some time ago, I was introducing Sylvia to a long-time friend as my boss and chair of the department. Sylvia quickly modified the introduction, stating that she was my colleague. She is trusted, level-headed, and insightful. She is demanding and supportive at the same time, whether with students, faculty, or the boards she directs.

One of Sylvia's former students, Cindy George, at the International College of the Cayman Islands, shared that the guidance she received from Sylvia enabled her to recognize her true value as a professional to any institution or organization. As a mentor, Sylvia encourages others to define what leadership is to them, not what is "expected" by the field. Her servant leadership, which embodies collaborative and transformative principles, guides her work. She rolls up her sleeves, listens to others' points of view, and builds opportunities to further strengthen and promote the counseling profession.

In reflecting on the influences on her leadership development and history of leadership, Sylvia has come to recognize and appreciate her skill set and disposition, which allow her to make a difference in the lives of others. She is appreciative of all the people (family, friends, professional colleagues, and students) who have been a significant part of her life. These are the people who led her to develop interactional and management skills and who dared her to take steps into the unknown and outside her comfort zone, to protect people when they were vulnerable and to support them in their own growth. She learned to listen to what people said about how they experienced her and what she does. She continues to pay attention to these perspectives to understand the ways she can be intentional in her endeavors. This is one of the characteristics that has most informed my own mentor-mentee relationship with her. When I was starting in the field of counselor education, if a thought came up, it came right out. Sylvia, in her quiet and unassuming way, fostered the valuable skill of stepping back to see the big picture, to slow down, and not to express an immediate reaction or response. At times, quick problem solving is essential, but far more issues resolve successfully when patience is part of the process. Patience allows for others to seek their own resolutions, to be creative, and to act as the expert in what works best for them and their situation. The people and organizations that gave her a chance to participate and contribute to their respective missions highlighted the need for an ongoing focus and direction. This is what continues to serve her in her leadership, asking "to what end and as defined by whom?" It must never be about her. She has learned to use her skill and disposition as the tool with which to lead, advocate, and serve.

To Sylvia, being a leader and an advocate is about being a change agent and being willing to lead from behind. Mahatma Gandhi famously said, "Be the change you want to see in the world." Sylvia takes that sentiment to heart. As she stated, "We live in a growing, complex society that is sometimes integrated very tenuously. It is isomorphic to the counseling profession. The mental health needs of society are complex and wide in scope, yet the basic human needs are still the same." She acknowledged that specialized training is needed to work with a wide range of client populations, yet the fundamental counseling principles and skills remain the same. "Both in society and in the counseling profession, we lose perspective by only looking at either 'the forest or the trees' and forgetting that we cannot focus on just one in the absence of the other."

Sylvia explained that leaders and advocates must be bridge builders:

> A bridge spans some sort of divide or chasm and connects two points to allow for movement from one point to the other. A bridge builder must first assess the divide/chasm, then determine the best structure that will most effectively connect the two points and be sustainable. The builder may never know or see the beneficiaries of that bridge. A leader in the counseling profession must assess what is separating us—philosophy, specialty practice, parity recognition—and determine what two points to connect. Each professional counseling organization has its own respective mission, but these missions are not mutually exclusive. Leaders seek to find the points of mutual interest and find ways to collaborate (the bridge) to allow movement across. The collaboration is what allows the movement to be to the mutual benefit of both organizations in the present and for the future. That is only the first step. Plans and action must then be developed and instituted that will allow for gains made to be sustained. Every sustainable bridge takes time and careful planning. The existence of the bridge is what's important, not who built it. Many bridges exist in this world that people recognize and can even name, but they are not always able to tell you who built it—and that's OK.

According to Sylvia, what others do not readily see is that leaders have a personal or organizational vision, and they have to patiently take small steps toward it while navigating the constant changes in society and staying within the structures in which they operate. Bridge building requires collaboration, negotiation, and compromise. A transformative leader must also have relational and transactional characteristics. As is true in working with clients, it is important that a trusting relationship is established, that clear goals are set with achievable objectives, and that the work is a social influencing process with the final outcome being sustainable change.

Sylvia pointed out another element that others may not see and that is the hardest to accomplish—to be transparent. Transparency is an ideal that is sought, but it requires both responsibility and vulnerability. When information is made available, the recipient has to determine how it is going to be used, and the source becomes vulnerable depending on how that information is used. Transparency can lead to better trust or further divide. Sylvia chooses to be transparent. "A philosophy and practice I live by is that I would never ask someone to do something I wouldn't do myself. Therefore, if I expect someone to be transparent, I have to be transparent first." For Sylvia, as a leader, setting direction must be a collaborative process, as identifying individuals' talents and paving ways for them to thrive ensures sustainability and transformation.

The Future of Counseling

Sylvia noted that the counseling profession emerged to meet a specific need, and the growth of specialized practice followed the same pattern of response to specific client populations and targeted societal needs. She believes that the more specialized the response, the more fragmented we became. Her concern is that "we have lost perspective by only looking at either 'the trees or the forest,' that is, specialties versus the counseling profession as a whole. Fragmented, we are weak and vulnerable to external threats; we need to continue in the direction of being a unified profession."

Therefore, Sylvia believes, we need to find the common denominator of who we are as counselors, be it in philosophy, mission, practice, or action. That common denominator will serve as the scaffolding and bridge between specialty areas of practice and professional organizations. Sylvia is optimistic that we can rediscover that common denominator and build new bridges or shore up the old ones. The difficult part, she thinks, will be to operationalize that, so that we are clear in describing who counselors are and what we do; what the national minimum standard of preparation for practice is; and how we regulate practice using an agreed-upon national core to include accreditation, credentialing, and a code of ethics. All components of this core already exist but are not similarly adopted across the country; therefore, no common denominator exists. "When this collective adoption happens," Sylvia predicts that "the counseling profession will be a stronger profession and will have a strong voice with legislators, a variety of third parties, and clients. This unified voice will allow the profession to be a change agent in the lives of not only clients but also in the lives of practicing professional counselors and counselor educators."

Words of Wisdom

Sylvia entered her master's program with a clear idea of what she wanted to do—be a counselor. She did not know with whom she would be working, because her plan was to return to Malaysia where counseling was not yet recognized as a profession. At the end of her master's program, she chose to continue into a doctoral program because she feared she would miss an opportunity if she were to return home at that time. Entering the doctoral program, she did not fully understand the scope of what was available to her and said that she could have used more information.

> Entering with the mindset of a practitioner, I expected that I was going to gain advanced knowledge and skills. What I wish I knew then was the variety of activities I could become engaged in other than a clinician, such as administrator, policy maker, consultant, or a trainer. I wish I knew then, that if I got into higher education, the choices I would have with regard to type of institutions with regard to teaching and research priorities, and the expectations of a faculty member besides teaching. I wish I knew then what it meant to be a focused researcher in terms of methodology and collaborations. I was fortunate that the professional service piece was very clear to me from every single one of my professors not only being engaged in service but also in leadership. Fortunately, many of my "I wish" statements are now built in to doctoral-level preparation because of the CACREP doctoral standards, the range of instructional and service delivery methods, and the maturing of the counseling profession.

Because a large part of Sylvia's career has been as an educator, she would first like to share words of wisdom with graduate students. She wants them to know that "who you are as a counselor and a leader is an embodiment of who you are as a person. While you are learning the theory and skill of the counseling profession, learn about who you are. Try things that push your own boundaries, take risks while you have faculty and supervisors to support you, and engage in activities that benefit someone else." She further urges graduate students to use their course assignments as a vehicle to research new topics and fully engage in experiential activities; use their practicum and internship to find their fervor for service and to which populations; and participate in professional and community service activities. She added, "Find your passion, whether it is a topic or a client population or an advocacy project."

Sylvia's words of wisdom to practitioners in the field are to remember that "you make a difference in the lives of individuals and families, and through your work you not only have a skill set but a wealth of knowledge. Share that knowledge through presentations and publications, connect with universities to be a guest lecturer, teach a course, or collaborate in research—you have much to contribute to the preparation of the next generation of counselors."

Sylvia concluded by sharing her advice for counselor educators. "Continue to sustain the passion that got you into higher education, continue to instill that same passion in your students, model for and partner with your students in scholarship and professional service, in spite of the institutional expectations of faculty that can be wearying." She urged leaders in the profession to "continue to stay true to your personal and professional vision and mission, always find ways to collaborate and support each other, create bridges and scaffolds so that the work you start will continue and sustain the profession. It is who we are and what we do that matters, not the position we hold."

The practices that have served Sylvia well as a leader are leading by doing, being transparent, encouraging others to try new things and not be afraid, making a difference in the system, always being collaborative and compromising, and creating building blocks and scaffolds through which others can thrive.

Christine Sacco-Bene's Final Reflections

Mentoring is all about learning and growing. This does not mean that a mentor has all the answers but that she has the experience to share to guide another. I was lucky to receive the gift of Sylvia Fernandez's mentorship. Sylvia and I had a bit in common when we first met at the beginning of my academic career: being mothers of young children, having fidelity to the Catholic faith, and wanting to see the field of counseling grow together and not apart. She shared her experiences and some stories, but mostly she shared her support and guidance. Although a mentoring relationship is often short-term, I have turned to Sylvia for direction at various times throughout my professional career. Now, I would be lying if I said that we never had disagreements. In fact, there were times when I would take a stand for students (or just because) that inevitably ended with my "hand getting slapped" by the administration. Her patience and tutelage helped me to step back, to look at varying perspectives, and to think through the implications of taking the stand as an immediate reaction. This is an important skill for a leader in learning to better engage and serve.

From the beginning of my journey as an educator, I was "coached" toward administration. My organizational skills and ability to see both detailed information as well as the "big picture" served me well in this area. However, because of Sylvia's encouragement and guidance, I engaged in working internationally and am now transitioning from an administrative focus in counselor education to more of a teaching and professional engagement role. As I start this next leg of my career journey, I know I can depend on my friend, colleague, and mentor to support and listen to me and offer guidance from time to time. I have come to understand leadership through my relationship with Sylvia. She works tirelessly to benefit the field of counseling, educators, students, and community, yet she gives credit to all those with whom she works and collaborates. She rolled up her sleeves to lead and serve. Her contributions have made significant changes in state, national, and international landscapes with regard to counseling practice and policy. Now she holds an integral role to continue these efforts as president and CEO of CACREP.

Her work has significantly influenced what constitutes leadership for me, especially in the field of counseling. As a leader in counselor education, I believe I have an ethical obligation to attend to the needs and concerns of those I serve: students, community, and profession. In so doing, advocating for one group should not be at the expense of another group, nor should it compromise the integrity of the profession. Sylvia learned from her institutions—family, school, and church—the importance of becoming and serving as a leader and of bringing in the personhood of the leader as a tool for connecting with others. It was from her mentors and through her experiences that she learned how to lead through action. My journey is my own, and I am so thankful to Sylvia for letting me know that it is OK to stay on my own path, to act in my own way, no matter my position.

Notable Accomplishments

1998–1999	President-elect and conference chair, Arkansas Counseling Association
1999–2000	President, Arkansas Counseling Association
2003–2008	Board of directors, NBCC International
2010–2015	Board of directors, Council for Accreditation of Counseling and Related Educational Programs (CACREP)
2013–2015	Psychology and Counselling Standards Committee, University Council of Jamaica, Kingston, Jamaica
2015–2017	CACREP-CORE merger implementation team
	Raising two wonderful sons

Chapter 9

Samuel Templeman Gladding

D. Robert Casares Jr.

Mentee's Introduction

Samuel Templeman (Sam) Gladding's mentorship has energized and encouraged me, D. Robert Casares Jr., throughout the 3 years we have worked together at Wake Forest University. As a new professional with a background in family counseling and an interest in advancing creative clinical approaches, I found that receiving guidance and mentorship from Sam is certainly fortuitous and surreal. Sam is generous, tenacious, and humble. His consistency and level of productivity are rare and undeniable, but the magnitude of his talents and achievements are routinely obscured by his unassuming demeanor and self-deprecating humor. Consequently, Sam has influenced my professional growth and development most profoundly through seemingly unremarkable moments and mundane circumstances. He arrives to work at the same time each day, filled with enthusiasm and optimism. Sam writes every morning (and most afternoons), unconcerned with word or page count. I used to ask myself how one person could publish more than 50 books, and looking out of my office and into Sam's one day, the answer was evident: one sentence, one paragraph, one morning at a time. More important, Sam values people over tasks. He is never too busy to listen, support, or affirm. He sees the best in each of his students and colleagues and, with warmth and humor, challenges each of us to be better. Inspiring by example and practicing what he preaches are the hallmarks of Sam's leadership style. Unsurprisingly, it is in the day-to-day duties and person-to-person exchanges where Sam's leadership and true greatness are on full display.

Samuel Templeman Gladding's Journey

Early Years and Career Path

Samuel Templeman Gladding, the youngest of three children, grew up in the Atlanta suburb of Decatur, Georgia. Sam's father, Russell, was a local businessperson, and his mother, Gertrude, taught fourth grade. His parents were hardworking and altruistic people who valued service and were actively involved in their local church and community. Sam credits his modest upbringing and his parents' example of humility and hard work as influences on his leadership philosophy and style:

> My family was less than affluent. However, before Robert Greenleaf coined the term "servant leadership," my family practiced it. They believed in giving to others because they thought it was the right thing to do. They did it through a number of formal and informal means. Both my parents had democratic styles and tried to teach by example. They emphasized to my siblings and me that we should go to college and give back to the world.

Soon after Sam was born, it was discovered that he had dislocated hips, and he spent a good deal of time during the first 2 years of his life in the nearby Scottish Rite Hospital, having a total of three operations to "wire" his hips back in place. Afterward, he had a somewhat adventurous life in the family's house on Church Street living with his parents, siblings, and maternal grandmother, the widow of Samuel Templeman, a Baptist minister for whom Sam had been named. He was described by his mother as "a daredevil," which Sam later reframed as "adventuresome." The end result, in either case, was that Sam needed emergency medical care twice before the age of 5, once after accidentally being hanged and once after knocking himself unconscious while trying to ride his tricycle down the family's front porch steps and landing headfirst in a cement barrel.

Sam soon faced another challenge due to a central auditory processing disorder that resulted in Sam being unable to hear distinct sounds well and thus not being able to pronounce words properly. A bit horrified that he could not pronounce the word "school," his parents almost did not let him go; they were resigned to the fact that Sam was a poor speller, reader, and speaker and could not sound out words phonetically. Nevertheless, Sam went to school and worked hard to keep up—he was what he called "persistent" and his mother called "stubborn." Sam liked people, and they liked him; and from an early age, Sam had a desire to serve as a leader.

Given his language disability, Sam was almost immediately confronted with the vulnerable nature of leadership, which required more than goodwill. Reflecting on the initial challenges he encountered as an aspiring leader, Sam stated:

> I realized early in my life, especially as a preteen, that leadership is hard work. You need to be prepared. It is not something you learn to do overnight. For example, the first time I got up to give a speech at age 11, a girl in the audience laughed. The next thing I knew, an adult leader was escorting me quickly out of the room because I teared up. After that experience, I learned to keep my cool and be well prepared. It paid off.

Sam made up for his deficiency in language by using a combination of rote memory and asking for help with pronunciations. He also remained flexible and developed a sense of humor. Later, in high school and college, his classmates recognized his work ethic and lightheartedness and elected him to positions of leadership in student government. Sam also took the initiative to work on campus publications.

Sam has always exhibited a deep reverence for history and, in particular, for the traditions and legacy of his ancestors, and his personal development and professional aspirations have been deeply influenced by the courage of his maternal grandfather. What Samuel Templeman did in life had a profound effect on Sam growing up, especially the story about how his grandfather stopped the lynching of an African American man in the Jim Crow South of the 1920s. He courageously stood in front of the jail with the sheriff and talked down an angry mob. The ethos of the Templeman family emphasized that life and leadership are about working for the common good and doing good.

Sam earned an undergraduate degree in history from Wake Forest University, and his desire to serve then led him to Yale Divinity School in hopes of becoming an ordained minister. His time at Yale in the late 1960s and early 1970s was marked by dramatic social change in the United States. This period was both influential and instructive, inspiring Sam to become active in various social causes, especially anti-war and civil rights struggles. Sam not only participated in marches but also went to Washington to talk to his senators about these matters. His actions eventually generated an unexpected realization. Despite his love for Yale Divinity School and all it stood for, he was not going to be a minister. It was not his calling. In the midst of wrestling with what was next, he took a counseling-related course. One of the requirements was to find someone who was in pain and to try to help in any way possible. One of his friends introduced him to a man whose son had just been killed in the Vietnam War. Every Monday night for a semester, Sam spent 2 hours with the man, listening and reflecting on his grief and pain. That experience was difficult, but it helped him realize that he had an interest in mental health.

Sam was unsure about which career path he should pursue, so he stopped at Wake Forest University on his way to Atlanta on spring break to talk with Tom Elmore (dean of students) who had befriended him as an undergraduate. "I gave him my twenty-something existential angst about what I was going to do next since I was not going to be a minister. He said, 'Why don't you try counseling?' I thought he meant try counseling as a profession. He actually meant I should get some counseling. My misunderstanding resulted in my enrollment in the counseling program at Wake Forest the next year. It was a perfect fit."

Sam's graduate studies at Wake Forest provided formative experiences and were instrumental in initiating his early career endeavors and successes. Sam expressed fondness and gratitude for Tom Elmore's positive influence in his life at that time. "He was a good teacher and helped me tremendously in writing my master's thesis and revising it, so the paper was accepted for presentation at the American Psychological Association conference in 1972 in Honolulu. Tom believed I could formulate questions worth exploring, research them, and write."

Sam completed his counseling degree in 1971 and began working as a counselor in rural Rockingham County, North Carolina. His early years as a novice clinician had their difficulties, moments of growth and insight, and a few laughs along the way:

> In a counseling situation early in my career, where I was struggling to help a resistant client make a change, I finally threw my hands up one day and told my client she had won. I then took off my shoes and gave her my socks. In the process, I told her that a counselor's socks were the equivalent of swords in antiquity that those vanquished in battle gave their adversaries. I had struggled, fought with all the counseling techniques I knew, but, alas, she had not changed and had been victorious.

The moment Sam handed her his socks, he recalled, changed the dynamic of their relationship—she was now in charge of her life in a way she had not been before. She was then able to laugh and cry and, eventually, to make some needed changes. Sam reflected on this insight: "The battle for structure, that we as counselors must win, was over; and the battle for initiative, that clients must win, had begun."

The next few years brought an array of personal and professional challenges but were incredibly productive and prolific. Even though Sam struggled in the aftermath of a broken engagement, he balanced the demands of his new clinical position with the training and responsibilities associated with his role in the Army Quartermaster Corps, when he was called up to fulfill his ROTC obligation in 1973. Sam credits his time in the Army with shaping some of his philosophy of leadership:

> In the Army was where, as an officer, I was involved in a number of leadership positions. Sometimes I struggled, since the troops I was in charge of did not always want to follow my orders. To combat the resistance, I practiced saying "we" instead of "me" or "you" whenever I could. For instance, I would jokingly say that the only time we used the word "you" was in talking about a female sheep, that is, a *ewe*. Humor helped break down resistance. I have found that to be true in a number of cases since.

After active duty, Sam began taking doctoral courses in counseling, psychology, and family life/human development at the University of North Carolina at Greensboro (UNCG). He transitioned from the mental health center, where he had returned, to becoming an instructor of psychology at the community college in Rockingham County in 1976. At the community college, he taught five sections of psychology each quarter, except for the summer. Although this work was demanding, he enjoyed it, and students seemed to like his classes. Twice they chose him to be their graduation speaker.

Sam earned his PhD from UNCG in 1977, and while taking classes, teaching classes, writing a dissertation, and playing tennis and sailing his Sunfish, he continued to publish numerous poems and a few articles in the *Journal of Counseling & Development* and elsewhere. Between 1979 and 1981, after a postdoctorate of 18 more semester hours in psychology at UNCG, Sam applied for dozens of counselor educator positions but received only three interviews and two offers. He was even rejected for an open position at Wake Forest University. Eventually, he accepted a position at Fairfield University and moved north to Connecticut. However, his first full-time position in counselor education was punctuated by departmental conflict and periods of loneliness and isolation: He did not know anyone, had unwelcoming neighbors, and it was a long, cold winter.

To combat the challenges he faced in the Nutmeg State, Sam played a game with himself. He pretended he was being held hostage, but his benevolent capturers had granted him paper and pencils with which to write every morning before going to work. He could also send his finished works off to an outlet for review. This is exactly what he did, and it was the start of his prolific rate of writing and publishing. In the 1980s alone, Sam had 40 refereed articles and 20 poems accepted in ACA journals, two new books published, and a film produced. Remarking on his ability to persevere and be productive during less than ideal times, Sam stated:

> I have always been optimistic within limits. I realized in high school I could never play football or basketball because of my size—5 feet, 2 inches, on a good day. I was also terrible at baseball, once telling friends that while my brother was a home run, I was strike three. However, I thought, "I can play tennis and I can swim." Therefore, I tried out and made both teams, lettering in each as well as being a manager for the football team. When one street closed, I would look for another avenue. That is what I did at Fairfield because other lanes were not open.

Traveling alternative routes has worked well for Sam. It has become his "go to" and his lifestyle. He believes in accepting the feedback he is given when he enters an activity. He evaluates it and then decides on his next steps. His optimism and determined style have had some funny moments, though. For instance, his oldest son, as a teenager, came to breakfast years ago, grumpy, frumpy, and lumpy, and said, "You know the problem with you, Dad?" to which Sam replied, "No." His son then responded, "Dad, the problem with you is you're too optimistic! You really think there is a pony in every pile of manure." This made Sam smile, confess the truth, and realize silently to himself that he had indeed found a lot of ponies.

When confronted with unexpected adversity, Sam has been quick to identify and acknowledge the blessings and bright spots in his life and to reevaluate and reframe these challenging circumstances. He recognizes that he has not experienced real hardships in his life, even though he has broken four bones, had a hip replacement, successfully fought prostate cancer, and survived an intestinal blockage that required two major operations. Sam recognizes real hardship as societal situations that leave people hungry, abused, or without opportunities because of the color of their skin or their gender. Sam has, however, navigated a number of challenges, such as being a clinician in an understaffed rural mental health center, working with his wife to raise three children when he was in his 40s and 50s, and being a mental health first responder after 9/11. All of these challenges have made him realize how fortunate he has been and how grateful he is for many aspects of life.

Sam does not take for granted his good health, a wonderful spouse, life energy, positive humor, and patience. He has come to see that life contains an abundance of possibilities, and he has found joy and a great deal of happiness. As he says with a grin, "I am not the 'smartest rabbit in the woods,' and I am not the Brad Pitt of men. However, somehow my life has been full of mostly good experiences. My glass has always been at least half-full. I am very blessed."

Pivotal Moments

Sam's professional accomplishments are particularly impressive and practically innumerable. He is quick to acknowledge, however, that others have played a huge part in his growth and success: "My favorite story growing up was *The Little Engine That Could*. I thought, like the little engine, that I could do almost anything. Thus, I kept working hard in school even though I was slow in processing information. I kept writing even though I could not spell. I was my own best self-advocate; I was not going to give up easily unless I found my goals impossible." Part of Sam's determination came from studying or hearing about people who had initial failures and kept trying, such as Thomas Edison or the Wright brothers. In addition to his belief in himself, other people believed in him before and after he entered the profession of counseling. As he has said, "I seem to have encountered a lot of people in my life who have been most gracious and affirming."

Sam's setbacks and missteps sparked many critical realizations and launched him on unanticipated pursuits.

> A story that illustrates an instructive misstep that taught me a major lesson occurred when I was on a panel at a conference. A woman in the audience came up afterward and said, "Who organized that panel?" I responded, "I did," to which she replied, "That was the worst panel I have ever heard." I was a bit dumbstruck and all I could do was apologize. While doing so, I thought, "I wonder what we could have done better?"

That moment helped Sam realize how foolish it is to take pride in presentations because they just might not go according to plan, and if they do go well, that is what should be expected.

Another of Sam's missteps occurred while he working full time at the mental health center and fell asleep while a client who had a monotone voice was speaking with him. He had no excuse other than that he was not totally engaged in the counseling process that day and could not seem to, as Sam describes it, "stay client-focused." His takeaway from that embarrassing experience was a resolve to be more active and confrontational and not to become sidetracked. Sam sees failure as a master teacher that instructs us in humbleness—but one we do not want to visit often. A better way to combat pretentiousness and to keep focused on what is important, according to Sam, is to remind ourselves regularly of what we are doing, what we are expecting, and what we have to do to achieve the best outcome.

Points of Pride

Sam has published an incredibly large number of poems and articles in refereed counseling journals, plus a plethora of book chapters. He is pleased with that achievement but also realizes it did not happen overnight, nor without a lot of effort. In reflecting on having published so prolifically, usually as either the first or the only author, Sam says part of the answer is in the game he started playing with himself when he was at Fairfield. He likes to write, and in his first two academic appointments, as a junior faculty member, he was assigned to teach more than 20 courses. Thus, he learned a lot about almost all aspects of counseling. He was thrilled and surprised to find that he was in the top 1% of contributors to the flagship journal of the American Counseling Association (ACA), the *Journal of Counseling & Development*, for the 15-year period from 1978 to 1993. Also noteworthy is that he has published 17 books, most of which are now in multiple editions and three are in their seventh and eighth editions. Overall, Sam has had 35 revisions of his texts. "I have especially fond memories of the years 1982 to 1987 when I had 31 articles (and 15 poems) accepted into refereed counseling journals and advanced from assistant to full professor in 6 years." Sam's scholarship is amazingly diverse and includes quantitative, qualitative, and conceptual pieces on a variety of topics: family counseling, group counseling, ethics, creativity, spirituality, social justice, and mental health.

Another of Sam's accomplishments is in cinematography. He remembers getting a grant for his first film in 1989 when he was at the University of Alabama at Birmingham (UAB; 1984–1990), his second academic institution after Fairfield

(1981–1984). He knew nothing about grant writing, but he came across a foundation he thought would give him a grant: "They did, and I made a film, *Uses of Metaphors and Poetry in Counseling*. Like most of my films outside of those I have made with ACA, this video is distributed by ProQuest. Although not an Academy Award contender, the film has good information. I made it in collaboration with the UAB School of Dentistry film crew (and no teeth were extracted in the process). I was inexperienced as a filmmaker and memorized all my lines, which were numerous." Sam has since written and produced about a dozen films, including the latest, a 25-minute humorous animated film titled *Adventures in Mental Health*. In this 2019 production, Sandy Dickson, in the documentary film program at Wake Forest, led him through the process. Sam says, "It was more fun than work, and the film is now in major libraries worldwide."

Another accomplishment about which Sam is delighted relates to his year as ACA president (2004–2005) when the conference theme was "Counseling: A Creative Force in the Fiber of Life." In 1975, William Fry said that "counseling and creativity are very much together." According to Sam, Fry was right. "My writing about counseling and creativity goes back to the 1970s too, and in 1992, ACA published my book on this topic, *The Creative Arts in Counseling* (now in its sixth edition). Likewise, they promoted the conference theme. I believe that, because of the hard work of ACA, a greater awareness was raised about the part creativity plays in counseling."

A final accomplishment in which Sam takes some pride is his consistency, flexibility, and growth as a scholar and a leader over the five decades he has been in counseling. He has held one or more major leadership position in every decade except the 1970s, when he was just beginning his career. These positions include service as president of ACA and three of its divisions (Association for Specialists in Group Work, Association for Counselor Education and Supervision, and International Association of Marriage and Family Counselors), and president of Chi Sigma Iota, the Association of State Counseling Boards, and Leadership Winston-Salem. He has served as chair of the ACA Foundation and editor of the *Journal for Specialists in Group Work* as well. He has transitioned from writing poetry to producing films, and his books have been translated into a number of languages, including Russian, Chinese, Korean, Malaysian, Polish, Turkish, and Spanish. In addition, he has made presentations on counseling in 30 countries outside the United States and has received two Fulbright awards to China and Turkey. He has done all of this while nourishing a 35-year marriage, actively raising three children, serving in two high-level administrative positions at Wake Forest University (assistant to the president and associate provost), chairing Wake Forest's Department of Counseling, continuing to offer counseling services, and teaching.

Leadership and Advocacy

Humility is a quality that Sam exemplifies in his interactions with his students, colleagues, and collaborators. It constitutes the cornerstone of Sam's approach to leadership and service. Sam also values diverse perspectives and is eager to learn from others. He is creative, compassionate, and committed to ongoing improvement. Sam affirmed, "As counselors, we realize every individual is unique. In leadership, we need to be aware that no two situations are the same. Groups we lead influence us just as we influence them, and what is happening in the environment has a bearing on what we, and those who follow us, do." Although some skills may carry over from one situation to another, Sam contends that being a leader is always a new experience. Thus, it is important to be prepared—to take forward the best of what you have learned about leadership from previous experiences—and to be flexible.

Humor and creativity are synonymous with the leadership and the legacy of Samuel Templeman Gladding. He loves the humor of Roy Blount Jr., who went to his high school, but also the wit of Stephen Colbert, Ellen DeGeneres, Tina Fey, Jonathan Winters, Erma Bombeck, and Mark Twain. "Humor has always inspired and delighted me. I love the way humorists play with words and make the serious light, manageable, and digestible. Humor gives us perspective and opens up possibilities."

Stories have also inspired Sam. Growing up in the South, a region rich in storytelling, his life was filled with stories. Many were about actual people, although some were fictional lies, and almost all were fascinating and entertaining. Sam believes that "life is a series of stories, and when we knit people's stories together, we find the persons behind them." Sam also loves music and the way lyrics convey what people cannot always articulate. He is inspired by memorable lyrics as well as melodies. Singer-songwriters, including the Beatles, Simon and Garfunkel, the Eagles, James Taylor, and America, constantly play in his mind.

> I find music helps me relax. It is also a medium I use when trying to learn new material. I put different words to melodies I am familiar with in the same manner Albert Ellis and Weird Al Yankovic would. Most music I listen to has an upbeat rhythm. When I have tried to do something and failed, music reminds me that the beat of life goes on and [that] instead of feeling discouraged, I need to try again and hit the right notes. Thus, I will play music by a group like ABBA realizing you cannot listen to ABBA and be lethargic or depressed!

Sam's leadership style has evolved because of what he has learned from others who left their mark on counseling leadership. "People we admire have set exemplary examples of what a counseling leader should be, and their examples need to be honored and emulated. They are what I call 'balcony people.' They call us to a higher standard than we might imagine and to be better yet than we are. I have always liked reading and studying the lives of counseling pioneers. They give us a lot to think about and to strive for."

At Yale, Sam took a course on Søren Kierkegaard. He liked what he heard and did everything he could to learn more about existentialism, including taking a course with Rollo May at the New School in New York City. He also read Paul Tillich and Dag Hammarskjöld. "Existentialism came to be important in my leadership style; that is, helping a group find meaning and purpose in what they were doing in the now. In my graduate studies, I came to like Carl Rogers. I thought Rogers's style and techniques had much to commend them. I particularly liked how Rogers actively listened, reflected, and helped individuals find answers within themselves." Thus, Sam's philosophy of leadership became a combination of existentialism and Rogerian counseling—listening to people, as well as his inner self, and using proven evidence-based techniques to do meaningful work in the moment.

A common denominator that Sam found in the theorists he embraced was storytelling. Kierkegaard told stories from the past with both subtle and obvious moral endings. Rogers had clients tell their stories in the present and come to conclusions about what they were doing and could be doing. Thus, Sam contends, "in counseling, and as counselors in leadership positions, I believe we should ask others and ourselves about the stories we have lived and are creating. Are they positive, purposeful, and altruistic? If not, how could we make them that way?"

Through mental health organizations and ACA, Sam has assumed leadership positions on a number of levels. All of these experiences have been different, but they have all taught him philosophically and practically that leadership is an ever-evolving phenomenon and that different situations call for different leadership styles. Sam added that he likes James McGregor Burns's concept of transformational leadership, but he recognizes that not all leadership needs to be transformative.

Sam also values ongoing reflection and acknowledged that effective leadership requires taking an honest look at oneself, and at one's relationship to the world and to others, and embracing the sometimes demanding task of implementing corrective feedback.

> I think self-awareness is developmental. If we are prudent, we learn from our actions through corrective feedback and focus on who we are and what we are doing. I think the best way to do this is to ask ourselves process questions such as "Who am I?" (intrapersonal), "Who are you?" (interpersonal), and "Who are we together?" (the whole group). We also need to ask ourselves content questions such as "What do we have to do?" and "What do we need to do to accomplish our goals?" If we constantly ask ourselves these questions, we are more likely to be self-aware and good leaders.

Sam credits his early publications and successes to generous mentors and supportive colleagues. His first accepted work was a poem titled "Reality Sits in a Green Cushioned Chair." It was published in 1973 in the journal that is now the *Journal of Counseling & Development*. The journal editor, Leo Goldman, was a noted researcher and was encouraging. Sam sent Goldman and his successor, James Barclay, many more poems. They published 21 of them.

Another influential mentor in Sam's life was Vikki Knight, who was editor of the counseling division at what is now Pearson Publishing (then Merrill Education). She accepted his first book proposal. It was a crucial moment, because Sam had gone to the leading publisher of the day and been turned down flat with a verbal shame attack. Vikki said, "Well, you seem like that ant who can move a rubber tree plant. I will send you a contract." In 1988, *Counseling: A Comprehensive Profession* was published. Kevin Davis followed Vicki's fine mentorship a few years later. Davis's dry wit and knowledge of publishing helped Sam reach new heights as an author.

Sam acknowledges many others who have provided instruction, guidance, and friendship over the years. Wes Hood, a professor at Wake Forest University, taught him a lot about career counseling in graduate school and also worked with him at the Rockingham County Mental Health Center as a consultant and advisor, and he later became a friend. Larry Osborne, a professor at UNCG, mentored Sam in how to be a counseling supervisor and taught him about groups and group counseling, and Mary Elizabeth Keister, a professor at UNCG, was his dissertation advisor and a diplomatic scholar of the highest order.

Sam also acknowledged some of his counseling colleagues, including Harold (Dick) Hackney, a professor emeritus at Syracuse University who asked him to make a counseling film for ACES and inspired Sam with the clarity of his writing. Barbara Okun, a professor emeritus at Northeastern, invited Sam to Boston to work with her in editing the first ACES monograph on marriage and family counseling. Donna Henderson, counseling professor emeritus and department chair at Wake Forest, was a fellow faculty member for 22 years with whom Sam wrote, presented, and collaborated. He described her as a gifted counselor, counselor educator, administrator, confidant, and good friend.

Thelma Duffey, a former ACA president and professor at the University of Texas at San Antonio also founded the Association for Creativity in Counseling and has been a creative inspiration to Sam. Courtland C. Lee, a professor at the Chicago School of Professional Psychology and also a former ACA president, taught Sam much about multiculturalism, and Sam has worked with Courtland both nationally and internationally. Sam recognized Theodore P. Remley, professor at the University of the Holy Cross in New Orleans, and Barbara Herlihy, professor in practice at the University of Texas at San Antonio and professor emeritus at the University of New Orleans, who have both taught him about the ethical nature of counseling. Others who have taught and inspired him include Art Lerner, a psychologist in Los Angeles who introduced him to poetry therapy, and Tom Sweeney, professor emeritus at Ohio University and the founder of Chi Sigma Iota International, who provided a model of counseling excellence. Jim Davidson, a statistician and Sam's former chairperson at UAB for 6 years, is also a member of that group. Jim gave Sam a lot of space and encouragement to be as academically productive as he could be.

It is not surprising that Sam would mention his writing friends, such as Allen Wilcoxon, a professor emeritus at the University of Alabama, with whom he has written a number of articles on family counseling and coauthored a book. He has also written creative pieces about scriptotherapy, stories, and humor with Melanie Drake Wallace, a professor at Jacksonville State, and has written about the healing power of poetry with Nick Mazza, a professor emeritus at Florida State University. In addition, he has enjoyed writing two ACA books with Kevin Alderson, a professor emeritus at the University of Calgary.

Sam has worked closely over the years with professionals at ACA. Two have played important roles in his leadership career; Rich Yep, ACA executive director, who supported him throughout his term as ACA president and taught him a lot about counseling and leadership in the process; and David Kaplan, former chief professional officer at ACA, who recruited him to be the facilitator of the *20/20 Vision of the Future of Counseling* project. Carolyn Baker, ACA's associate publisher, has suggested edits to the book manuscripts Sam has sent to the ACA into works worth reading and is also someone he reveres. Sam said of Carolyn, "I have never known a better editor or anyone easier to work with."

Sam includes in his shout-out of important people some of the counselors with whom he has worked. He worked in private practice in Birmingham, Alabama, with Jim Cotton, Robbin McIntyre, and Marian Cosper. They were as "competent as the day is long" and taught him a great deal about the art and science of counseling. When Sam was working at his first counseling position in mental health in Rockingham County, North Carolina, Frank Hedges (a social worker) and Nancy Isaacs (a psychiatric nurse) mentored him and taught him how to be effective in demanding clinical situations. Kevin Cox, a professional writer for the Wake Forest news bureau for 30 years, helped him see what good writing could be, although he never edited Sam's work. Finally, Sam's support systems include Claire, his wife, "who has been a wonderful life partner in raising our children and supportive of all my activities from writing to administration throughout our marriage."

Many of Sam's accomplishments have been due to timely opportunities and a willingness and readiness to serve. For example, he did not expect to return to his alma mater, but when the president of Wake Forest called in 1990 and asked him to be his assistant, Sam quickly accepted. Likewise, he did not plan to become president of ACA, three ACA divisions, Chi Sigma Iota, or the American Association of State Counseling Boards, but when asked, he said yes and did not look back. George Washington purportedly said, "Great moments in war and great moments in love should always be made the most of, for they never come again." Sam believes that these words apply to counseling as well. He is grateful and humbled for what has happened. He did not see it coming.

The Future of Counseling

Sam has experienced and influenced the growth and advancement of the counseling profession over the past five decades, and his leadership and writing have helped shaped generations of counselors. He remains upbeat and optimistic in his hope for the future of the profession.

> Counseling is strongest when it stresses wellness, relationships, development, and prevention. I would love to see us, as evidence-based practitioners, go even deeper and stronger into all of these areas. Helping people grow and mature at different ages and distinct stages of their lives is something counseling can contribute to the world. We need to help individuals and groups connect socially in the multicultural society in which we live. We, as counselors, should be on the frontlines and in the positive mental health trenches of practice, because we have a lot to contribute. We need to stress our uniqueness in emphasizing who people can be.

Second, Sam hopes that counseling will become more united as a profession and stop the political infighting. He hopes that the artificial barriers set up for licensing across state lines will be broken down, because many individual state requirements are not necessary to protect the public. According to Sam, "unification is uneven." He would love to see that change.

Sam's third hope is that "we, as counselors, will own our identities better. Usually, when I speak, I say, 'My name is Sam and I am a counselor.' We have a great tradition. We need to emphasize what we bring to the table of integrated mental health care; for example, an emphasis on relationships, wellness, human development, and prevention. That is an identity of which we can be proud."

Words of Wisdom

Sam concluded our conversation with these reflections on the nature of counseling and leadership:

> Collaboration is crucial to being a counselor and a leader. As the Beatles lyric says, "I get by with a little help from my friends." The "I" should be "we." I like being around people and value them. I look for how I can be a friend or colleague and bring out the best in others; that is, how I can be a mentor. The importance of respect and collaboration is grounded in the spiritual base of my life. I think there is a divine presence in all life. As Martin Buber wrote so eloquently in his book, *I and Thou*, we need to honor that presence and not treat people or any living creatures as if they were objects.

Leadership is being responsible to others, being responsible to yourself, and being accountable to society. William Butler Yeates wrote that writing poetry was harder than breaking stone. Sam agrees: "I think being a leader is more difficult than breaking stone or doing physical work. We do not sweat physically in leadership. However, we sweat internally as we wrestle mentally. Leadership is always a struggle because there are always decisions to be made, and many of them are hard."

Sam stresses that counseling leaders should value the right to struggle, just as we give that right to our clients. Choices are before us, and when the answers are not clear-cut, we have to ask ourselves what is best for the most people. "I think the challenging aspects of leadership are answered by asking ourselves ethical group process questions such as 'What am I doing? and Why?' and 'How is what I am doing going to affect others?'" If what we are doing as leaders is not headed in a positive direction, we need to be responsible and make changes. That may mean trusting the power and competence of the group of people we are leading. Asking followers to help us can be wise, for those in the group may have different and effective ideas. There is strength in numbers, especially in airing thoughts and considering as many viable concepts as possible.

Leadership is a challenge, and internal challenges are often as important as external ones. Sam advises aspiring leaders to take their professional pulse regularly and challenge themselves to be reflectively thoughtful of what they can do and not to be discouraged by failure. Generate at least three responses to situations you encounter, and explore available options and opportunities. Leadership is a lifelong process of learning and hard work. Plenty of opportunities exist to make significant contributions in the field of counseling. Do not run the race before the starting bell has sounded; let life develop and unfold rather than trying to make things happen. Listen to what you are hearing inside yourself: What do you really want to do and why? Remember that reflective behaviors involve all of our senses. Realize that what we are best at makes a difference in what we do and how we live our lives as leaders. Finally, be ready for some surprises because they will happen.

D. Robert Casares's Final Reflections

Writing this profile of the life and legacy of Samuel Templeman Gladding has been an honor and an instructive experience, not for the new details I learned about Sam but for the age-old adages that he embodies and affirms: Disappointments and setbacks are inevitable. Never lose hope, failure is not final. You can be bitter, or you can be better. Do the right thing. Work hard, play hard. Persistence pays off. Dream big, and give yourself to something great.

Notable Accomplishments

1988–1992	Editor of the *Journal for Specialists in Group Work*
1989–1990	Licensed clinical mental health counselor and a member of the counseling licensure boards in Alabama
1989–1990	President of Chi Sigma Iota
1990–present	Produced several counseling films
1993–1994	President, ASGW
1996–1997	President, ACES
1997–present	Published numerous books, articles, and poems on counseling
2001	A first mental health responder to New York City after 9/11
2003	Established the Department of Counseling at Wake Forest University
2004–2005	President, American Counseling Association
2007	A first mental health responder to Virginia Tech shooting
2008–2014	Licensed clinical mental health counselor and a member of the counseling licensure boards in North Carolina
2010–2011	Chair of the ACA Foundation
2010	Funded ACA's Unsung Heroes Award to recognize exemplary counselor practitioners
2018–2020	President, IAMFC

Chapter 10

Barbara Herlihy

Anita M. Pool

Mentee's Introduction

I am Anita M. Pool, and I have known Barbara Herlihy since I began my doctoral studies at the University of New Orleans in 2013. When I entered the doctoral program, a new acquaintance (and now a dear friend) gave me some of the best advice I received throughout my time in the program. Her advice was this: "If Dr. H offers to take you under her wing, let her." I politely thanked her and tucked away that bit of advice, although I was not quite sure what she meant or how it would transpire. Most of all, I had no idea how significant that advice would become for me, both professionally and personally.

I already had "stars in my eyes" in Barbara's presence on campus, but it was not until I attended my first conference with her that I truly realized the extent of her celebrity-like status. Barbara would vehemently deny having this status, but those of us who watched people waiting for an autograph or a photo opportunity would say otherwise. From our interview, I learned that Barbara has difficulty even identifying as a leader. Those who know her recognize Barbara as an advocate, an educator, a mentor, an advisor, a researcher, and a prolific writer—and, yes, a leader. In addition, those who have been "under her wing" refer to her as a "dynamic force in this world," a "consummate professional," and a "counselor educator savant," just to name a few descriptors. Regardless of how she defines herself or how others label her, Barbara is without a doubt one of the most grounded, humble, and influential individuals in the field of counseling. She has left her indelible mark on the profession as a whole and on many individuals as well. I am immensely grateful to have been taken "under her wing" and for the many benefits I received from being there.

It is no wonder that Barbara is an inspiration to many. She is an accomplished professional who has also mastered the art of living. She is a compassionate mother and friend who values connection and truly enjoys life; the perpetual smile on her face and the positive attitude that goes with it are proof of this. She has an unparalleled zest for life, an appreciation for unique cuisine, and a deep love of international travel. It is not uncommon to hear her talk of her most recent travels, which often include her son. Whether hiking mountains, seeing historic landmarks, or tasting the local cuisine, she enjoys her trips abroad to the fullest. She makes the most of being on the other side of the world and often stays for weeks at a time. She does not allow fear or her age to hold her back and is always ready for the next adventure. We could all take a page from Barbara's book about having a can-do attitude, taking advantage of every moment, and living life with gusto.

Barbara Herlihy's Journey

Early Years and Career Path

Barbara's propensity for advocacy may have been evident at a very early age and is recounted in one of her favorite childhood memories, which she describes as "a little snapshot of who I was going to grow up to be!" She was surprised when this particular memory emerged during an Adlerian "early recollections" activity several years ago: When she was 5 years old, her mom took her on a road trip from Ohio to Florida to see the ocean. Barbara had spent many hours sitting in the car and had become annoyingly restless, so her mom stopped at a public park near Atlanta so young Barbara could "run off her energy." She played and had a wonderful time, and then it was time to get back on the road. She recalls telling her mom, "I'm thirsty, and I want to get some water from the fountain." She ran ahead to get in line. She remembers her mom arriving at the water fountain a few minutes later with an awful, embarrassed look on her face. She vividly recollects her mom saying, "You can't stand in that line. You need to get your water at the other fountain under the White sign." Young Barbara did not understand why she needed to do that, so she refused to move. As she clearly recalls, "I was intrigued. . . . I wanted to see the colored water . . . because that's what the sign said." After a garbled explanation from her mom about what the sign actually meant, she remembers throwing a temper tantrum and saying, "That's not fair! That's not fair! That's not fair!" "I did not notice that I was the only pale-skinned person in the line . . . that's not what a 5-year-old is seeing!" Thus, she jokes that her inclination toward human rights and social justice commenced that day in Atlanta. She still speaks out when something is not fair, but she would like to think that she has found better strategies than throwing a tantrum.

Barbara grew up in upper-middle-class "suburbia" and left her "cocoon of privilege" to pursue her bachelor's degree in French and psychology at Miami University in Ohio. It was when she went away to college that she first understood how truly encapsulated she had been, realizing that the "world was a bigger place and wasn't composed solely of White, Protestant Republicans." She believes she could not have come of age at a better place or time because the world was "changing so rapidly in ways that were exciting" to her. She recalls the energy surrounding such a changing society and the increasing recognition of human rights. Those were exciting and influential times, and Barbara "jumped right in" and participated in significant historic events, including the civil rights movement, the women's rights movement, and the anti–Vietnam War movement. Her direct involvement in these notable events greatly influenced her and further shaped her into the person and the professional she would become.

Barbara describes her educational journey as "serendipitous." As a result of her early exposure to historic and impactful events, she knew she wanted to "do something to change the world and make it a better place." Career options for women at that time were limited primarily to nursing or teaching, so she decided that teaching was what she would do. Planning to complete her bachelor's degree in May of her senior year, she accepted a teaching position in California, which seemed like a "happening place" to be at that time in the United States. Then a "glitch" occurred that would prove to be life-changing. Barbara flunked her 1-credit course in bowling and thus did not graduate on time. She had to attend summer session, so she decided on a whim to take a few graduate courses in counseling in addition to what she laughingly called "remedial bowling." With those few courses, she was hooked on counseling! At the end of the summer, she received a full-ride scholarship from the counseling department head and decided to stay and complete her master's degree rather than accept the teaching position.

After earning her master's degree in counseling and guidance from Miami University, she practiced as a counselor in several different settings, including a school, a men's prison, an agency, and private practice. While working at her first job as a school counselor, she became pregnant and remembers hiding her enormous belly behind a tall file cabinet when the superintendent was in the building because pregnant women were required to resign when their pregnancies became visible. This proved to be another event that would further influence her affinity for feminism.

After her son was born, she sought a part-time job and was hired at a nearby university as an administrative assistant to the chair for the teacher education department. One day about a year later as he was discussing the need to find an adjunct for an undergraduate educational psychology course, Barbara recalls saying, "Can I try?" and his subsequent laughter. The chair returned to her later, though, and offered her the position. She remembers him saying, "I don't know why I didn't think of you. Go ahead and teach the course!" It was after she taught that first course that she knew exactly what she wanted to do, university teaching—not to train teachers but to train counselors. She went on to earn her doctorate in counseling psychology from Northwestern University.

Barbara regards her mentors as among the major influences on her career and the resulting professional she has become, although she doubts that many would consider themselves "mentors." Nonetheless, it is important for her to acknowledge those individuals and their impactful role in her professional journey:

> There have been so many people who have encouraged me and supported me along the way. I wouldn't be who I am if someone hadn't believed in me. . . . There were people who encouraged me and said, "You can do that!" and I would say, "Aww, not me!" You hear that often enough, and people give you opportunities to try on those new roles, and you find you can do it. I'm just so grateful to the people who saw something in me and helped draw it out.

One of Barbara's first mentors was counselor educator Vernon Lee Sheeley. As a beginning assistant professor, Barbara was attending a professional conference and a very nice gentleman held the elevator door for her as she sprinted toward it. She thanked him and mentioned her fear that she would be late for a presentation on privileged communication in counseling. He smiled and responded, "Relax, you won't be late. I'm the presenter." This began a collaboration of several years in researching and publishing about confidentiality and privileged communication.

Other mentors came later and have evolved into friends and colleagues. Notable among them is Gerald Corey, who kept encouraging Barbara to help him write a chapter on feminist therapy for his theories book. Barbara "ducked and wove" and put him off, intimidated beyond belief at the idea of writing with such a prolific author. But Corey, who is nothing if not persistent, wore her down. The feminist therapy chapter in his book paved the way for the inclusion of a feminist chapter in other theory textbooks as well—a result that she has been delighted to see. After years of collaborative writing and presenting with Barbara, Gerald Corey states:

> She is a wonderful writer and editor, an exceptional teacher and mentor, and a true leader in the field. In addition to being a highly competent professional, she is a caring, compassionate, and supportive person. She has mentored thousands of students, many of whom are now making major contributions to the counseling field. Barbara Herlihy is a true inspiration for her students and colleagues and her influence will continue to be felt for many years.

Another of her mentors, and now a friend, Courtland C. Lee recounts:

> I have known Barbara Herlihy for 30 years as a colleague and dear friend. I have had the pleasure of collaborating with her on writing projects and presentations over those years. One of the things that has always impressed me about her is her unwavering commitment to ethical practice, multicultural competence, and social justice. She has been passionate about feminism and advancing the role of women and people of color in her many leadership positions within the counseling profession. Unlike many, Barbara tends not to seek the spotlight. However, her words, both written and spoken, and her actions are powerful and have made her one of the preeminent experts in the profession on counseling ethics. I have been with Barbara at conferences and watched scores of people approach her with compliments and praise for her work. She handles this adulation with both humility and grace. Barbara has been and continues to be one of my role models and mentors.

Pivotal Moments

Although Barbara's involvement in the civil rights, women's rights, and antiwar movements greatly influenced her as an advocate for human rights, it was Hurricane Katrina that affected her in the most profound way. When she showed up and protested at earlier historical movements, she considered herself a "visitor . . . in the way that people with privilege can go picket and then go home to a warm, safe environment." As a resident of New Orleans during Hurricane Katrina, she was "no longer a visitor" in a world that was terrifying. She, like many others, evacuated before the storm, lived as a displaced person without knowing what had happened to her home, committed to returning to New Orleans and helping to rebuild, and experienced a long road to recovery. It was after returning home to

New Orleans, however, that she recalls being "smacked" with her privilege when she saw those around her struggling. She owned a car, which enabled her to evacuate; she had insurance that would assist with home repairs; she never missed a paycheck; and she did not lose her job. This was not at all the same experience as that of the majority of New Orleanians.

This new understanding affected her profoundly, and she found herself on a mission to tell people's stories. She realized from her place of privilege that the effects of Hurricane Katrina were far more profound than what was being revealed by published statistics or PTSD prevalence studies. Her fellow New Orleanians were real people with untold stories, including: true accounts of being rescued from roof tops; families losing everything; being trapped in the Super Dome; and the resulting mental health issues. Those who were lacking in resources before Katrina had even fewer resources after the hurricane, yet they endured and recovered. Their strength and tenacity were amazing and a testament to the human spirit. Barbara's work in helping to develop a mental health program in the schools after Katrina led to a lifelong friendship with another mentor, Dr. Milton W. Anderson, section head of Child and Adolescent Psychiatry at Ochsner Health System of New Orleans. Working with the team he assembled to create a multidisciplinary approach to providing mental health services within a school system that was broken, within a community that was impoverished and still devastated, expanded her vision exponentially and led her to connect with the resilient citizens of New Orleans whose stories she told in book chapters and presentations.

Points of Pride

The contributions Barbara identifies as her most valued include the obvious and the not-so-obvious. Although her list of accomplishments is extensive, her proclaimed list of most-valued contributions is brief: the profession's more nuanced understanding of ethics, her multigenerational influence as a mentor, and her coveted "Katrina stories."

She is best known for her work related to ethics, which is evident from her professional writing and contributions to the scholarly literature, as well as through her numerous speaking engagements. As Barbara states, "If I have contributed to our profession's understanding of ethics as foundational to best practice, I feel really good about that." One does not need to search very hard to locate one of her numerous publications, nor look very long through a professional conference program to find one of her keynote speeches or session presentations on ethics.

Perhaps the least known of her professional contributions, yet work she is particularly proud of, are her Hurricane Katrina stories. As a "storyteller at heart," it is some of the writing she feels best about. She affectionately describes the Hurricane Katrina stories as opportunities to illuminate the "remarkable resilience of human beings who are sometimes forgotten in our society."

Leadership and Advocacy

Although Barbara does not identify as a leader or "someone out in front," she does embrace the roles of educator, mentor, writer, expert, and advocate. In those roles, she has influenced not only those in her immediate sphere but also others around the world. Her notable contributions to the field of counseling are abundant.

Throughout her career as a counselor educator, many students at various universities have had the good fortune of having her as an educator and mentor. Her first 5 years as a counselor educator were spent as an assistant professor at the University of Wisconsin at Whitewater. She would go on to become an associate professor at the University of Houston at Clear Lake and then to teach at Loyola University of New Orleans and the University of New Orleans. During her time at the University of New Orleans, she earned recognition as a university research professor. Her reach as an educator extended internationally to universities in Mexico, Venezuela, and Malta. She is currently a professor in practice and doctoral program director in the Counseling Department at the University of Texas at San Antonio, and she remains a professor emerita at the University of New Orleans.

As an expert in the field, Barbara has conducted research, produced scholarly literature, and presented on a variety of topics related to counseling. Her primary focus, however, has been on ethical issues in counseling, feminist therapy, social justice and advocacy, and multicultural counseling. A prolific writer, she has authored and coauthored approximately 100 written works, including books, book chapters, and journal articles. She is best known for her contributions to our profession's understanding of ethics and, with Theodore P. Remley, has literally "written the book" on ethics, now in its sixth edition. She has also coauthored (with Gerald Corey) two other current textbooks related to ethics. True to her humble nature, she modestly admits that she did not think she would ever write a textbook.

In addition to the books, chapters, and a plethora of refereed journal articles on ethics, she has also shared her expertise as an invited keynote speaker and panelist at numerous professional engagements across the United States and has participated in more than 100 refereed conference presentations nationally and internationally. Her presentations have been attended by hundreds, if not thousands, of people and her work has greatly influenced our profession. One of her students, Angela James, recalls attending a conference presentation involving an ethics case that would transform the ethical guidelines for counselors:

> Barbara was the lone female presenter in a group of heavy hitters in the field of counseling. The room was a packed house; the case had gotten national attention, so it was certainly all the buzz at the time. Yet, here she was, calmly discussing it with the ease of chatting about her favorite piece of art or a book she recently had the pleasure of reading. No pretense, no sesquipedalian words. . . . There was a way in which she spoke that let you know of her brilliance.

Barbara's leadership extends beyond her teaching, research, and publications to the professional organizations of which she is a member. During the course of her career, she has served in various leadership capacities for the American Counseling Association, Chi Sigma Iota, and the International Association for Counselling, among others. Her name has become synonymous with "Ethics Committee," and she continues to work diligently to provide guidance to counseling professionals around the world. In addition, she remains committed to advocacy for individuals who are disenfranchised and underserved through her continued outreach and service to the profession.

Further evidence of Barbara's leadership is found in her service to Chi Sigma Iota International. Her contributions to excellence in counseling include serving as a chapter faculty advisor for over two decades at two different universities, as well as serving as president in 2017–2018. She continues to share her wisdom and expertise as an invited guest speaker at CSI initiation ceremonies.

Barbara believes that mentoring is a crucial aspect of leadership, and she is gratified to think of her multigenerational impact as a mentor. She readily identifies with the role and enjoys "paying it forward." She joyfully admits:

> Definitely, seeing my students develop into counselors and counselor educators who are competent, confident (this one takes a while longer), and impassioned about their work has been most rewarding. I am grateful I have had the opportunity to contribute in small measure to that development and to have stayed in the profession long enough to see it become intergenerational.

When asked how the mentor-mentee relationship begins, she acknowledges that, in some instances, mentees find her, but she also tends to seek out the people who are like her. In her opinion, those individuals may not see themselves as having leadership potential or may feel intimated by being in a doctoral or master's program. She looks for those who are "kind of lurking in the corner," and she "gently nudges [them] out of the shadows." She has the keen ability to see the potential in others before they see it in themselves.

Students who have been fortunate enough to be Barbara's mentees attest to the powerful influence of her relationship. According to Angela James:

> She gives encouragement without platitudes or overinflated words of affirmation. She lets you know what she sees and gives you opportunity. From there, if that uncertainty overshadows the potential, she doesn't dismiss it. Rather, there is an acknowledgment that the belief is still there, and when you are ready, she will be too. How remarkable of a gift is that—to know that once she decides to cultivate, even if the full bloom isn't apparent, she doesn't discard you. Your journey is your journey. When it leads you back to her, she is there, ready. . . . I am sure my experience is not unique to me. She is generous in how she shares knowledge and opportunities. There are a few flowers in her garden: We are all acutely aware of and are bonded in how she allowed us to stand in her light, and we are able to cast a light of our own. What strikes me is that she always seems continuously surprised that the thing that brings her joy is also the thing that brings her praise.

Others readily acknowledge the impact Barbara has had on the trajectory of their careers. Melissa Deroche identifies several "defining moments" that stand out to her, including Barbara's encouragement for her to present at professional conferences and take on leadership roles.

> Dr. H has a keen ability to see the strengths, gifts, and talents of students, often before they see them in themselves. She identifies these strengths and presents opportunities to assist students and professionals in their growth and development. At the same time, she does not seek credit or accolades for her work. . . . I have both observed and benefited from her ability to allow others to find their own direction. . . . Although it is sometimes easier to just show or give others the "answers" or tell them what they cannot see, it is more empowering to allow them to make the discovery on their own. This is what Dr. H does so well!

Kristen Dickens also describes Barbara's influence on her career. Through their multiple relationships, including advisor-advisee, professor-teaching assistant, professor-graduate assistant, and dissertation chair-student, Kristen describes Barbara's way of mentoring students.

> Her effortless ability to connect with students really struck me, and though it was intimidating to work with and learn from her at first, she had a way of putting me at ease. She truly embodies the heart of feminist therapy and never places herself in an overbearing or expert role. Instead, she found a way to acknowledge my interests in research and teaching and helped me cultivate skills that would ultimately aid me in my current role as counselor educator. . . . She always encouraged me to be true to myself and not to put on airs for people, especially if it is not authentic to who I am. . . . So much of who I am as a counselor educator came from my "formative" doctoral years learning under Barbara's tutelage. That time is gold to me, and I'm honored to call her my friend.

The Future of Counseling

Barbara's vision for the future is a "hopeful" vision, which, according to her, is "the only one I have, because that's who I am." In her vision for the future, she imagines the following:

> I see us spreading our work globally, and because we have worked hard to reach a better level of cultural awareness, we are less likely to be going out there colonizing. I think we are really going to be out there contributing to an incredibly diverse meld of professional helpers—whether or not they are called "counselors"—who will not look anything like us or work in a way that is similar to us, but we will be doing the same thing, which is helping and healing. I see that going global.

Barbara believes that spreading our work globally requires us to use our own experiences and to share those experiences with others, whether it's through writing about them, talking about them, or literally embarking on the experience with others. As Barbara points out, "It's useless if I just hold it inside me."

Some of the ways that she has shared her experiences with others include taking doctoral students with her to teach in Malta, writing about her experiences, and her involvement with the International Association of Counselling (IAC). She is continually engaged in outreach as she works to engage others in global efforts. Her connection with IAC was the result of an invitation from one of her valued mentors who has become a friend and colleague. In 2008, Courtland C. Lee, who was IAC president that year, invited Barbara to give a keynote presentation at the IAC conference in Malta on lessons learned from Hurricane Katrina. She was so energized by her interactions at that conference with counselor educators from all over the globe that she found renewed excitement and a new direction for her work. She has come to believe that to have a greater impact we need to "be less parochial and broaden our vision." It is in getting "caught up in what's going on in our very narrow little world" that we forget to "look out there."

Looking to the future, she reflected on the current coronavirus pandemic, and she recognizes that we are all "interconnected and interdependent, on a global scale." When the pandemic is over, Barbara anticipates that grief and trauma will exist worldwide:

> As was true for Katrina, those who had the fewest resources to survive it will bear the largest burden. More than ever before, counselors will be needed everywhere on this planet, and the opportunities for us to contribute will be limitless. Now is the time for us to work hard at growing in our cultural humility and transcultural competence.

As evidenced throughout her life and career, Barbara continues to find opportunities during unprecedented events to advocate for and help others.

Words of Wisdom

Before offering her words of wisdom, Barbara first reflected on the wisdom she would have loved to have received throughout her life. She began with her childhood and wished that "someone had told me you don't have to stand in the 'correct' line. You can go where your heart leads you." As a young woman in the most radical phase of her feminist development, she wishes someone had told her that "men and women can both be tremendous mentors and friends."

> By and large, my male mentors have encouraged me to "do" things I thought I wasn't capable of doing, and my female mentors and friends have encouraged me to "be" my authentic self—notable among them are Dr. Harriet Glosoff, my sister-with-different-parents, and Dr. Thelma Duffey, who provided me with the opportunity to "un-retire." I am grateful to all of them.

She also wishes that someone had told her that a day would come "when females and people of color will be sitting in the full professor's chair, that things are going to change . . . back then, it didn't leave room for a lot of aspirations for people like me. . . . But that's not realistic, wanting someone to have told me something they had no way to know."

It is not surprising that the spirit of giving, connection, and advocacy are evident in Barbara's words of wisdom. She believes in the "butterfly effect" and points to how the COVID-19 pandemic has shown us that everyone on the planet is interconnected:

> A person falls ill in Wuhan, China, and the world is changed. A counselor makes a connection with a person who is hurting, and that person is changed. That person pays it forward . . . and so it goes. Whatever you choose to contribute, you make a difference. Believe in yourself and get out there and do it!

Although she is a woman of few words, what she has to say embodies how she lives her life. As a true reflection of her character, Barbara encourages people to reach their potential and values the contributions of everyone.

Anita M. Pool's Final Reflections

Barbara is a person I wish I had known all of my life. Although I have known her for less than a decade, the things I have learned, and continue to learn, are the kinds of things that are life-changing: Mighty can come in small packages; humility is one of the most important and attractive characteristics a person can possess; a few words can go a very long way; and recognizing and encouraging the potential in others is transformative. She has not only been my mentor, teacher, and dissertation chair, but she has also been a rock for me during some of the most challenging times of my life. Both professionally and personally, Barbara continues to share her invaluable wisdom and comforting support, for which I am eternally grateful.

Some of what I learned happened in the classroom, but much more learning took place off campus. During the years I have known her, we have spent time together at conferences in sessions where we presented together, and other times socializing with the University of New Orleans delegation at restaurants in various cities around the country. We have worked on numerous CSI activities together in various locations, and some of my favorite times have been at her home in New Orleans for CSI social functions. Although all of these were special in their own right, my most cherished moments are the meals we enjoyed in Malta, just the two of us. Of course, we discussed professional issues, but we also had intimate conversations about the similarities in our upbringing, shared stories about our children, and talked about traveling the world. I cannot recall all of the details of our conversations, but I do remember exactly how I felt—honored and content, and yes, a little star-struck. I went to bed each of those nights truly appreciating the gift I had been given.

Years later, I continue to be grateful for our special relationship and the benefits I have received from being under her wing. Some people come into our lives, make a significant impact, and leave an indelible mark. Barbara is absolutely one of those people for me, and I know she is for many others as well. She is a special human being and an incredible professional whose influence will continue to benefit individuals and the entire counseling profession for many years to come.

Notable Accomplishments

	American Counseling Association Fellow
1987–1989	American Counseling Association, chair/cochair of the Ethics Committee
2009	Southern Association for Counselor Education and Supervision Courtland Lee Social Justice Award
2009	Association for Counselor Education and Supervision, Distinguished Mentor Award
2009–2013	American Counseling Association Foundation trustee
2011–2012	American Counseling Association Foundation chair
2017–2018	Chi Sigma Iota International, president
2018–2019	American Counseling Association, chair/cochair of the Ethics Committee
	Coauthor with graduate students and former graduate students of numerous journal articles and book chapters
	Coauthor (with Theodore P. Remley) of *Ethical, Legal, and Professional Issues in Counseling*, and (with Gerald Corey) of *ACA Ethical Standards Casebook* and *Boundary Issues in Counseling*

Chapter 11

Gerard Lawson

Corrine R. Sackett

Mentee's Introduction

I, Corrine R. Sackett, have known Gerard Lawson for 12 years. He was my mentor throughout my doctoral program in counselor education at Virginia Tech. I am lucky to continue to call him a mentor and now a friend. He was my dissertation chair, and we have since collaborated on research and writing. It has been a pleasure to watch him be a force in the profession. I feel incredibly fortunate to have Gerard on my team, in my professional development and in my life in general.

Gerard Lawson's Journey

Early Years and Career Path

Gerard Lawson was the fourth of five children in a Catholic family. He grew up in Detroit and moved to Virginia at age 12. Both of Gerard's parents were heavily involved in service to the community, school, and church. His dad had been in the Marine Corps and worked for the City of Detroit and Fairfax and Prince William Counties in Virginia, and his mom was very involved in the school and community. Being involved in service was part of the Lawson family identity, and Gerard grew up thinking that everyone was working for the greater good. His first job was as a paperboy, starting at age 10 and continuing through adolescence, and he served as an altar boy in his church in Detroit. Both of these roles helped shape his work ethic at a young age. He had to be up at 5 o'clock in the morning to deliver papers, and being one of the youngest altar boys meant he was assigned the less desirable shifts, such as the 6:00 a.m. mass in Latin and the 7:30 a.m. mass in Polish. Because he didn't understand either language, he learned to read nonverbal cues as a way of understanding relationships and his place in a larger system. Upon reflection, Gerard attributes those early experiences to helping shape the way he approaches his work, service, and leadership roles.

Virginia Tech was part of Gerard's formative years as well, and its motto, *Ut Prosim* (That I May Serve), reinforced the idea of service throughout his college years. Combined with his childhood and family context, this identity paved a path for him to seek a career in which helping people and service for the greater good were at the forefront.

At Virginia Tech, Gerard and found his way to a major in human development in the family and child development program. During that time, he attended a presentation by Elisabeth Kübler-Ross and was thoroughly impressed with her. He was awed by her work with hospitalized children who were terminally ill and by her stories of the unexplainable wisdom they exhibited. This sparked Gerard's interest, and he started volunteering with Hospice. He provided respite for families whose loved ones were in hospice care, which he found to be meaningful work. Being with individuals during their loss and grief helped Gerard realize that he could be present with people through the difficult times in life. This experience helped foster a sense of a broader purpose in life and showed him that there are many ways to serve others.

Gerard's leadership philosophy revolves around serving others, and he began to volunteer in helping roles at a young age and continued to do so in high school. Although Gerard didn't necessarily know what counseling was at that time, he was poised for a career in it even so. Following graduation from Virginia Tech, he worked in child protective services (CPS), and then for the juvenile court system as a juvenile probation counselor. In both of those roles, Gerard began to ponder "How can I be an agent of change?" and "How can I be the person here that's helping to move the process forward?" He began to bump into some of the systemic issues that keep people stuck and realized that families who are involved with CPS aren't involved by choice but because things got out of control and were beyond their current coping abilities. He recognized that this was largely due to systemic issues.

When Gerard was leaving his role with the juvenile court system, the director of the local social services said to Gerard's boss, "Please stop hiring activists because it's too much work." Gerard had been recognizing and pushing back against systemic barriers, attempting to change things for the better, but the system was resistant to change. Realizing that there are two ways to do this kind of work was a clarifying moment for Gerard. He could go through the motions and keep the peace, but if he chose this route, people who were stuck in the system would continue to be stuck. Alternatively, he could do the job in a way that is transformative and help people get unstuck. This required changing the system, leveraging it in different ways, and trying to help people overcome challenges by changing pieces of the puzzle. Gerard enjoyed the advocacy aspect of his early roles because he needed to be creative in his thinking instead of just doing things the way they had always been done. Gerard's leadership theory and philosophy were evolving with the recognition that if this work is to be transformative, it requires more than an 8-hour workday in the traditional role. It requires us to think more broadly and more creatively to answer these questions: "What are the issues that people are facing today?" "How do we predict some of the issues that are coming down the pike?" "What are some of the things that we can do to help to prepare now to meet those challenges when they arrive?"

Gerard vividly remembers one of his first cases as a CPS worker. As he was leaving his first home visit, he thought he was ill-equipped to do this work. He didn't feel he had the training he needed to help families overcome the challenges they were facing. He began thinking about how he could improve. Once he learned about counseling, and how that was different from social work or psychology, the next step in his career began to make a lot more sense. Counseling, with a focus on wellness, strengths, and systemic change, felt like a good fit. After working for years with CPS and probation, much of what he learned in the beginning of his counseling program was intuitive. As he moved into higher levels of learning in his program, things came into clearer focus.

For Gerard, becoming a counselor educator was more accidental than intentional. He enrolled at the College of William & Mary to fulfill needed licensure hours, and he was encouraged by the faculty to apply to their doctoral program. He found that he really enjoyed counselor education, including research and supervision. As he was finishing the doctoral program, he applied for and secured a faculty position at Virginia Tech as a counselor educator. He was moving on in his career, but Gerard experienced a grieving process in leaving clinical practice. He realized that he had to lose something to grow as a professional. He remembers telling families with whom he had been working for years that he was leaving, and one of them remarked that he would now need to train counselors to do the kind of work that he had been doing so well. This person's ability to separate from her own needs really touched Gerard, and she said, "All right, now you get on the next generation so that they are good at this." He keeps this expectation at the forefront as he works to prepare counselors he would feel comfortable sending to help somebody he loves, which is a high bar.

Gerard believes that we lead by serving, and he has approached every one of his roles in this way. Some people look for leadership opportunities to advance their careers or because these roles will help them secure something else and move toward another strategic goal. But for Gerard, leadership has been more about opportunities for him to contribute in a meaningful way.

Pivotal Moments

When he was a new faculty member at Virginia Tech, Gerard recalls a pivotal moment that helped him crystallize the importance of the gatekeeping role in counselor education. Two students who were not well suited for the profession didn't show up on the faculty's radar until they were entering practicum, and Gerard advocated for the students' dismissal from the program—"counseling them out of the profession" was the phrase used at the time. Over the years he had worked with counselors, social workers, and psychologists, he encountered individuals who were burned out and were no longer effective and others who were laboring with vicarious trauma. This experience of gatekeeping helped him realize that he was now in a role that made him responsible for catching some of these problems on the front end. Around that same time, a call appeared in *Counseling Today* for people to serve on a task force on counselor impairment. Gerard took the opportunity, and David Kaplan, the American Counseling Association (ACA) president, asked Gerard to chair the task force. When Gerard expressed hesitation because he was so new to being a counselor educator, Kaplan assured him that it is helpful to have new people who can navigate the process with a fresh perspective.

This was Gerard's first official role within ACA, and it happened to be a leadership role. Even if he hadn't been chairing the committee, Gerard said it still would have been a leadership role, because the people who are willing to show up and serve on committees and task forces provide the kind of leadership on which the counseling profession is built. "It's not always the person at the front of the room or the person on stage that's the leader. So much of the work that is required is done behind the scenes, and that's leadership in every bit of the same way."

Gerard remembers that first committee experience as beneficial for many reasons. He was able to work with some incredibly talented people who had been in the field much longer than he had and with people relatively new to the field who had much more practical experience with counselor impairment than he had. This committee decided early on to rename themselves the Task Force on Counselor Wellness and Impairment as a way to broaden the scope and to include wellness and how to prevent impairment. Some of the resources they generated were so helpful in identifying risks and how to mitigate those risks that they are still on the ACA website today, more than 14 years later. For Gerard, this committee work also opened a line of research that he may not have otherwise pursued. Finally, he held onto Kaplan's perspective that the counseling field needs new people in service and leadership roles who are willing to dedicate their time and talent to efforts to move the profession forward.

Along with realizing where he could contribute meaningfully, Gerard was learning through experience that he was less effective in other areas. He made peace with the idea that he had a skill set that would not be all things to all people, and he learned to be selective about the opportunities he pursued. He believes professional counselors can help in many ways, and it would be a waste to dedicate their time and their strengths to something they would neither enjoy nor contribute to effectively. He urges those who hope to become leaders to find work that speaks to their passion and to use their skills where they can make a meaningful difference.

Points of Pride

Legislative advocacy for counselors and clients has been an important part of Gerard's professional work. He is proud of many accomplishments that have stemmed from his advocacy over the years. One example is a student project that took place several years ago. When students are in their first semester of the master's program at Virginia Tech, Gerard has them engage in an advocacy project. One year, several students teamed up to propose a "good Samaritan" bill. In a situation in which two people were using alcohol or other drugs and one person overdosed, the bill proposed that the other person could call emergency services to get help without worrying about being arrested for possession or being under the influence of drugs or alcohol. The students found that other states had similar laws, and a number of models were working well. The students met with their legislators individually and wrote letters advocating for the bill. At the end of the semester, seeing what a nice job they had done, Gerard encouraged the students to take the bill forward to see if they could get it passed. He talked with a state senator he knew, and as the General Assembly session grew close, the senator reached out to tell Gerard that he had introduced the students' bill. He asked Gerard to engage in outreach with newspapers to help the community understand the issue, which he and the students did. Gerard gave a number of interviews and testified before the General Assembly. The bill eventually passed, and the students were able to see the governor sign their bill into law. Gerard related this as a nice example of effective advocacy efforts. He readily admits that, at times, it can be a much longer process, with not as much success.

Another of Gerard's advocacy efforts has been focused on advancing research related to disrupting the school to prison pipeline. Individuals and communities bear a huge cost when youth are sidetracked from their educational careers because of disciplinary issues in school. That disciplinary action often leads to students being suspended or expelled, which then leads to legal trouble in the community and may ultimately lead to court and jail. Gerard has been engaged in research and advocacy around these issues to help people understand this problem more holistically. When you look closely at the data, it is clear that Black students and students with disabilities are incredibly overrepresented compared to the total school population. He is in communication with the departments of education, juvenile justice, and criminal justice regarding how to work on these disparities and help ensure that every student has the same opportunities to be successful, to stay in the classroom, and to stay out of the courtroom. He is proud that his efforts around these issues have had an impact, and he points to guidance from his research that appeared in recommendations of the Select Committee on School Safety and Research and were adopted in the General Assembly. Gerard believes leadership is about finding an injustice, being curious about it, and figuring out how to help rectify it.

Gerard is proud of how the Virginia Tech faculty have grown their counselor education program, including the services their students provide in the training clinic and their outreach in the community. Although difficult to acknowledge as a source of pride, he is fulfilled by the leadership and service he has been able to provide around recovery from the shootings at Virginia Tech on April 16, 2007. This work has continued to be at the forefront for him more than a decade later. He was trained as a disaster mental health volunteer by the Red Cross after 9/11, so he was in a position to provide support to the families of students who were killed, faculty members who had lost colleagues, and the larger community of Virginia Tech grieving in the wake of the shootings. He is incredibly proud of the university's work in response to the mental health needs of the community, helping build a solid foundation from which to start recovery.

Leadership and Advocacy

Gerard remembers a time as president-elect of the Southern Association of Counselor Education and Supervision (SACES) when he was at an Association of Counselor Education and Supervision (ACES) board meeting. Gerard was vocal about a topic they were discussing and felt confident that he had inadvertently alienated many in the room. He remembers leaving the meeting and thinking, "I'm probably going to be sitting alone at dinner tonight." Then the president-elect of ACES, Tom Scofield, came over and said, "I think you made some good points today. It was a conversation that needed to be had." Scofield asked Gerard if he had ever thought about running for ACES president. This was a pivotal moment for him, and Gerard continues to believe strongly that individuals need to speak up even when their message is unpopular. Whether what he said was right or wrong, he realized that the group needed to have the conversation to arrive at a place where everyone had considered the issues thoroughly and then could make a more informed decision.

From that time forward, Gerard has worked hard to be sure that people participate and that no one in the room is silent. He believes it is leadership malpractice to have failed to express why you believe what you believe and then move the process forward, one way or the other. He believes in the need to have an opportunity to engage and have a conversation about the strengths and weaknesses of everyone's arguments so that everyone has a thorough understanding of the issue. For example, later when he was ACA president, he would say to the new governing council members, "Now that your division or region has sent you here with a purpose, you forfeit your right to remain silent. You have to come and share. You have to come and participate. You need to provide your perspective. You need to read and engage with this material before you come to the table." He explained that leadership is needed, not around the issues on which 80% of people agree but when only 40% of people are in support of something but it is the right thing to do. Leadership is required to figure out how to build on that 40% and bring more people along to a place where the group can move forward.

Gerard has been at the forefront of many controversial discussions involving the relationship between accreditation by the Council for Accreditation of Counseling and Related Educational Programs (CACREP) and licensure. He believes a direct line exists from making graduation from a CACREP-accredited program a part of the licensure process to getting recognition for counselors under Medicare. He sees this straight line as an existential problem for the profession. In today's political climate, if the concept of Medicare for All were to become policy, but counselors were not included in Medicare coverage, there would be a seismic impact on the profession as there would no longer be third-party payers. He argues that every other profession has moved forward by having an educational standard in place for licensure. He believes this idea is actually more popular than it appears to be, because the opposition is a very vocal minority. Gerard's general philosophy is that what other people think about him is none of his business, and this attitude has helped him when he was often under attack for his position in this debate. Gerard's position is that individuals should be trained as counselors, including a consistent set of educational and ethical standards, if they are going to be licensed as counselors. He believes that accreditation is the foundation for licensure.

Leadership requires patience to see things through, along with the ability to recognize that the initiatives one works on may be so far reaching that one never sees them through to actualization. Gerard recalls that he was warned about this when he was president-elect-elect of ACA. Leadership is often about planting seeds that will finally come to fruition 2 or 3 years after the leader has left office. It is often about laying the groundwork and trusting that the process will work, along with being faithful to the direction prior leadership has given to you to continue.

Given his experiences at Virginia Tech, it is not surprising that Gerard advocates for the need for more counselors to be trained in disaster mental health work. As president of ACA, he initiated a task force for disaster preparedness and response, with a focus on how to get more counselors involved and ready to respond if a need arises in their community. For example, the state of Virginia encourages more involvement through a regulatory change that allows licensed professional counselors who engage in training and volunteer work with the Red Cross to count their time toward continuing education credit hours. This is an important incentive for counselors to dedicate their time. Gerard conducts trainings with the Red Cross to contribute to building a workforce of disaster mental health volunteers. In collaboration with the Virginia Counselors Association, he helped lead a day-long training for counselors to get up and running as mental health volunteers with the Red Cross. He also continues to answer calls for deployments with the Red Cross, being most recently deployed after the shootings in Virginia Beach in 2019 and, before that, in Florida after Hurricane Irma.

Gerard initially wondered if disaster mental health work was too close to home for him after the shootings at Virginia Tech. However, he soon realized that he had much to offer because of his experiences and he is able and comfortable doing so. He remembers the remarkable ways that Virginia Tech was supported after the shootings in 2007, and he wanted to be part of that support for others moving forward. Not everyone would feel comfortable and safe contributing in this way, and he encourages people to help only as they are able. Relatedly, he has collaborated on research and outreach around how counselors can care for themselves after disasters and traumas. He has found himself contributing in ways that require a level of leadership, but he also greatly appreciates the value of a team.

Counselors do not need to run for elected positions to become leaders. The majority of leadership is not on stage or at the front of the room. Most of the leaders in the counseling profession work behind the scenes on committees and task forces, lead trainings, and advocate in their communities. All leadership requires is for counselors to show up and do the work. Gerard points out that leadership is most needed when there is not yet momentum one way or the other, or when the right thing to do is the unpopular option. Leaders put energy into getting people to see the concern, to understand the issue from a new angle, and to develop a proposal to address the concern.

This profile would not be complete without highlighting Gerard's achievements related to licensure and professional identity. Licensure standards in Virginia once allowed counselors to provide supervision after holding the licensure for 2 years, without training in supervision. The Virginia Association of Counselor Education and Supervision (VACES) had begun a process while Gerard was in his doctoral program, culminating when he was president of the Virginia Counseling Association (VCA), that required 20 hours of continuing education or a graduate-level course in supervision for people to provide clinical supervision toward licensure. The association then faced the challenge of getting supervisors up to speed on the new regulation, and Gerard and his colleague Laura Welfare began providing trainings through VCA. He is proud of the work that VACES did on the front end, getting the regulatory change, and then training approximately 1,000 licensed professional counselors (LPCs) in Virginia over the course of 8 years so they could gain the competencies they needed.

A related accomplishment in which Gerard takes pride is establishing that only counselors can supervise other counselors toward licensure in Virginia. At one time, psychiatrists, psychiatric nurses, psychologists, and social workers could provide half of the supervision counselors needed toward licensure. Gerard saw this as a professional identity and ethical issue, and he introduced a petition for a rule change stating that counselors working toward licensure needed to be under the authority of the board of counseling. Gerard was pleased to see that regulation passed, because it was increasingly evident to him that clearly establishing the professional identity of counselors was the way forward for the field. Counseling needed to establish an identity separate from psychology.

During his time as president of ACES, Gerard pushed for clearer standards for accreditation for the counseling profession. At the time, many programs were identifying themselves as "CACREP-aligned" or "CACREP-equivalent." These programs were not CACREP-accredited and did not have the oversight and accountability that comes with accreditation. ACES formulated a statement recognizing CACREP as the accrediting body for the counseling profession, and this was passed by the ACES governing council the following year. Rehabilitation counseling was the exception because, at the time, it was still separately accredited through the Council on Rehabilitation Education (CORE). This created a good bit of controversy, but Gerard believed it was important for the profession to get behind a single accrediting body if counseling was to be recognized as a profession equal to the others in the marketplace in services provided and accessibility. Psychology, social work, and marriage and family therapy each have a single accrediting body. These professions also have written into their state laws that one must be a graduate of their accredited programs to be licensed in their respective disciplines.

Later in his ACES presidency, Gerard started working with the National Board for Certified Counselors (NBCC) on a position statement regarding licensure portability. It had taken 33 years for counseling to achieve licensure in all 50 states, and Gerard saw the next step as moving forward to consolidate what it means to be a counselor. Today, 50 different sets of standards exist for counselor licensure, and considerable variation remains in the number of required hours of supervision and in what qualifies as educational experience. Gerard advocates for counselors to consider how to get 50 states to either start using the same standard or get closer to the same standard. His position has resulted directly from feedback from federal legislators who have voiced concerns about some states having very low requirements for obtaining licensure as a counselor. Gerard wants consumers to know that when they go to see an LPC, they will receive the same professional quality no matter where they are located.

The licensure portability efforts that Gerard undertook with ACES, NBCC, and the American Association of State Counseling Boards were important first steps in that direction. Later, when Gerard was on the governing council for ACA as the representative from ACES, the governing council brought forward a similar proposal. ACA now recognizes CACREP as the accrediting body and the standard educational requirement for licensure as an LPC, and Gerard hopes this movement will continue to gain traction as more and more states adopt this standard.

As Gerard was wrapping up his time as ACA president, he reached out to the Council of State Governments, an organization that works on interstate compacts. Rather than changing the regulations in all 50 states, this council directs its effort toward convincing states to sign on to and agree to abide by a compact. For example, if Virginia and South Carolina both signed an interstate compact on portability, a counselor able to meet the compact standards in one state could practice in the other state as well. This approach is much more efficient than attempting to change the laws in all 50 states or requiring individuals to apply for licensure in multiple states. It also eliminates the problem of not being able to practice in border states (for instance, counselors in northern Virginia are very close to and may practice in Washington, D.C., and Maryland).

Gerard initiated discussion of interstate compacts at the end of his term as the ACA president, and the governing council has made a significant commitment to getting them formed and operational, including signing states. As an ongoing result of Gerard's advocacy in this arena, the ACA is currently working on a viable interstate licensing compact and making good progress.

The Future of Counseling

Gerard predicts that what happens with the Affordable Care Act and Medicare for All will have a significant impact on the future for counselors. It appeals to him to think of universal health care for every American; however, if counselors are not included in Medicare reimbursement when that happens, a huge drop-off in mental health services will occur.

Gerard believes that the future of counseling is tied to the integrated care components of the Affordable Care Act, which have started health care moving in that direction. Counselors will need to partner with general practitioners and doctors' offices to ensure that mental health services are available on site. Gerard hopes this will lead to a breakdown of the artificial barrier between physical health and mental and emotional health, which could make an incredible difference in people's overall well-being.

The counseling profession also needs to determine how to influence distance counseling so that it can be useful to the people for whom it is appropriate, which he doesn't believe is everyone. Populations for whom distance counseling could be appropriate are individuals with disabilities who confront barriers to getting out to see a counselor and people with conditions involving severe anxiety, such as agoraphobia. Essentially, distance counseling would be used appropriately when the choice is to get help online through distance counseling or to get no help at all. Gerard stressed the need for ongoing assessment regarding the best way to counsel in those situations and how to evaluate the next step in the client's recovery. Ultimately, it is important to consider whether clients are choosing distance counseling out of convenience or necessity. He also notes the importance of counselors being trained in distance counseling before providing it. After the onset of the coronavirus pandemic, we saw how distance counseling can be effective in an emergency situation, but no research has been published about the impact of client care as a result of moving services online. Gerard believes that this is an evolving area for the profession that could continue to redefine how we do our work.

In thinking about the future, Gerard stresses the importance of developing a pipeline of the next generation of leaders and supporting those interested in participating in leadership roles. He believes this process should begin in counselor training programs. Counselor educators should be talking with students about advocacy and leadership as part of the counselor's role, and they should have related expectations for students. During his regular visits to the Hill on Legislative

Day in Virginia, legislators have been enamored with the counseling students who come to advocate. Gerard's vision is that the connection between counselors-in-training and legislators will solidify so that future work can be done. Not only does Gerard go to Legislative Day with an "ask" for legislators, he also wants legislators to know that if they could use some help in tackling a mental health concern, he is a resource for them. Gerard envision this process as a two-way street that benefits everyone.

Gerard believes that the leadership of ACA has become more reflective of the demographics of the membership over time, but it still has a way to go. He argues that the ACA could do a better job of reaching out and making sure counselors feel welcome in the leadership. Leadership is often invitational, and Gerard believes we do a disservice to the field if we say "I think you'd be good at this" only to people who look like them. A deeper, broader, more diverse pool of people should be invited to participate, and it should be easier for them to engage. Practicing counselors, not just counselor educators, are needed in leadership roles so leadership stays in tune with what counselors and clients need.

Words of Wisdom

For Gerard, leadership in counseling is all about relationships, both with people who agree with us and with people who disagree with us, and with people from whom we need something and those who need something from us. For example, with respect to professional advocacy, he advises counselors get to know their legislator before they need something from that legislator. He argues that none of us will get things done by ourselves. He urges leaders to trust others to do their jobs, understanding that we each have a role in the process. He asserts that we exist in a system made up of parts working together toward a common goal. This understanding should help prevent burnout for leaders.

When asked to reflect on what he wishes someone had told him when he was in graduate school, Gerard says that he wishes he would have known that counseling is a unique and powerful profession, that there is something special about the work that counselors do that is different from psychology, social work, or marriage and family therapy. He is careful to say this is not to denigrate the work that those disciplines do or to inflate the work that counselors do but to recognize the reality that we approach things differently. Part of the role of a counselor is to advocate for clients beyond their immediate needs in the counseling room so they will be able to navigate the world more successfully. Gerard wishes those kinds of conversations had been more explicit in graduate school. The clearer we are about that, the easier it is for people to want to be engaged in the profession.

Corrine R. Sackett's Final Reflections

When I entered the doctoral program at Virginia Tech, Gerard was already established as a leader in the field. However, I didn't fully grasp his impact and had little interaction with him, and I experienced him as being fairly reserved. Then, during my first SACES conference in 2008, I vividly remember hearing him speak at the Emerging Leaders event. Gerard had the entire audience captivated and laughing hysterically. Some of my new peers and friends from other programs looked to me between laughs and asked, "Is he always like this?" And I responded, "I don't even know who this is!" I went back to Virginia Tech after that conference realizing that Gerard had a lot to offer in the way of mentorship and that I wanted to soak up as much of it as I could. I did just that.

As I got to know Gerard better, I benefited a great deal from his intelligence, humor, and genuine caring nature. These characteristics were critical throughout my development, but especially during my dissertation and academic job search process. Best of all, I still benefit from Gerard's mentorship and continue to look to him in my evolution as a counselor educator. I don't hesitate to call him for consultation in navigating academic politics, program issues, or research conceptualization. Just knowing he is in my corner as I continue to develop as a counselor educator gives me a certain amount of peace and security. He is always present, caring, honest, and wise in what he has to offer.

Writing this leader profile of Gerard has left me reflecting on what more I could be doing in terms of advocacy, and it has felt like a supportive challenge. It would be easy for future leaders to feel overwhelmed with the gravity of all that Gerard has contributed and continues to contribute to our field, but the reality is that Gerard consistently leverages his strengths to benefit others and our profession. And we can all definitely work to do more of that.

Notable Accomplishments

2002–present	Professor of Counselor Education, Virginia Tech
	Fellow, American Counseling Association
2003–2006	Chair, ACA Task Force on Counselor Wellness and Impairment
2009–2010	President, Virginia Counselors Association
2010–2013	Chair, ACA Crisis Response Planning Task Force
2011–2013	President, Association for Counselor Education and Supervision
2013–2016	Governing Council Representative, ACA
2017–2018	President, American Counseling Association

Chapter 12

Courtland C. Lee

Marja Humphrey

Mentee's Introduction

I, Marja Humphrey, met Courtland C. Lee during my interview for admission into the doctoral program at the University of Maryland at College Park, where he served as the program chair. Later, when students were critical of the textbook for his doctoral-level Multicultural Counseling course, he challenged us to write a better one. The next week, he walked into class with the outline of a book proposal, and *Elements of Culture in Counseling* was born. Courtland mentored us through the entire process. We never imagined we would write a textbook as doctoral students. A year later, as we reviewed the book layout and proposed covers, we were all still in disbelief, yet we had become better scholars and counselor educators and were a more close-knit cohort. Our work had superseded who we were as individuals. I doubt that any of us has ever criticized a textbook again.

That was not the last time any of us would publish with Courtland. He routinely pulled in doctoral students to write with him. He taught us in the doing, through on-the-job training. It was always an invitation, but it was never optional. We referred to it as being "voluntold." Looking back, I realize that this exercise instilled confidence in me that I had not possessed at the time.

One semester, I served as Courtland's teaching assistant for the master's-level Multicultural Counseling course. He was masterful. I marveled at how, every week, he recounted a story of his experience in a different place around the globe working with diverse people. The desire to teach had long solidified in my bones, but lecturing without notes, who did that? How could I bring words to life and have students understand themselves within the context of these ideas? Most important, how might I as an educator inspire counselors-in-training to help others, not according to their own agenda but in ways that honored their clients' cultural identities and traditions?

Courtland C. Lee's Journey

Early Years and Career Path

Courtland C. Lee was born in Philadelphia, Pennsylvania, into a working-class family. His early years provided many positive experiences and opportunities for leadership capabilities to emerge and develop within his family, school, and community. The seeds of a future counseling career were planted: listening, leading, helping, advocating. Courtland credits his mother with much of his subsequent success. For further information on Courtland's childhood, please see an earlier profile expertly written by Gladding (2011). Courtland completed the rigorous curriculum at Philadelphia's Central High School and went on to college at Hofstra University on Long Island, New York.

His first position after graduating with his bachelor's degree was as a fourth-grade teacher in the Bedford-Stuyvesant neighborhood in Brooklyn, commonly referred to as "Bed-Stuy." The school served mostly Black and Puerto-Rican children from lower socioeconomic backgrounds, and Courtland saw the effects firsthand of the intersection of poverty and race in the neighborhood. Courtland spoke of his time there as developing his sense of the importance of understanding cultural diversity and social justice. His transition into counseling occurred as a result of his work with these students. After 4 years of teaching in Brooklyn, he moved into a position as a school counselor in East Lansing, Michigan, while completing his doctorate at Michigan State University (MSU).

Courtland spent 2 years as a school counselor in East Lansing, having been thrust into a community that was the polar opposite of Bed-Stuy. This solidly middle-class school served the children of the professors from MSU. Here, Courtland found it imperative to advocate for the Black and Brown students from Detroit who were also in the school system.

Pivotal Moments

A pivotal experience that influenced Courtland's professional journey in counseling came when he was a master's student at Hunter College in New York City and met Alfred Pasteur. Pasteur was a founding member of the Association of Non-White Concerns, a division of what was known then as the American Personnel and Guidance Association (now the American Counseling Association [ACA]). As a graduate student, Courtland had never had a Black professor, and as the only Black student in class, he was "mesmerized" by Pasteur. Courtland whispered to himself, "I want to be like him when I grow up." An organic relationship evolved as the two rode the subway together: Pasteur talked, Courtland listened. This mentor-mentee relationship grew as Courtland accompanied Pasteur on multiple consulting engagements. Pasteur set Courtland on his career path, opening up a "whole new world" in which there was a place for Courtland as a Black person in this profession. One thing Courtland remembers as particularly inspirational was how Pasteur, a professional singer with an amazing voice, incorporated Black art forms into individual and group work with clients. Later, Courtland would conduct his own research on how to use Black music and poetry with Black boys in counseling.

Courtland recalls that Pasteur "told me under no uncertain terms [that] I was going to get my doctorate." Courtland enrolled at Michigan State, where the urban counseling program was funded by a grant from the National Institute of Mental Health to train counselors of color and advance new notions of counseling with attention to social justice issues. With a focus on cultural competency, Courtland learned alongside giants of the field: Joe White, the father of Black psychology; Robert L. Williams, who examined cultural bias in testing; and Thomas Gunnings, who wrote about systemic counseling, now termed social justice advocacy.

Courtland identified a second pivotal moment as his appointment at the University of North Carolina–Chapel Hill (UNC-CH) in the College of Education. In 1979, Courtland was one of very, very few Black faculty members. UNC-CH was White, southern, and racist, which precipitated the exodus of most of the faculty of color. Courtland recalled that his White colleagues saw him as a token affirmative action hire and that the students thought they were brighter than he was, which, admittedly, was intimidating at first. "The seven of us [faculty] who came in at the same time, we supported each other." Courtland earned tenure within 5 years, contrary to the expectations of many of his colleagues. Black students across campus began flocking to him, and he started to write, expanding on ideas from his training under Pasteur. As his name began to "get out there," he accepted leadership roles in several state and national counseling organizations.

After transitioning from UNC-CH to the University of Virginia (UVA), Courtland began accepting calls for more travel and speaking engagements. He became editor of the *Journal of Multicultural Counseling and Development*, the journal of the Association for Multicultural Counseling and Development (AMCD), at a time when the journal was in bad shape. With the help of the editorial board, Courtland turned it around, laying a foundation for the excellent journal it is today. Simultaneously, he was encouraged to branch out, broadening his work beyond AMCD, so he began working with other journal editors. He became the chair of the Council of Journal Editors, primarily composed of White males, which led to even more firsts. Courtland, "a Black face," served as a representative, a door-opener.

With his name now known and his reach extended, Courtland became involved with the Council for the Accreditation of Counseling and Related Educational Programs (CACREP). People "were beginning to see me as someone who transcended the multicultural division." The assistant director of ACA, Barbara Brown Robinson, a friend of Courtland's from his hometown of Philadelphia, introduced him to Carol Bobby. Courtland describes Barbara, the only African American ACA staff person at that time, as "an anchor person in my life." Later, Bobby asked Courtland to consider running for the presidency of Chi Sigma Iota. Through his various activities in ACA and CACREP site visits all over the country, Courtland met David Capuzzi, Gerald Corey, and Tom Sweeney, other "giants in the field."

These colleagues began encouraging Courtland to consider leading ACA. He had not thought about running for ACA president but recognized that "in some respects, I had been training for this my whole life." He ran twice, winning the second time. This was a "true pivotal and salient moment." Courtland was the third African American but the first African American male to serve as the ACA president. This role challenged and tested what he knew about leadership as well as his leadership philosophy. It was a challenging time for ACA, and there was tension and bad blood. Courtland chose to emphasize the importance of the unity of the profession. "We have many specialties, but we have to be able to speak with one voice." He used this pulpit to talk about issues of multiculturalism and diversity, convening the Multicultural Diversity Summit with all the stakeholders: division presidents, CACREP, the National Board for Certified Counselors (NBCC), and the Insurance Trust.

During this time, ACA was interested in getting more involved internationally with other counseling organizations. Courtland attended a joint conference with the British Association for Counselling (BAC). The theme of the conference, held in London, was Cultural Diversity, and Courtland sat on the conference planning committee. The conference was a success, and Courtland met more colleagues and maintains contact with many of them today. Next, the International Roundtable for the Advancement of Counselling Conference was held in Finland. Courtland submitted a paper on African American male development, which was accepted. This was the beginning of his international work. He began traveling internationally several times a year, conducting workshops and trainings. Later, he was awarded a Fellowship with the British Association for Counselling and Psychotherapy (BACP, formerly BAC); to date, he is the only American to have this honor.

Courtland found that other countries were roughly 10 to 15 years behind the United States in terms of their multicultural counseling thinking, and many were still fighting the colonized mentality. Enter Hans Hoxter, who escaped from Germany during the 1930s, when Hitler came to power, and helped to start counseling in the United Kingdom, founding the International Association of Counselling (IAC). Hoxter took Courtland under his wing with the words, "I think you have a big future in international counselling." Courtland was elected secretary of the IAC, and he helped to "keep the organization going between conferences." He was then elected president of the IAC. Although it was never said overtly, Courtland could tell there was some real resentment from the Brits and the Canadians, but he garnered great support from the African and Caribbean members. He later became a Fellow of the ACA and was promoted to full professor at UVA. At this time, there were no more than three or four African American full professors in counseling, and Courtland used his position to be "a really powerful voice to speak about multicultural and diversity issues" in counseling.

For Courtland, all of these pivotal moments have an existential component. Being in this profession is about "facilitating and promoting human potential, one of the most important parts of counseling." According to Courtland, this becomes even more important with Black students. As a counselor educator, he wants students to have a powerful experience. He spoke of an intangible sense he has when meeting students, one that fuels him to advocate for them. It is the recognition of their potential.

A final pivotal moment of which Courtland spoke took place in July 2003 when he married his long-time friend and colleague, Vivian Ripley. To those of us who came to know her, she was quickly titled "Dr. Mrs. Lee." An accomplished counselor educator in her own right, she was a noted scholar on school counseling. Vivian was soon traveling with Courtland to national and international conferences where they often presented together. Courtland invited Vivian to contribute to several of his books, most notably a chapter on promoting a culture of positive peace in the third edition of *Counseling for Social Justice.* This provocative chapter challenged Courtland to expand his thinking about the concept of social justice and the role of counseling in general. This chapter did not just rehash old thinking about social justice and counseling; it took social justice counseling in important new directions. One in particular was that counseling, as both a profession and a process, could be a force for promoting peace on many levels by advancing mental health and social well-being.

Vivian and Courtland opened their house to students each December to celebrate the holidays. Vivian was a gracious hostess who welcomed us and made us feel like family. At these gatherings, amid the fun and socializing, both of the Lees would offer students guidance and encouragement in dealing with the challenges of graduate school. It was obvious to all of us that "Dr. Lee" and "Dr. Mrs. Lee" were a dynamic team who loved and supported each other. Sadly, Vivian passed away in 2020, and her loss has affected Courtland deeply:

> I am a better human being because she was in my life. She was a fierce and passionate social justice warrior who abhorred violence and social injustice in all of its many forms. It was her mission in life to make the world a more just and peaceful place. She committed herself in her life and work to the principles of cultural humility and social justice. Her life commitment is a challenge to me to continue working as hard as I can for peace and social justice.

Points of Pride

When Courtland was asked to consider the professional accomplishments in which he has the most pride, he quickly noted his publications. Although writing and publishing are not easy, it is a talent with which Courtland was gifted. He enjoys the challenge. He reflected on his upbringing—"thanks to my mother"—where learning and the written word were prized. Having learned to write well in high school, Courtland has gone on to produce numerous articles, and his most popular multicultural counseling textbook, *Multicultural Issues in Counseling: New Approaches to Diversity* (Lee, 2019) is currently in its fifth edition. He shared that "seeing your name in print is really powerful." Although he acknowledges how lonely it can be to sit in his office writing, he experiences the impact of his work when meeting others who have read his books and articles. Other than publishing, seeing his "children" (i.e., students) do well is Courtland's proudest professional accomplishment, and it is a testament to his legacy in the counseling profession.

Leadership and Advocacy

Courtland's leadership philosophy developed from two perspectives. He quotes Lao Tzu, a Chinese philosopher and the founder of Taoism: "Of the good leader, when the work is done, we will say we did this ourselves." Perhaps Courtland's research around multiculturalism enabled him to readily embrace an Eastern perspective. "I came across this quote early in my career and as I reflected on this statement, it made perfect sense. And that is what I have done." According to Courtland, to be a leader is to help empower others to do their best and develop their talents, to help others do it on their own.

Second, Courtland learned about leadership principles through Chi Sigma Iota, the international honor society of professional counseling. The emphasis on giving back and being a servant leader permeated his approach to each leadership position he undertook. "We are to serve the organization, not for our own benefit but to benefit the organization." This theme of contributing to the greater good of others seems to have been born in Courtland, the oldest of four children. He was constantly organizing activities for the other children in his Philadelphia neighborhood. He was always the leader of something, getting a group of people together to do things. "Somehow, I got the notion early on that leadership was not about me, it was figuring out a way to get everybody involved."

Courtland reflected on the challenges of serving when you are the "first" to occupy a position of leadership. Having watched what Barack Obama experienced as president of the United States, Courtland said that he went through some of the same "stuff," although on a much smaller scale. This parallel was drawn because Obama was the first African American president, as Courtland was first in many of his experiences as a leader in the counseling profession nationally and internationally. Courtland spoke of understanding the current of resistance and racism that a person of color faces when taking on a leadership role. Specifically, as the first Black president of the IAC, Courtland said, "in opening doors, you have to expect that." The work of a trailblazer is difficult, but there is a responsibility as a leader to pave the way for those who will come after you.

The salient events in Courtland's leadership journey have fueled his drive to advocate for his students. It has always been important to him that his students have the kind of experience that he had as a graduate student with Pasteur. Seeing their potential is the impetus behind his publishing and presenting with students. He has said more than once, as he was similarly told, "You are going to get your PhD, and you have no choice in the matter." Courtland believes in reaching behind to bring the next group of folks along as Pasteur instructed him to do, which includes students as well as junior faculty members. He sees himself as a mentor, taking others under his wing to guide them in their careers. "This is the whole notion of being a servant leader. Using your power and influence to help other folks. It is important that I am a role model and a mentor as well." Courtland offered a distinction between the two: Role models offer great examples; mentors offer personal support. This personal touch seems to have made all the difference for many of his former students.

Advocacy work is often hidden. Despite all the public work of a leader, much of their impact happens behind closed doors. What others do not see is all the behind-the-scenes work that a true leader does. Courtland contrasted two types of leaders. The position of the servant leader is that nothing is beneath you. The "diva" leader just looks around and asks why the conference room is not set up, whereas a true leader starts setting up the chairs. "You roll up your sleeves and do whatever needs to be done." Currently, Courtland serves as faculty advisor for the Counseling Student Organization at the Washington, D.C., campus of The Chicago School of Professional Psychology. He provides much needed "encouragement" to his students in their current studies as well as a few "mandates" to pursue a doctorate. The behind-the-scenes work is what advances someone or a cause—going the extra mile for another's benefit.

Courtland has had an impact on counseling graduate students for several decades now. One student who has followed his footsteps closely, while carving his own path in the profession, is Carlos P. Hipolito-Delgado, associate professor of counseling in the School of Education and Human Development at the University of Colorado, Denver. Carlos was pleased to share his experiences as one of Courtland's mentees. Carlos first encountered Courtland through his textbooks: "Dr. Lee got me thinking that I could exist and occupy a space that felt white and be an advocate for people of color." Although Carlos had not planned on pursuing a doctoral degree, he began to consider the possibility while working as an academic advisor, when he officially met Courtland. Courtland was conducting training at the University of California, Los Angeles, because Carlos's supervisor had a grant with ACA. Carlos remembers two specific things that Courtland said. One was that people of color needed cultural validation, especially in White spaces. The second was an exchange between the two about cultural identity development models and how Carlos felt they promoted Americanization. Courtland's response, which sparked even more inquiry within Carlos, was that there were a lot of folks who didn't think that way at all. This exploration of identity and political action continued as the two became mentor and mentee at the University of Maryland. Carlos remembers "how confident and unapologetic" Courtland was. Carlos told himself that if he was going to learn something, it was going to be from him.

Courtland's modeling then has had an impact on Carlos's own leadership journey and his mentorship of early career faculty. He spoke resolutely: "I learned a lot from watching him. First, the need to always be professional and conduct myself responsibly." Wearing a shirt and tie was a necessity so that, as a man of color, the way "I look doesn't give you a reason to discount me." Looking professional must be accompanied by conducting oneself in a professional manner: "Because there are not a lot of men of color in counseling, we have an obligation." Second, Carlos spoke of how Courtland prepared him for the profession and academia more broadly. He remembers the "young, idealistic me" and all that Courtland taught him about politics, the importance of involvement in professional organizations, and the need to constantly write. "It makes sense in retrospect. Particularly now, as I mentor young faculty of color, I am trying to pass along these lessons." As Carlos prepared to step into the presidency of the AMCD, a position Courtland had previously held, a conversation with Courtland "forced me to think clearly about what I wanted to get done. What were the goals for my term? What impact could I make? What was my strategy?" Carlos concluded, "this man has impacted my life, my thinking, and my profession. We are here to support the next generation; he modeled that."

Another mentee, Lauren Brown, is a resident in counseling with the City of Alexandria, Virginia. She began her graduate studies in counseling at The Chicago School of Professional Psychology (TCSPP) in 2016. Courtland was the instructor for several of her courses: Diversity and Multicultural Counseling, Research Methods, and Counseling Theories. Lauren recalls, "I loved that class [Diversity]" because Courtland was a "fantastic professor." Lauren also enjoyed the weekly journal assignments that chronicled her growth as a counselor-in-training. Lauren said that Courtland "cares about his students, he is fair and challenging, his classes have changed my life in so many ways."

A month into the course, Courtland pulled Lauren aside to provide some feedback. "He said, 'You are a fantastic writer.' A professor at TCSPP had never before sought me out like that, especially to give me such a meaningful compliment. Then he said, 'I have a project for you,' and so began my coauthorship of a chapter in his third edition of *Counselors for Social Justice*." With Courtland's encouragement, Lauren was soon at her first counseling conference, giving her first poster presentation. The following year, Lauren traveled internationally with Courtland and "Dr. Mrs. Lee" to present her research on identity negotiations at the Euroscicon Clinical Psychology and Neuroscience Conference in England. Courtland and Lauren's most recent collaboration was a presentation accepted for the 2020 ACA conference. Lauren shared, "I admire and look up to Dr. Lee. As my advisor, he always checked on me, professionally and personally. In those moments when I shared my humanity, he has shown his humanity as well. I so much value his presence in my life."

The Future of Counseling

As we moved to the end of our conversation, I asked Courtland to share his perspective on where he sees the counseling profession going in the future. He spoke of the counseling profession broadening internationally so that all counselors are engaging in the global context. There is still a need for understanding "cultural competence as a crucial foundation of counseling practice. We need to demonstrate cultural competence as a part of being a credentialed counselor, particularly as we see (and need) more people of color in the profession." Courtland would like to see counselor training at the master's and doctoral levels become less theory based and more infused with real-world realities, because many of our theoretical notions do not reflect contemporary life. He hopes that counseling will have parity with other mental health professions, such as psychology and social work.

Courtland encourages future leaders in the counseling profession to "be more global in their thinking and get beyond lip service to cultural competency, ensuring that cultural competency is embedded in lifelong, ongoing professional development." He emphasizes that we must take steps to ensure outreach to underrepresented groups and recruit them to the profession. Counselor educators and counselors need to stay current and maintain their involvement in professional organizations at the state, regional, national, and international levels.

Words of Wisdom

Reflecting on his journey thus far in the field of counseling, Courtland offered these words of wisdom.

> Again, it is important to reach back and bring the next generation along. Never, ever take yourself too seriously. You must not lose the ability to laugh at yourself. Practice humility. This is really important. Have balance in your life. It cannot be all about your profession. Read a novel, a biography, watch something on Netflix. If you are pursuing leadership, think about why. The right reasons should be to help empower other people and serve the profession. Do not do it for your vitae or ego. Finally, learn when to take a bow and exit stage right. Let go instead of recycling yourself through leadership positions.

Courtland often shares these words of wisdom during CSI initiation ceremonies. Clearly, Courtland has not only shaped the field of counseling but has allowed himself to be shaped by his work and his colleagues.

Looking forward and looking back provide perspective. Kierkegaard said, "Life can only be understood backwards; but it must be lived forwards." Courtland started his graduate studies in counseling at Hunter College at the City University of New York. As he looked back to that time, he wished someone had told him, "This profession is going to be very good to you, but don't let it consume you." This goes back to the balance question. Honestly, Courtland said, it has cost him a marriage and connections with old friends. "Part of it was getting tenure; part of it was spending weekends on the road with ACA. No balance." Courtland is quick to admit that one will make mistakes in the career development process; however, he embraces chance theory, noting that "sometimes it is not always a matter of choice, things just unfold."

Marja Humphrey's Final Reflections

Over the years I have presented with Courtland C. Lee, published with him, and enjoyed UMD program holiday celebrations at his home. More than that, he has encouraged my professional career through service opportunities with Chi Sigma Iota and ACA and has written recommendation letters on my behalf. It was an honor to interview him. To be honest, I thought I already knew his story. I was wrong. I got to know him all over again, in a deeper, richer way. Over a decade removed from our Maryland days, my perspective has shifted now as an early career professor, and Courtland has logged many more miles across the earth, contributing even more to the profession. The legacy of Courtland C. Lee continues.

Notable Accomplishments

1995–1996	President, Chi Sigma Iota
1997–1998	President, American Counseling Association
	Fellow, American Counseling Association
2006–2012	President, International Association for Counselling
	Fellow, British Association for Counselling and Psychotherapy
2008–2009	Chair, American Counseling Association Foundation Board of Trustees
2012–2013	Chair, American Counseling Association Foundation Board of Trustees
	ACA Foundation benefactor, Courtland C. Lee Multicultural Excellence Scholarship Award
	Author, editor, or coeditor of seven books on multicultural counseling and three on counseling and social justice

Chapter 13

Spencer G. Niles

Patrick Akos

Mentee's Introduction

I am Patrick Akos, and Spencer G. (Skip) Niles was my professor and dissertation advisor at the University of Virginia. He has continued to be my mentor and friend for the past 20 years. Skip was a major influence in my path to professor in the School of Education at the University of North Carolina at Chapel Hill. I am honored to share his story and am excited to share reflections offered by many significant others in his journey.

Many tales could contribute to understanding Skip as a person. His early abbreviated cross-country running prowess, bike rides in Vancouver constructing hope career theory, karaoke in Korea with career practitioners, leading study abroad in Rwanda, chasing away bats with a comforter in Ireland, the meaning in the passing of his mother, executive development work at Harvard, debating saunas as the secret reason to the Finnish success in the Programme for International Student Assessment (PISA), his passionate support for Penn State football . . . these are all aspects of his interesting personal character.

From a professional perspective, Skip is one of the preeminent voices in career development and counseling. Donald Super helped him understand that a career is much broader than what you do for a living. It is about living a meaningful life. Skip has led a meaningful life. To Skip, leadership and advocacy are synonymous with helping others construct a meaningful life.

Spencer G. Niles's Journey

Early Years and Career Path

Skip comes from a long line of educators (siblings, parents, grandparents). He studied elementary education at Bloomsburg University and considers education the family business. His interest in counseling emerged from his childhood experience growing up with a divorced mother at a time when counseling wasn't considered as an option. During this impressionable period, Skip wondered how people were to make sense of their life experiences. He found that one way to do this was through the lens of cultural diversity and cultural humility.

His mother was a high school Spanish teacher in rural Pennsylvania who worked multiple jobs to save enough money to send him and his two older sisters on an annual trip to Mexico City. Throughout her career, his mom took sabbaticals to both the University of Madrid and the University of Granada. These opportunities allowed Skip to develop a diverse lens on life. He concluded that people make sense out of experience through the context of their lens and the resultant life philosophy and personal theology that emerges. This led him to enroll in a liberal Protestant graduate theological seminary with a rich Black church and social action tradition (Crozer Theological Seminary). This cultural enrichment again shaped his life path. The main church in which he was involved threw him out for advocating for the ordination of members of LGBTQ+ populations, and he realized the traditional church setting was not for him.

Indeed, throughout these early years, transitions held both challenge and opportunity for Skip. Leaving the seminary led him to seek career counseling for himself for the first time. He was desperately seeking some direction in his life but experienced the stereotypical "test-and-tell" career help that was practiced at the time. It was a mechanistic, disengaged process that relied on standardized assessments to inform him of what he "should do." His experience as a client was so awful (including his career counselor literally falling asleep) that it led to an epiphany—there had to be a better way to help others in career counseling.

Enter counselor education (Lehigh University and Penn State University), the ideal preparation Skip embraced so that he could learn more. In his first-semester career development course, he learned quickly that people make career choices as a process of making meaning out of their own life experience. He shifted from an orientation steeped in the "psychology of possession" (how much one possesses relative to aptitudes, interests, values, etc.) to a "psychology of use" (how one chooses to use what one possesses to make meaning out of life experiences). This new lens provided the clarity he needed. Skip believed this orientation reflected life in the way that most people live. Rather than thinking about our location on the normal curve, we strive to make meaning out of our life experiences and translate that meaning into a career direction. This foundation for career intervention, grounded in positive psychology, helps career counselors give clients a structure in which their basic roles of living allow for a life they find more meaningful. Helping others find meaning was the type of advocacy that gave Skip purpose.

Pivotal Moments

Skip is quick to highlight the important influence of others and key mentors who stoked his passion for career development as an area of research and intervention. Starting with Edwin Herr, significant individuals also include Mark Savickas, Donald Super, John Krumboltz, Norman Amundson, James Sampson, Courtland C. Lee, and many others—including most of the outstanding faculty colleagues with whom he has worked.

Ed Herr was Skip's advisor throughout his graduate training in counselor education at Penn State University. Ed provided Skip with opportunities to direct a vocational assessment center, work in a developmentally oriented career center, and secure his first position teaching a master's course in career development. A particularly salient moment during his first semester as a doctoral student occurred when Ed invited him to coauthor a journal manuscript. Skip panicked. He believed he could barely write letters home. He told Ed, "Thank you very much but I don't know how to do that," and Ed replied, "That's OK, it's a developmental skill and I can teach you." That response changed the course of Skip's life. Ed Herr, an amazing leader in counseling who was the ACA (then American Association for Counseling and Development) president at the time and author of literally several hundred publications, believed in him. At the time, Ed was the first distinguished professor of education at Penn State. Twenty years later, when Skip was named a distinguished professor at Penn State, his first phone call was an emotional one, telling Ed it would never have been possible without his mentoring. This example of caring, compassion, and concern for others shaped Skip's calling to care about the careers of others, especially when they might have difficulty mustering the confidence to take on important career development tasks.

Several experiences in Skip's first academic job at the University of Virginia (UVA) were critical to his career. This was his first opportunity to teach career counseling at the doctoral level. He was 33 years old and rather intimidated by the prospect of teaching and advising doctoral students. Some of his doctoral students were older than he was and had more experience, but he sought to learn from and with them, and he partnered with them on many writing projects and conference presentations. He quickly found he loved working with them. This was when Skip's research blossomed. He joined Donald Super's research team, focused on developing his Career Development, Assessment, and Counseling (C-DAC) model, and became licensed as a professional counselor, all while directing a career counseling center for adults in the Charlottesville community. During this same period, he began to take on leadership roles, both in the Virginia Career Development Association and the National Career Development Association (NCDA). From newsletter editor to more prominent roles, his work on the editorial board of *The Career Development Quarterly* (*CDQ*) was a significant lesson in leadership. Paul Salomone gave Skip this initial opportunity with *CDQ*, and Mark Savickas became an instrumental mentor who helped him refine his ability to write for publication. Mark's mentoring and help from many others led Skip into roles as the editor of *CDQ* and the NCDA president (the first time) in 2003–2004.

Returning to Penn State to become the coordinator of their counselor education program proved to be another pivotal moment. Here, he battled to create their first CACREP-accredited doctoral program, with the help of Brandon Hunt and Jerry Trusty. As he had experienced in his own doctoral program as a student, many faculty and administrators viewed counselor education at Penn State as "less than" a new counseling psychology program. His colleagues from that time report some extraordinary leadership and political advocacy within his academic unit, overcoming resistance to changing a DEd to a PhD and adding a clinical mental health program. This challenging environment in his coordinator role taught him the value of advocacy for the profession as a whole. His steadfast belief in professionalism and national standards (CACREP) provided the department with resources and support to create and sustain a tremendously successful counselor education program at Penn State.

Skip extended this notion of advocacy in his role as editor of the *Journal of Counseling & Development* (*JCD*), president of Chi Sigma Iota, and eventually chair at Penn State. His goal was to elevate *JCD* while using the scholarship as an advocacy tool. He inherited a 3-year backlog in accepted manuscripts, with no easy way out of that situation. As might be expected, Skip credits "amazing" editorial board members (Rick Balkin, Paul Peluso, Sylvia Nassar, Brandon Hunt, and others) who helped the journal recover and transition into Balkin's outstanding editorial leadership. In fact, as his associate editor, Balkin noted that Skip "bridges the scholarly nature of counseling with the humanistic aspects of our profession flawlessly, so I experience an authentic moment with someone who willingly shares of himself, and I grow as well."

Jane Myers's invitation to run for president of Chi Sigma Iota was also instrumental to engaging in advocacy through leadership for the counseling profession. Skip is quick to note that it provided him with an opportunity to learn from amazing counseling advocates such as Craig S. Cashwell, Tom Sweeney, Jane Myers, Vicki Kress, Donna Gibson, Holly Moorhead, and many others. Kress, who recruited Skip to run for president, noted that "what really makes him stand out is his character . . . anyone who knows him will tell you he is kind, authentic, genuine, down-to-earth, open, vulnerable, transparent and compassionate . . . sadly, qualities I rarely see in leaders."

These experiences and his experience as chair at Penn State University helped Skip develop a disposition toward advocacy and a drive to strengthen the profession and led him to pursue a position as dean. This role challenged and sharpened his talents as a leader and provided the platform for Skip to advocate on a broader scale for all programs within the School of Education.

Points of Pride

Of all the contributions Skip has made, the one he values most is mentoring. His impact on the counseling field is obvious, but the largest impact Skip will ever have is on the students and colleagues with whom he has worked. Not only did he find meaning in others, but others also became his life purpose. He embodies one of our core conditions in counseling—a genuine, caring relationship.

Skip has surely made Edwin Herr proud. As David Monk noted, Skip "patterned himself after his mentor, Ed Herr . . . what stands out is his commitment to high quality mentoring." Bradley Erford (Skip's first doctoral mentee) validated that "Ed was very proud of Skip and all that he accomplished, but Ed also told me that he was most proud to see how expertly Skip was mentoring the next generation of counseling professionals." That Skip has emulated the mentors he most admires is evident in these words of impact from former doctoral students. Bradley Erford, now professor and program director at Vanderbilt University, states that Skip "creates serendipity. . . being in orbit around Skip has led to some of the best opportunities in my professional career and personal life. The most valuable lesson I learned from Skip was to always be your genuine self and be proud of who you are! Skip is the mentor we all hope to emulate."

Other former students made similar observations. Gary Goodnough, now professor at Plymouth State University, stated that "Skip valued my feedback while also mentoring me . . . and has continued to provide mentoring, collegiality, and friendship (30 years later)." Brandon Hunt, now professor at Georgia Southern University, attested to Skip's influence as a mentor and role model: "His mentoring and unwavering love and support have helped me to be the counselor educator I am today, and he continues to be a model of the person I work to become every day. He has many amazing qualities, but his sense of humor is what I love the most about him." Hank Harris, now professor at the University of North Carolina at Charlotte, notes that "what I remember most about him was his work ethic, encouraging attitude, and humbleness."

Skip's mentors, especially Edwin Herr and Mark Savickas, were selfless in their leadership styles. They worked to build up others and realized it was important to pay forward the mentoring they received by providing that sort of mentoring to others. Skip exudes gratitude for their excellent examples of servant leadership and carries this notion of mentoring, a commitment to pay it forward, as perhaps the most important part of his legacy.

Leadership and Advocacy

Skip's leadership contributions are too numerous to adequately cover, but those that stand out most are his impact on the departments and schools he has led, his international collaborations, and the NCDA. He worked hard to elevate the quality of the counselor education programs at UVA, Penn State, and William & Mary through outstanding faculty hires (including Jerry Trusty, Richard Hazler, JoLynn Carney, Julia Bryan, Daniel Gutierrez, Patrick Mullen, Natoya Haskins, and Craig S. Cashwell) who care about the profession and their students. His first job was as an assistant professor at the University of Virginia, where he rose to the position of assistant dean due to his leadership. At Penn State, in addition to creating the CACREP-accredited PhD program in counselor education, he led the creation of the career counseling master's degree program. During Skip's time on the faculty at Penn State, the counseling program was ranked in the top ten by *U.S. News and World Report* and continues to experience high rankings.

Skip has influenced counseling internationally and continues to do so. His initial work at the University of Lisbon as a visiting scholar led to substantial collaboration with the Danish Ministry of Education. He provided training in Denmark and brought Danish counselors to the United States for training. His leadership in bridging cultures continues in his international work in over 30 countries, including as a Fulbright Scholar in Finland at the University of Jyvaskyla and leading William & Mary students to Rwanda for study-abroad experiences. Raimo Vuorinen, who sponsored Skip's Fulbright in Finland, noted that "I have learned from him the importance of looking beyond one's own perspective. . . . Spencer has a unique skill to combine his extensive academic research and the ability to engage all the participants into a constructive dialogue." International leaders and scholars (from China, Turkey, Korea, and other countries) continue to come to the United States to study and learn from Skip.

His role as dean of the School of Education at William & Mary has resulted in a legacy within and outside the counseling profession. President Katherine A. Rowe noted: "During his time, Dean Niles successfully expanded the school's reach, growing the school's online footprint substantially, and led the development of new and impactful partnerships. I am deeply grateful for his leadership."

Among Skip's accomplishments, he started online master's degree programs in clinical mental health counseling, school counseling, and counseling for veterans; initiated online programs in curriculum and instruction and higher education; expanded executive education programs in educational leadership; and increased the size and diversity of the faculty. His leadership around equity and inclusion includes mentoring programs for underrepresented doctoral students, awards for student research in social justice and diversity, scholarships for STEM teachers in high-need school districts, and bringing in significant speakers (e.g., Pedro Noguera, Freeman Hrabowski, and Deborah Ball) when he launched a Diversity Speaker Series.

Skip is one of the few counselor educators nationally to lead as dean of an entire academic unit and to do so in a way that elevated counselor education and all programs and faculty in the school. Provost Peggy Agouris described his impact: "Dean Niles is an excellent example of the power of vision and leadership to move an institution forward. In my brief time working with him, I have already found him to be an accomplished scholar, a distinguished leader in education innovation, and a respected colleague."

Skip understands that position power does not equate to leadership. Skip has empowered others through shared governance and decision-making as well as providing the right balance of autonomy and support. Rick Gressard, chancellor professor of counselor education, described Skip's leadership this way:

> [Skip's] faculty-centered approach to leadership ensures that each faculty member feels heard, is supported in the projects about which they are genuinely enthused, and can trust that their work will matter to the School of Education and William & Mary. He's fun, he's an inspiration, he's one of the best counselor educators in the history of the profession, and he's one of the best friends I've ever had.

Other colleagues in the counselor education program have also commented on Skip's unique style of leadership. Patrick Mullen shared that "he naturally empowers those around him to pursue and achieve their passion," and Craig S. Cashwell stated that Skip "did what he did for me because he cares deeply both about the welfare of our profession and, perhaps, more important, the people around him. That is the mark of a true leader." In just his third year as dean at William & Mary, Skip was identified in a national survey as the 11th most influential dean of education in the United States.

Skip's impact in higher education is substantial, but perhaps his most meaningful and longest leadership contribution has been to NCDA. Collaborator Rich Feller noted that "Skip is a major influencer I turn to . . . being an NCDA board member with him became a lesson in leadership. I know no one who does not learn, enjoy, and become inspired by being with Skip Niles." The executive director of NCDA, Deneen Pennington, summed up both his impact and his humanness, noting that "Skip is a genuine colleague, trusted mentor, and supportive friend. Besides his incredible intellect, his friendly personality and team approach to leadership make him one of NCDA's most influential past presidents. He helped to expanded NCDA's brand beyond the U.S. borders."

Skip feels honored to have served as the only two-time president of NCDA (2003–2004; 2018–2019). He was the first NCDA president to organize a joint

NCDA/IAEVG (International Association for Educational and Vocational Guidance) international symposium, which was held before the 2004 NCDA conference. That year had the largest attendance in NCDA's history, topping 1,000 participants. In fact, Binnur Yesilyaprak, who was a visiting scholar from Turkey at Penn State, noted that "I owe great thanks to Spencer for his contributions to the improvement of career counselling in Turkey. For me, as a person who feels herself in love with counselling and finds meaning of life in this field, I think Spencer Niles is not only a distinguished professor and an important leader in this field but also is an advocate in counseling mission; he is a saint." His service as editor of *CDQ* (6 years) and as a member of the NCDA board of directors (approximately 25 years) are unparalleled.

Skip reports that he has received far more than he has given, and he feels privileged to have been mentored by Mark Savickas, Rich Feller, Mark Pope, Jane Goodman, JoAnn Harris-Bowlsbey, Martha Russell, and so many others. He believes strongly that the community of NCDA is unmatched globally and that the accomplishments of the members, since 1913, are incredible. He is honored to have called NCDA his professional home for so long.

When Skip speaks about accomplishments, it is always about others. For example, the awards he has received from NCDA and ACA are most meaningful because they were initiated by former students and his colleagues. He notes that "we have each had help . . . there are *no* self-made persons. Anyone who accomplishes anything has had assistance. This should keep us humble and committed to providing similar assistance to others."

The Future of Counseling

Skip's hope for the profession is that we continue to increasingly engage in advocacy for our clients, our students, our programs, and our colleagues. He asks us to "make the tent big—declare strongly what we as a profession bring to our communities, our nation, and the world. We make an incredible difference. Other helping professions do this as well, but we are unique and important. We should be very proud of that and remind others of our important influence." He continued with this exhortation:

> Advocate, advocate, and advocate . . . through research that is effectively communicated to policy makers, through being present at the table providing solutions to crucial societal problems, through direct service, and through excellence in counselor preparation. We are incredibly powerful as a profession when we each engage in these ways.

Skip believes we need to double down on our investment in the next generation of counselor educators. He wants us to elevate their research training, prepare them to be competitively engaged in acquiring research grants, and ensure they are trained in the most recent developments in the learning sciences, especially neuroscience. He feels strongly that we each have a responsibility to be advocates for licensure, licensure portability, the creation of policies that support the provision of counseling services across settings, the generation of evidence-based practices, the increased diversification of the profession, and the capacity of our profession to serve more clients and more diverse clients across the life span.

> We cannot become complacent. Nor can we settle for mediocrity. The human development needs are too great for any of that. Empowering others coping with addiction, family and relationship issues, career concerns, depression, anxiety, suicidal ideation (the list goes on) is a never-ending call to action for professional counselors. That said, I do think (and Jane Myers would agree) we need to give greater attention to wellness—in general, and within ourselves in particular. Creating space for human *being* is just as essential as our focus on human *doing*, maybe more so.

Words of Wisdom

Each of Skip's major accomplishments represents an instance when he felt stretched to do something he wasn't entirely sure he could do. Each, he believes, reflects his effort to carry forward the faith his mentors had in him, even when (or especially when) he didn't have that faith in himself. His advice is to "believe in yourself. Stretch and learn. Don't focus on whether or not you will be successful as much as what each opportunity has to teach you about yourself and the world. And when you receive help, remember to pay it forward. When you do, assuming the positive in others, you will develop the powerful collaborations and mutual understanding that empower us to take on the complex challenges people experience in living today."

Patrick Akos's Final Reflections

I have been fortunate to experience part of Skip's legacy, and in 2002, soon after I completed my doctoral program, I shared these thoughts about Skip as he received the David Brooks Award for Excellence in Mentoring from ACA.

> What made Dr. Niles most significant to me was his ability to make me feel more like a colleague than a student. Whether supervision, research, classwork, dissertation, or serving as my advisor—he always challenged me to think and then listened intently to my opinions, my thoughts, and my passionate feelings about counseling. I have not found many individuals who combined the national reputation he has as a scholar [with] the personable, supportive manner he has with people. I know that I would not have the knowledge, confidence, or ability to pursue my career goals without the influence of Dr. Skip Niles.

It has been nearly 20 years since I was his responsibility as a student. But since then, his support and empowerment of me has only grown. He was there to talk about my own anxiety as a new assistant professor and imposter syndrome, to celebrate and commiserate fatherhood, to applaud my first publications, to guide and encourage my tenure process, and to interrogate and challenge me when I lost confidence or ventured astray. He is still there to empower my voice as a full professor, there with nurturing support amid health challenges, there to debate society and cultural aspects of life, there to listen to my wonderings around leadership, and there to talk about midlife and the struggles and meaning and purpose that make us whole. He has the same impact on me that Ed Herr had on him. I am only one of many who has experienced his compassion and leadership in counseling, and I am eternally grateful.

Finally, Skip's impact would not be complete without mentioning his family. Both of his children have also landed in the counseling profession, and they clearly reinforce who Skip is and who he has become. At the 2019 NCDA conference, Jenny and Jonathan had this to say about their father:

> Our dad grew up seeking meaning, validation, and hope; words that have become important elements of his work. We've been by his side through difficult experiences and watched as he's transformed those challenges into deeper meaning. We are proud of you—for your accomplishments but, more important, regardless of your accomplishments. Thank you for teaching us to be kind and compassionate to others, to follow our hearts and do work that we love.

Notable Accomplishments

1998–2003	Editor, *The Career Development Quarterly*
2003	ACA David Brooks Award for Excellence in Mentoring
2004	Fellow of the National Career Development Association
2007	Eminent Career Award, National Career Development Association
	Fellow of the American Counseling Association
2008–2013	Editor, *Journal of Counseling & Development*
2012	Fulbright Senior Specialist
2013	ACA Thomas J. Sweeney Award for Visionary Leadership and Advocacy
2019	ACA Hohenshil Award for Excellence in Scholarly Contributions to the Counseling Literature
2020–present	Editor, *Counselor Education and Supervision*
	Author or coauthor of approximately 150 publications and 150+ presentations at international, national, and regional conferences

Chapter 14

Theodore P. Remley

Alexander T. Becnel

Mentee's Introduction

I am Alexander T. Becnel, a doctoral student studying with Theodore P. (Ted) Remley Jr. at the University of Holy Cross. We first met in August of 2014. It was Ted's first semester at the University of Holy Cross, and he was excited to be returning to New Orleans after spending 8 years at Old Dominion University in Norfolk, Virginia. Similarly, I was excited to be starting my master's program in counseling. During the graduate program orientation, I happened to take a seat next to Ted without knowing who he was or what his presence at the university would mean for me. As both of us are sociable, southern folks, it was natural to strike up a conversation. We traded jabs about him being a University of Florida Gator and my being a Louisiana State University Tiger before finishing the orientation and saying our goodbyes.

Several semesters into my master's program, I received an email inviting me to one of Ted's study abroad courses in Italy. I had never traveled abroad, and I was encouraged by the woman who is now my wife to seize the opportunity. Soon I was off to Reggello, Italy, to study play therapy. A year later, Ted invited me to join him in Le Mans, France. Once again, I said yes to the opportunity, and I was off to study the counseling profession in France. At the time, I thought these trips were just a fun way to earn credits; however, they gave me the chance to know Ted in a more personal sense. It was also during these trips that Ted encouraged me to apply to the doctoral program. Although getting a doctorate had been my distant dream for many years, it was never a goal for which I envisioned a realistic pathway. Several years later I am a committed doctoral student and proud to call Ted my mentor.

Theodore P. Remley's Journey

Early Years and Career Path

Ted Remley was born in Florida and raised in a blue-collar family. His father had an eighth-grade education, and his mother was a high school graduate. "Statistically speaking, I probably should have never made it to college," said Ted, "but this background really colored my career." Because he was one of the first people on either side of his family to attend college, he was not aware of all the options available for his education: "I went to college because my high school English teacher said I should apply. So, I did. When I asked her about which college I should attend, she said University of Florida, so that's where I went." When it came time to pick his major, Ted chose English because his English teacher was the person who sent him to college. Even though he did not have aspirations to become a teacher at the time, he took some teaching certification courses so he could get a job when he graduated. "Looking back, that decision really had an influence on my career choice."

Even though he was not always sure what his path might look like, Ted had a strong, internal drive to be in charge. At the University of Florida, he was involved in student government, edited the student newspaper, and was vice president of his fraternity. One of his more significant roles was his leadership in the student union organization, which was responsible for bringing speakers and entertainers to the university. Toward the end of his undergraduate years, Ted thought it might be possible for him to make a career out of event planning and organizing at the university. When he inquired about the possibility, he was told that he needed to earn a master's degree in student personnel services to get the job. He applied and was accepted at several universities, but ultimately Ted chose to remain at the University of Florida where he was offered a fellowship.

On the first day of class in his new master's degree program, Ted was surprised to hear some news that would change the entire trajectory of his career. The department chair announced that the student personnel services program was being renamed the counselor education program. Ted was shocked at the change. He did not know what a counselor was, nor did he know what counselors do.

Ted's fellowship was intended to prepare counselors to work in community colleges. Community colleges were a new concept at the time, and Ted was excited about the opportunity. Although he still did not see himself as a clinical counselor, he embraced the idea of helping students develop their vocational goals as a career counselor. He graduated from the University of Florida with a master's degree in counselor education in 1971.

Ted was ready to begin his career as a community college counselor, but he had participated in the Reserve Officer Training Corp (ROTC) during college and needed to fulfill his military obligation. He accepted a job as a school counselor temporarily as he awaited his military orders. In March 1972, Ted reported for Army basic training at Fort Sam Houston, Texas, where serendipity and opportunity once again arrived at his doorstep. "When we first arrived, they told us that we're going straight to Vietnam. Halfway through training, they asked if anyone would like to go into the reserves for 6 years instead of deploying. So I raised my hand." The Vietnam War was winding down, and Ted served in the Army Reserves for 6 years as he began his career as a community college counselor at Blue Ridge Community College in Weyers Cave, Virginia.

Ted spent the next 7 years in Virginia near Washington, D.C., and continued working in community colleges. These years arguably were some of the busiest years of his life. After his time in the military, Ted had kept in contact with his former roommate who had attended Harvard Law School. One day, his friend suggested that Ted should attend law school because he thought Ted could become a great lawyer. "Prior to that conversation, I had never considered attending law school. I had fraternity brothers who became lawyers, but I never considered it for myself." Much like when his English teacher suggested that he should go to college, Ted took the advice he was offered and decided to attend law school. He applied and was accepted to law school at Catholic University in Washington, D.C., which was a 4-year evening program.

During his first year in law school, Ted was contacted by one of his professors from the University of Florida. "He told me that he was retiring and that I needed to come back to complete my doctorate. When I said that I was in law school, he said that it didn't matter because I could do both." Once again, Ted decided to take the advice of a trusted advisor and enrolled in both programs. During his second year of law school, he went back to Florida to complete his PhD courses while earning credits toward his law degree at the University of Florida. During the final two years of law school, he went back to Washington, D.C., to complete law school while he wrote his PhD dissertation. In 1980, he graduated from both programs. Ted admitted that earning both degrees simultaneously was unusual and quite unplanned.

Although many people think of Ted as one of the nation's foremost leaders in counseling law and ethics, this area of expertise was not his original intention. Ted planned to create a career in criminal law, and after he completed his education, Ted began practicing law. He also taught counseling courses part time, first at George Washington University, then at George Mason University. After 7 more years of the balancing act between law and counseling, Ted came to a crossroads. He was offered a job with a large law firm in Chicago, and he was offered a full-time job as a professor and department chair at George Mason University. "It was sort of a turning point for me, but I decided to take the university job. Being a professor was just a natural fit."

Shortly after beginning his career at George Mason University, Ted was again given a chance to grab a rare break. Only three professors worked in his department, and there was no program leader because neither of the other two professors would accept the job. Ted, having a persistent desire to be in charge, gladly accepted the role. "From the very beginning, I was a program leader," he said. He was able to gain that position by stepping up when others would not. That quality would continue to serve him well throughout his career.

Once Ted committed himself to counselor education, it became obvious that he should capitalize on his legal background. From that point forward, law and ethics became his specialty, and the majority of his research and writing focused on risk management, or helping counselors understand their liability and how to protect themselves. "I didn't set my sights for that," Ted says. "I didn't say that I was going to become an expert in counselor ethics. I just did it because it was natural, and it made sense."

Ted's early years are painted not only with some luck but also with an ability to take advantage of the moment. Even though he had not intended to become a counselor educator, he was able to evaluate his circumstances and to act on opportunities. "I was a first-generation college graduate. I didn't know what I was doing when I went to college, I didn't know what I was doing after college, I entered the counseling field accidentally, and I embraced it." He did not expect to become a lawyer either, but he listened to the people who believed in him, and he figured out his journey along the way. His early career path developed in unexpected ways because he was open to new and interesting opportunities and had a willingness to say yes.

Pivotal Moments

Several moments throughout Ted's career influenced both his professional journey and his leadership style. One such moment was accepting a role in 1990 for which he is perhaps best known, executive director of the American Counseling Association (ACA). He was the first counselor educator to hold the position, and he saw a potential to make a significant impact on the profession. However, Ted considers much of his time in the role a failure. "If I were to do it over, I wouldn't have applied for the job." His experiences during those 4 years significantly altered his view of himself as both a leader and an advocate for the counseling profession. Recalling the beginning of his tenure as ACA executive director, Ted said, "My vision was to have ACA be the spokesperson for the profession of counseling, much like the American Psychological Association (APA) is for psychologists and the National Association of Social Workers (NASW) is for social workers." Quickly, he realized major barriers existed that would prevent this vision from becoming a reality. At the time, the counseling profession was desperately trying to establish itself as a recognized mental health profession. Social workers and psychologists had long been perceived by political entities as the trusted mental health practitioners. Counseling was still a new field, and counselors had not yet learned how to navigate legislation and advocacy.

As counselors were trying to prove that they were competent to practice independently and that they should be reimbursed by insurance companies for their services, Ted believed that a single, unified voice was needed to speak for the profession. He was not aware, however, of the structural issues that would prevent ACA from leading the entire profession. ACA's governing board was made up of representatives from various ACA divisions, and these divisions often had interests that were separate from the interests of ACA as a whole. Each division attempted to pull ACA toward its own goals, disrupting any meaningful progress toward goals to benefit the profession as a whole.

Another issue Ted faced as executive director was the structure of ACA leadership. In ACA, the spokesperson for the entire association was the elected president, not the executive director, and Ted's role was more of a manager than a leader. This structure was also problematic for the organization because the elected leader was replaced every year, leaving no time to achieve long-term goals. Ted made a career-changing realization. "I think, at that point, I decided that I could not be in charge of the entire profession of counseling. So, that's when I decided that I had to make my contributions in other ways."

Leadership and Advocacy

Ted has always been a leader, and he believes that leaders are born, not trained. The Army's philosophy was that anyone could be a leader if they were taught the appropriate behaviors and techniques, but Ted disagrees. "I believe leadership is more about personality. People have to have an inner drive to be in charge, and they have to be personable in a way that other people will accept them as leaders." He believes that these qualities cannot be taught. The military was teaching his entire platoon to lead, but only a few people who had these innate traits were successful. "You need to be sensitive to other people, and you have to have a drive to be successful." Ted explained that leaders cannot simply dominate others and stampede their mission to the forefront. Leaders have to understand how to assemble others around them.

Ted learned early in his career that finding leadership opportunities is easier than most people expect. "You just need to raise your hand or let someone know you're interested. There are so few people willing to volunteer for a leadership position." What sets Ted apart from others who simply say yes is his ability to follow through on those commitments. "I'm going to do whatever it takes to make something happen. I'm not going to let the project fail. I'll include other people and delegate duties to them, but they need to be reliable." Even when others are not reliable, Ted is not afraid to pick up their work and finish it. To him, it is crucial that leaders see their projects to the finish line. Leaders who do not fulfill their obligations are likely to struggle.

Ted reflected on how his leadership style interacted with his career. When he was an assistant professor at George Mason University, he became the leader of the counseling program during his first year because his colleagues did not want the extra responsibilities of the job. His experience at George Mason allowed him the opportunity to become department chair at Mississippi State University 4 years later. And in September 1990 he seized opportunity again and became executive director of ACA. In all of these moves, Ted saw an opportunity for growth and took control of his circumstances.

After his time as executive director, Ted began focusing his work on counselor licensure boards. As a young counselor, he was involved in getting one of the first licensure bills passed in the United States, which set in motion the passage of similar legislation across the country. These licensure bills transformed the practice of counseling into a legitimate and recognized mental health profession. Ted believes that he is the only person in the United States to have served on four state licensure boards: Virginia, Mississippi, the District of Columbia, and Louisiana. He was also one of the creators of and the founding president of the American Association of State Counseling Boards, which provides a forum for all state licensing boards to come together and share ideas. It is also where the idea of licensure portability first arose. This is one of the biggest challenges the counseling profession faces today. Ted believes his licensure board work is his most meaningful and important accomplishment.

Ted believes that his next largest contribution to the profession was the textbook he coauthored with Barbara Herlihy: *Ethical, Legal, and Professional Issues in Counseling*. They realized that there wasn't a textbook that covered law, ethics, and professional identity and decided to create the ultimate textbook that covered all three topics. With respect to the success of the text, Ted says, "I think we're educating a generation of counselors who know more about law and ethics than before the textbook came along." Ted believes that this comprehensive textbook is used by a majority of counselor education programs in the United States.

Ted is also responsible for establishing a series of international counseling institutes. As is true of much of his storied career, the creation of these workshops was an accident. "My nephew was working for the United Nations in Geneva on a 1-year appointment, and he wanted me to visit him. He thought that we should try to visit another country while we were already in Europe, so we went to Italy." During his time in Italy, his colleague Pat Thomas suggested that Ted visit Paul Krieg, who was her former classmate during her doctoral program. Paul was running a retreat center called Casa Cares in an old church in Reggello, a small town in the Tuscany region near Florence. Ted immediately loved Casa Cares and asked Paul if he could organize a trip for counselors to visit.

Ted took his first group of counselors to Casa Cares in 2003, and by 2019, Ted had taken groups to Italy, Ireland, France, Argentina, Bhutan, and Malawi, with annual institutes occurring in Italy and Ireland. Pat Thomas accompanies Ted on many of these institutes and stated, "I have seen many lives changed as a result of Dr. Remley's efforts in this area." During these international institutes, counselors have an opportunity to learn about the counseling profession in another country while observing and discussing the similarities and differences to counseling in the United States.

Ted has also played a role in advocacy for the counseling profession. In 2008, he was nominated to participate in a TRICARE committee whose purpose was to study the viability of licensed professional counselors (LPCs) as providers of mental health services. TRICARE is the health care program responsible for providing health benefits for active duty, retired, and dependents of military personnel. Before 2008, TRICARE only reimbursed psychologists and social workers for mental health services. Counselors had argued for many years that they were adequately trained to provide services to this group, but TRICARE's view remained rigid until the U.S. Congress passed legislation forcing TRICARE to review the eligibility of LPCs to provide services. The committee of which Ted was a member was called together as a result of that legislation.

Over the course of a year, this committee met several times to discuss how to make LPCs providers for TRICARE members. Ted argued that counselors' education, training, and state licensing processes showed that they were capable mental health providers. Eventually, the committee agreed to allow LPCs to provide mental health services to TRICARE members as long as LPCs graduated from a CACREP (Council on Accreditation for Counselor Education and Related Programs)-accredited university and counselors passed the National Clinical Mental Health Counselors Exam (NCMHCE). Ted initially thought these stipulations were major setbacks. "I thought we had lost. I didn't think people would actually take the exam and be able to counsel military personnel." To his surprise, many counselors have complied with the new rules. Because of his efforts on this committee, counselors can provide affordable services to members of the military. Ted considers this feat to be one of his biggest accomplishments.

One of Ted's most recent contributions to the profession is the creation of the Law and Ethics in Counseling Conference. After publishing the textbook with Barbara Herlihy, Ted realized that it would be valuable for scholars and practitioners from around the United States to come together annually and share ideas and discuss the current trends in law and ethics in counseling. When Ted accepted a faculty position at the University of Holy Cross in New Orleans, he saw an opportunity to start the conference. His colleagues were supportive of the idea, and they thought people would like to visit New Orleans each year. In 2020, the fifth annual Law and Ethics in Counseling Conference was hosted, attracting about 250 participants from across the nation.

A lesson that can be learned from Ted's experience is that leaders need to be curious about new paths and open to exploring unfamiliar territory. Taking chances on opportunities with unknown outcomes is risky. Ted did not know what it would be like to pursue a law degree and a PhD in counseling at the same time, but he proceeded anyway. Ted's career path demonstrates that leaders need to be open and flexible but also to have confidence in their decisions and commit to walking their chosen path to the end.

Ted's career path shows that leaders must be ready to capitalize on opportunities when the circumstances arise. Ted's visit to Casa Cares led to developing his first international counseling institute. Similarly, when Ted moved back to New Orleans, he saw an opportunity to establish an annual conference and took steps to create it. Ted believes one of his greatest strengths as a leader is his ability to follow through. When Pat Thomas of the University of Holy Cross thinks of Ted's leadership and contribution to the field, she says that "two areas in particular come to mind, both of which are indications of a quality I admire: his ability to see potential in situations and then his knowledge of how to bring life and energy to these situations." Potential leaders need to be ready to act when unique circumstances present themselves.

Sometimes leaders just need to make the best of the situation at hand. Plans deteriorate and conditions can change quickly. Ted's story demonstrates the merit of his ability to grin and bear it. He found himself studying to become a counselor when his graduate program changed course unexpectedly. Rather than giving up, complaining, or quitting, Ted embraced the change, committed himself, and has flourished in a career that had never landed on his radar. Future leaders can learn from Ted the value of rolling with the punches.

Ted also made a habit of leading by doing. He is not afraid to pick up extra work from others when a project begins to falter. His willingness to do whatever it takes to see a project to the end comes from a deep love and appreciation of his work. Mary Hermann, Ted's former student and mentee, who is now an associate professor at Virginia Commonwealth University, recognized this trait in him as well. She says, "He models a strong work ethic and encourages us to enjoy the work that we do."

The Future of Counseling

Ted believes the future is bright for the counseling profession, especially in light of the advances that counselors have already made. When Ted first entered the field, counseling was a new mental health discipline with little support. Counselors had to advocate for themselves and were often at odds with psychologists and social workers about their place in the world of mental health. "We won the battle against all odds. We're recognized by insurance companies, we're licensed in every state, and counselors are seen as well educated and capable mental health professionals. I think we are the mental health profession of choice." He is also proud of the way new counselors are being educated in CACREP-accredited programs and is glad to see the success of the National Board of Certified Counselors. "I see a bright future for counseling because it's going to continue to grow and continue to be a profession that makes a difference in the world."

An area of concern for Ted is the current state of ACA. With the departure of both the American School Counseling Association (ASCA) and the American Mental Health Counselors Association (AMHCA), ACA lost its two largest divisions. Ted believes that the splintering of ACA further divides the profession: "ASCA and AMHCA are now working against ACA. It's a very disturbing moment in the profession for me, and I don't see a solution."As the ASCA and the AMHCA continue to grow, Ted predicts that ACA will diminish. For the future of the profession, Ted would like ACA's board of directors to be comprised of a small group of elected leaders who would then re-create a place for school counselors and mental health counselors within ACA. "Hopefully those new divisions would compete with ASCA and AMHCA, put them out of business, and reunite the profession." Realistically, however, Ted thinks that the ACA, ASCA, and AMHCA will continue to remain divided.

Ted believes one of the biggest challenges counseling professionals face today is licensure portability. Because counseling licenses are regulated by individual state governments, each state legislature has to agree to modify its rules before counselors can practice across state lines. Ted noted that "some states aren't interested in doing that. The reality is that we're a mobile population and people move from state to state." He believes that licensure portability will happen in the future, but current and future leaders in the profession need to continue to lobby state governments and advocate for this important change.

Ted urges future leaders to focus on changing job classifications within governmental agencies. Counselors are currently classified as social workers or psychologists, but counselors cannot meet the educational criteria for classification at higher levels. The current classification system not only mislabels counselors but also prevents them from being promoted and becoming leaders in these agencies. This problem is similar to the issue of licensure portability in that each individual entity must be addressed in every state in order to resolve this issue. "It's a monumental job, and nobody is doing it right now. Nobody is in charge. So I think it is something that future leaders need to figure out."

Future leaders need to be aware of state laws and legislative issues as well. Leaders of the counseling profession must ensure that laws that encroach on the work of counselors are not enacted. "When states pass laws that say counselors can't diagnose or that counselors can't test, our practice capabilities become more limited." These issues arise frequently in state legislative discussions because of efforts by other mental health professions. "Counselors usually prevail in these situations, but somebody has to be watching." Future leaders need to be vigilant for potential threats and ensure that we maintain our place in the mental health community.

Words of Wisdom

Looking back on his early career, Ted reflected on one thing he wishes he had done differently. "I wish someone would have told me how to plan a career as a professor. Actually, my professor tried to tell me, but I wish I would have listened." At the University of Florida, Ted studied under Robert O. Stripling, one of the creators of the committee that would become CACREP. Stripling tried to help Ted understand the importance of scholarship in the world of academia. "He told me that most people will tell you that there are three parts to being a professor: teaching, research, and service. But really, it's research, research, and research." Had he listened to Stripling, Ted believes he would have had even more success in his early career.

Ted advises anyone who wants to be a leader in the counseling profession to listen to their mentors. The people who have already walked the minefield often have valuable information about your projected path. "I wish I had listened to my professor, but I didn't realize what he was trying to tell me." Ted admitted that he took the hard route at times, which resulted in learning from his experience rather than from other people. When he did listen to his colleagues and confidants, however, his career often blossomed as a result of their advice and suggestions. Becoming a leader is not a singular journey. The progression often requires collaboration and an open ear to others.

Ted also advises, "Lead positively, not negatively." Get involved in leadership because you have something to add, not simply to criticize or correct. "See yourself as a change agent rather than someone who is going to fix everything that's wrong." Leaders need to be sensitive to others to be accepted as leaders. Those leaders who look only to point out wrongs will isolate their constituents. Leaders who use their creativity and charm to generate new ideas and build on the existing strengths of others will rally others around them.

As Ted's journey illustrates, anyone who wants to be a leader needs to say yes. At many times in his career, Ted became a leader simply because nobody else was ready to volunteer. Ted did acknowledge that it may not always seem easy to say yes. "When I was younger, it was sort of frowned upon to want to be in charge. Sometimes people thought it meant you were egotistical." Nonetheless, he urges others to embrace themselves as leaders. "See it as a positive thing and don't be embarrassed about it. Don't deny yourself." Leadership requires self-recognition and the bravery to step forward when others will not.

Ted's final advice to others who would like to become leaders is to remember to be a good follower as well. "When someone else is in charge, I'm that person's best advocate." Leaders should not compete with each other. "You don't have to get rid of a leader to be a leader. There are plenty of leadership opportunities around for everyone." All leaders benefit when there is a collective desire to succeed. Sometimes stepping aside and becoming a cheerleader for others is the best way to lead.

Alexander T. Becnel's Final Reflections

After interviewing Ted and reflecting on my time knowing him, I am now more aware of how Ted has influenced me, both professionally and personally. First, he showed me the importance of encouragement. Many of the opportunities I pursued in my educational and professional path were the result of conversations we had in his office. He encouraged me to travel with him to Europe for the international courses, he told me that I should get my doctorate, and he has pushed me to undertake numerous scholastic enterprises. His encouragement ignited my vision and turned ideas into reality. It is my hope that I will be able to inspire confidence in others in this same manner.

Ted taught me the value of professional generosity. Personally, I have benefited from this generosity because he has continuously found ways to help me build my career. In our interview, Ted said that there is no reason to hoard leadership opportunities: "There is plenty of leadership to go around!" That mindset goes beyond leadership for him. Whenever Ted sees a chance for one of his students or colleagues to make a beneficial move or to participate in a meaningful project, he passes on his knowledge and connects them to the appropriate resources. "Throughout my master's and doctoral programs, I noted how he generously shared his knowledge and experiences with his students," said Mary Hermann. "Ted is incredibly supportive."

Most important, Ted has shown me the impact that a leader's personality has on the people around them. "At conferences, so many former students are excited to see him, it is as if he taught the entire profession," said Mary Hermann. Although it would be expected that Ted knows many others because he has been in the field for so long, the difference is that many of these counselors feel personally moved by him. His open approach and often humorous outlook make him accessible to others. In turn, others accept him as a leader. David Capuzzi, a longtime colleague, stated this best: "Ted Remley role models what it means to be a counselor and counselor educator because of his capacity to respect the needs and worldviews of every person he encounters, and he does so with grace, humor, and inclusiveness."

Notable Accomplishments

1981–1982	President, Virginia Counseling Association
1981–2005	Service on four state licensure boards and chair of two
1985–1986	Founding president, American Association of State Counseling Boards
1986–present	Chaired 80 dissertation committees in counseling to completion
1990–1994	Executive director, American Counseling Association
2001–2019	Coauthor, *Ethical, Legal, and Professional Issues in Counseling*
2008–2009	Member, TRICARE Committee of the Institute of Medicine
2016–present	Founding chair, Law and Ethics in Counseling Annual Conference

Chapter 15

Martin Ritchie

Amber Lange

Mentee's Introduction

I am Amber Lange, and I still remember the day I met Martin Ritchie, although it was almost 20 years ago. Martin was among the individuals who interviewed me for admission and an assistantship in the counselor education doctoral program at the University of Toledo. At that time, students were able to take advantage of a loophole whereby they could complete doctoral work in counselor education and use their coursework to apply for psychology licensure. This loophole, seemingly lucrative and beneficial to the student, failed to advance the profession of counseling. His interview question to me was, "Is dual licensure your intent?" I vividly remember my response: "Why would I do that? My intention is to be a counselor educator." Martin simply nodded and sat back in his chair and smiled. Counselor professional identity mattered to Martin, and although I did not know it at the time, it was the moment our relationship began.

Martin was tireless in his efforts to teach me and my cohort of doctoral peers in the profession of counselor education. He encouraged association membership as well as roles on various counseling boards and attended association meetings with us. He even drove us to association meetings. He presented at conferences with us and supported us emotionally. He tirelessly advocated for the counseling students and the profession of counseling. He not only taught it but lived it too.

One of the hallmarks in my doctoral career was attending the American Counseling Association (ACA) leadership and advocacy training in Washington, D.C. When I returned from this training, I was excited because I had learned a great deal about counseling and advocacy for the profession. Martin was an enthusiastic supporter, and we spent many hours in his office talking about professional identity, political advocacy, and the advancement of counseling.

For me, like many doctoral students, the final years of the degree were the hardest and the most crucial for success. It is easy to become isolated, to try to regain a personal life, to accept a full-time job; all life experiences that can greatly jeopardize completion of the degree. Martin never let that happen. He continued to prompt me, remind me, maybe even sometimes chastise me to get my work done, to stay connected with others, and to persist. His ongoing message to me was "don't be someone who falls through the cracks. Amber, the modal number of students who complete their PhD is zero. Zero, Amber." Those words scared me, motivated me, and annoyed me all at the same time. They also led to my graduation, so I count them as some of the best words I know.

Martin Ritchie's Journey

Early Years and Career Path

Martin was born and raised in rural western Maryland. He attended the University of Virginia (UVA) in Charlottesville. He enrolled with the intent to major in astronomy and physics but barely passed his physics classes. He soon discovered psychology and "was hooked." Like hundreds of other undergraduate students, he earned his BA in psychology but learned that he could not become licensed without a doctorate. This was his first introduction to the importance of professional credentials.

Martin's psychology advisor informed him that his grades were not sufficient for him to be accepted in a doctoral program in psychology and suggested he look into counselor education. He was accepted into the master's degree program in counselor education, and his career-long engagement with the professionalization of counseling began. At that time, counselors were fighting for licensure in Virginia. His advisor, William Van Hoose, was involved in the struggle and enlisted Martin's aid as a graduate assistant. Martin searched the law library for court rulings that might support establishing counseling as a separate profession. By studying how professions are established and witnessing the passion of his advisor and other counselors, he began to see the importance of legal recognition for all counselors. Virginia became the first state to gain licensure for professional counselors. Martin was part of that success, and he has never forgotten the persistent effort and advocacy needed to make it happen.

Martin earned his MEd in counselor education at UVA and applied for dozens of positions as a school counselor, but he received no offers. At that time, most states required teacher certification and 3 years of teaching experience to be certified as a school counselor. As he later learned, school counseling was a "captive profession," meaning that one could be credentialed only by first being credentialed in another profession. That didn't make sense to Martin. He would have to go back to school, earn a degree in education, become a certified teacher, get 3 years of teaching experience, and only then be eligible for certification and employment as a school counselor.

Luckily, Martin's advisor William Van Hoose agreed, and he and other counselors lobbied the Virginia legislature to drop the teaching requirement. The law was changed, and Martin was among the first school counselors without teaching experience to be employed as a school counselor in Virginia. He literally had to take a copy of the law to his interviews. Martin went to work as a school counselor in rural Virginia and loved his job. He didn't have any ambition to continue graduate study at that time.

However, the Spanish teacher at Martin's school was enrolled in the master's program in counseling and was commuting to the University of Virginia twice a week. Martin sometimes rode with him to keep him company and eventually decided to enroll in some courses he hadn't taken as part of his master's degree program. Martin's advisor, Van Hoose, saw that Martin was taking classes, and he arranged for Martin to get a scholarship if he would enroll in the doctoral program. Although Martin was content with his school counseling position, he thought this was an opportunity to move beyond his comfort zone. As Van Hoose told him, leaders must be willing to take chances and risks. Martin returned to UVA and was guided through his studies by his advisor once again. Martin was interested in what constitutes a profession and how professional recognition is achieved, and he wrote his dissertation on this topic.

At that time, the Association for Counselor Education and Supervision (ACES) was testing voluntary training standards developed by Thomas J. Sweeney and others. These standards would eventually evolve into the Council for the Accreditation of Counseling and Related Educational Programs (CACREP). Martin was excited and felt that he was witnessing the professionalization of counseling. He felt ready to inspire and train others to become professional counselors, but his professional journey took an unexpected detour.

Upon graduation with an EdD in counselor education, Martin applied to more than 30 universities for a position as a counselor educator without success. His lack of experience and his inability to become licensed as a psychologist seemed to be barriers for him at that time. Van Hoose insisted that Martin go to the American Personnel and Guidance Association (APGA; now ACA) annual conference in Washington, D.C., to look for a faculty position. After 3 days of rejection and frustration, Martin met a professor from The University of Queensland in Brisbane, Australia, who was in the United States on sabbatical and had come to the conference to recruit someone to help develop a school counseling program in Australia. Martin was offered a position as lecturer at The University of Queensland. His colleagues told him that it would derail his career, but Martin's advisor once again urged him to take a chance and learn about the profession from a new perspective. Martin accepted the position, and he learned. Martin worked with another American, Sam Beavers, training guidance officers (a combination of school counselor and school psychologist). It was a rigorous training program with highly selective admission. Beavers and Martin incorporated the evolving CACREP standards into an Australian cultural context. He met his wife, learned to play cricket and snooker, and was quite content in his career.

However, Martin's advancement was hindered because he was not licensed. Counselor licensure did not exist in Australia, and he was not able to be registered (licensed) as a psychologist. He learned that his actual training meant less than who controlled the training/accreditation standards. The picture of what needed to be done to achieve professional recognition became clearer to Martin, be it in Australia or elsewhere.

Martin returned to the United States and accepted a position as an associate professor at Ohio University, and he later moved to the University of Toledo. After 26 years at the University of Toledo, Martin retired in 2013.

Pivotal Moments

A pivotal moment in Martin's career occurred when he earned sabbatical leave from The University of Queensland and spent part of that time back in the United States. He presented at the Association for Counseling and Development (now ACA) conference where he learned of a faculty position open at Ohio University. Thomas J. Sweeney was the department chair and had been instrumental in helping Martin with his doctoral research. Martin applied, accepted a position, resigned his position in Australia, and moved to Ohio with his wife to begin a new chapter in his life. It was another big risk, but he again saw it as a challenge and an opportunity. He was at Ohio University for only 2 years, but during that time he received a crash course tutorial in professional politics from Sweeney and others.

Sweeney had just established Chi Sigma Iota, the international honor society for counselors. This really resonated with Martin. When he was an undergraduate psychology major, he was a member of Psi Chi, the International Honor Society in Psychology, and he had felt like he was becoming part of a profession. But when he was in the master's program in counseling, no such honor society had existed. Chi Sigma Iota filled a much-needed gap in our professional development (and continues to do so).

One day while having lunch with Sweeney, Martin asked him why there was no ACA division for marriage and family counselors. In typical Sweeney fashion, Tom said that was a great idea and "we should establish one." Before Martin had a chance to reconsider, he was laying the groundwork for a new association. Sweeney did the heavy lifting and PR work while Martin worked behind the scenes, and within a year, they had cofounded the International Association of Marriage and Family Counselors (IAMFC). Marriage and family therapists, psychologists, social workers, and some counselors opposed forming this new division, and Martin was tutored by Sweeney in the importance of recognizing and respecting opposition while building cooperation and coalitions. These were lessons he would need in future leadership roles.

During Martin's time at Ohio University, he became familiar with the CACREP standards and how to implement them. He took the training and became a CACREP on-site visitor. Then opportunity knocked again. He accepted a position at the University of Toledo with an emphasis on his specialty in school counseling. The master's and doctoral degree programs were not yet CACREP-accredited at Ohio University. With the help of colleagues—most notably, Nick Piazza—Martin secured CACREP accreditation for these programs.

At that time, graduates of the doctoral program could apply for licensure as psychologists, which was allowed under the psychology licensure law. When Martin became department chairperson, he tried to close this option and modify the curriculum to strictly adhere to CACREP standards. Not everyone was happy with the direction Martin was trying to take the program, including the dean who decided to relieve him of his chairperson position. Although quite upset at the time, Martin had time to reflect on how meaningful change takes persistence, time, collaboration, and compromise. Eventually, a new dean reappointed him as chairperson, and by then Martin had secured the support needed to close the psychology "back door" and fully embrace a professional identity as a doctoral program for counselor educators and supervisors.

Another salient moment in Martin's career arose from his appointment as editor of the *Counselor Education and Supervision* journal. He stated that it was a distinct privilege to be privy to what counselors and counselor educators were researching. Also, it was an awesome responsibility to know that his decisions to publish or reject often had a very real impact on people's careers. He learned to trust the judgment of his editorial board members who were incredibly dedicated to fairly and thoroughly reviewing manuscripts. Martin felt that some manuscripts submitted dealt with trivial or obvious topics and the research methodology used was often fatally flawed. He was somewhat discouraged to think that counselor educators and supervisors were not fulfilling their duty to conduct meaningful research to advance knowledge and improve practice. Looking back on this experience today, he believes there is still room for improvement.

Points of Pride

Martin is proud of having trained professional counselors for more than 35 years. He feels privileged to have been able to encourage and sometimes inspire students to achieve the confidence and skills needed to help others, and to have been part of a noble profession. He is most proud of the fact that he missed only one graduation ceremony in all of those years. He is both honored and humbled that a scholarship has been established in his name at the University of Toledo. He can think of no better way to further his passion for training counselors than to assist students in their quest to become professional counselors.

The CACREP board established an Award for Excellence in Advocacy in Martin's name. Although he believes many others who served on the board during his tenure are equally deserving, it gives Martin great pride to have been recognized and see that recognition bestowed on others. Martin believes that advocacy is essential to the growth of our profession. Being a recipient of the Chi Sigma Iota Thomas J. Sweeney Professional Leadership Award is especially meaningful to Martin. Tom Sweeney was a mentor and an inspiration to him while he was a doctoral student and throughout his career.

Leadership and Advocacy

Toward the end of his career, Martin applied and was accepted to serve on the board of directors of CACREP. He had begun his professional journey learning of the importance of professional training standards, and now he was in a position to oversee their implementation. Over the years he served as a CACREP on-site reviewer, he helped write several CACREP self-studies. Now he found himself reviewing CACREP applications from diverse programs located all across the country. Standards were evolving to reflect changes in professional training, such as multiple campus sites and online or distance-learning programs. He found it both stimulating and challenging.

Being elected chair of the CACREP board is one of the highlights of his career. Twice a year the CACREP board of directors met to review and vote on the accreditation status of dozens of programs. Each program is different and has a unique approach to meeting the standards. Teams of board members review all the documentation for each program and make their recommendations to the full board. As Martin stated, "I was continually impressed with the integrity of board members in assessing programs fairly. Even if a program failed to meet a standard, the board made specific recommendations as to how they might meet the standard in the future. Unlike a policing action of 'I gotcha,' it was more an exercise of 'how can we assist this program in meeting the standards?'"

During Martin's tenure, CACREP was dealing with political issues. Martin had long argued that, for a profession to achieve full recognition, it must have mandatory training standards leading to accreditation and that accreditation must be required for legal recognition or licensure. Although the number of programs seeking CACREP accreditation was growing precipitously, accreditation was not a requirement for counselor licensure in any state. This began to change during his tenure on the board. Through the tireless efforts of board members, counselor educators, and, most notably, Carol Bobby, the CEO of CACREP, state licensure boards began requiring CACREP accreditation for counselor licensure. Just as the first licensure law in Virginia drew critics and political enemies, so did the CACREP requirement. But, as Martin noted, "through patience, collaboration, and compromise, we were achieving our goal. Then the federal government began recognizing licensed professional counselors as approved providers if they graduated from a CACREP-accredited program. This was the legal recognition we had been striving for over several decades." Martin acknowledges that our profession still faces many challenges, but he is confident that we have achieved professional status by recognized criteria.

When Martin was asked to describe how his leadership evolved, he responded, "I wish I could tell you that I devised a plan early in my career for my professional development and leadership roles and followed it throughout my career. The truth is, I was a very fortunate victim of circumstances. At pivotal points in my career, I was lucky enough to be in the right place at the right time, surrounded by the right people. My leadership derived from seeing opportunities, taking risks, and enlisting the support of others to advocate for what we believe in."

Martin acknowledges that leaders can possess many characteristics, some better than others. Some leaders are overly ambitious and self-serving. When they rise to positions of power, they feel entitled and use their position to manipulate others and advocate for themselves more than for others. Effective leaders don't aspire and maneuver to attain leadership; they are thrust into leadership roles by colleagues and constituents who recognize their competence, respect for others, and integrity. They view leadership not as an entitlement but as an honor and as a responsibility to advocate for others.

Martin believes that the best preparation for leadership is through observing and listening, without judgment, to learn what is needed, how change is likely to occur, who can assist, and what role one can take. "Leaders must not be content with the status quo. They must be able to see an opportunity and take a risk. They have to be able to take criticism and learn from their mistakes. I believe patience is a virtue for leaders."

Although it helps to be somewhat visionary, Martin believes leaders become effective not so much for what they know but for how they inspire and mobilize others.

> Leadership is not simply an exercise in persuading others to accept your vision. I found that by actively listening to other points of views and suggestions I often discovered more effective plans of action than I ever imagined. As professional counselors, we are trained to be active listeners. I believe that active listening is a prerequisite to effective leadership. Counselors are trained to advocate for others. I have found more satisfaction in encouraging and assisting others than in personal accomplishments.

The Future of Counseling

As Martin reflected on the future of the profession, he began with a broad perspective and then focused on more specific concerns about school counseling and the state of research.

> As the youngest mental health profession, counselors must continue to fight to protect what we have earned. Because there are other competing mental health professions, we must remain vigilant in protecting and expanding our licensure and scope of practice. We must continue to revise our professional training and ethical standards to adequately reflect the needs of our clients. CACREP needs input on standards as they periodically revise them. It is important for counselors and counselor educators to be active in their professional associations. Professional associations need input on the effectiveness of ethical standards.

Martin continued by expressing his concern for the future of school counseling. He believes school counselors are facing some important decisions about their practice and identity. "Although school counselors receive training in interpersonal and group counseling, some school counselors do very little counseling. Instead, their roles have evolved to include administrative and secretarial duties that are not part of their master's degree training. If these duties are the backbone of their job description, then the training they receive should better prepare them. If they want to spend more time counseling, however, they will have to demonstrate their effectiveness to students, parents, and administrators."

> When a crisis occurs in a school, such as a shooting or suicide, mental health counselors are often called in to assist the students. If they are there to supplement the counseling role of the school counselors, fine and good, but if they are called in because the school counselors are too busy to offer counseling, I believe that is a shame. Effective school counselors know their students and earn the trust of students and parents. In a time of crisis, they should be best positioned to offer counseling assistance.

Martin pointed out that the new CACREP Standards for school counselors require a 60-semester-hour master's degree program including increased requirements for mental health training. "It will be up to the newly minted professional school counselors to educate their school systems about their enhanced training, and they will have to advocate for a new, improved role in the schools."

Martin also expressed concern about the quality of research in counseling. "I mentioned that when I had the privilege of serving as editor of *Counselor Education and Supervision* I was disappointed sometimes in the quality of research manuscripts we reviewed. A profession is grounded in a knowledge base that is driven by research. In some of the 'harder sciences,' such as medicine, there is consensus about the most important issues that require research. Teams of researchers from different institutions collaborate on methodology to maximize effectiveness and avoid duplication of efforts. They present and share the results of their research in online journals and at conferences to advance the knowledge base of their profession." He acknowledged that it is difficult to compare a social science discipline with medicine, but he believes lessons can be learned about how best to conduct research and further our knowledge base.

Martin offered further reflections on the current state of research in our field.

> Judging from publications and conference presentations, it sometimes seems like the important research agendas are the current "flavors of the month," and the preferred methodology involves online surveys. This is particularly true of doctoral dissertations. It is my hope that professional counselors will identify research issues that will have a practical and direct effect on our training and practice. I hope to see more rigorous qualitative and quantitative methodology employed and more collaborative research efforts.

Martin acknowledged that advances in medicine and pharmacology will continue to affect the way we view mental health and mental illness. Some psychological disorders once seen as moral weakness or as the result of faulty parenting are now understood to be chemical imbalances that can be treated with medication. But Martin believes professional counselors also perform a necessary service, providing comfort and help throughout our lives. "I am confident this trend will continue; however, it does not mean that interpersonal counseling will become unnecessary. While drugs can treat chemical imbalances, people's behaviors still need to be modified. Some conditions like grief are not conducive to taking drugs. People need to be able to express their feelings and be accepted. They need to learn to trust their ability to cope and grow. Professional counselors are trained to offer these skills. Counselors will always be needed."

Telemedicine is emerging as a new service delivery model, and Martin believes counselors should embrace this as an opportunity to reach clients who would otherwise not see a counselor. Accreditation and ethical standards of practice will need to accommodate this growing trend.

Martin is optimistic about the future. "Overall, I am very confident in the integrity and longevity of our profession. As long as counselors are committed to helping others and some are willing to assume leadership roles, I believe we will continue to be a positive force in the mental health field."

Words of Wisdom

Martin reflected on what he wishes he had known when he first decided to become a counselor. He wishes he "had been told more about the importance of accreditation and the requirements for certification and licensure. In fairness, when I entered my master's degree program, accreditation and counselor licensure did not exist. I'm sure I was told that to be certified as a school counselor in Virginia required a teaching degree and 3 years of teaching experience, neither of which I had. However, I know that my advisor told me that he and other counselor educators were in the process of trying to change the law. In fact, I became involved in the effort to my immediate benefit. I became involved in the push for counselor licensure as well." Martin did not know how important advocacy would be when he began his graduate studies, but he learned quickly, out of necessity.

Martin also emphasized the importance of accreditation. "Although accreditation did not exist on the program level, the fact that my program at the University of Virginia was using the ACES-approved standards (which would evolve into CACREP) taught me the importance of national accreditation."

Amber Lange's Final Reflections

After I completed my doctorate under Martin's tutelage, I moved into higher education as a faculty member. I love teaching students about counseling and professional advocacy. Most of all, I desire to give students what Martin gave to me, a passion for counseling and counselor education. I want all students to know why the profession of counseling is important, unique, and necessary. I want to help students persist.

After decades of service and leadership, Martin has retired. He has been honored with lifetime achievement awards, fellow awards, and all sorts of recognitions from leaders in the profession. He spent his final days in counselor education working with CACREP and instituting critically needed changes to support the counseling profession. During his initial retirement years, we would meet for coffees and lunches and Martin would sing the praises of retirement. I would complain. I complained about the lack of progress we were making in the profession, about professional issues that remained in limbo year after year, and about administrative issues in higher education. Martin would slowly nod his head up and down, and smile.

We continued to meet for several years, and Martin continued to sing the praises of retirement. As time passed, my complaining subsided and turned to concern. I was concerned about students' education and completion, the passage of legislation to help licensed pofessional counselors, and the direction the profession was moving. Martin would nod and smile. As a matter of fact, it was the same nod and smile I had seen the day we met and the day I graduated. It was the same smile I saw when I was a new faculty member, a seasoned faculty member, and even now as a department chair. His nod and smile meant this: "You're on the right path, keep going, you can do it. Don't give up. Hang in there. You'll make it through."

Martin's passion and desire to train individuals in counseling and counselor education has had a profound impact on me. He trained students to have a heart and soul for the profession, to be passionate advocates, and to persist. Martin has supported me, encouraged me, taught me, and mentored me in my pursuits for almost two decades. He believed in me when I didn't believe in myself. He has been a cheerleader in my personal and professional life. Just the other day, I was talking with a new doctoral student and found myself smiling and nodding as I said, "Just keep on going, you can do it. Persist." If that is not the most amazing mentorship anyone could ever have, I just don't know what is.

Notable Accomplishments

1986	Cofounder, International Association of Marriage and Family Counselors
1994–1997	Editor, *Counselor Education and Supervision*
2007	Chi Sigma Iota Thomas J. Sweeney Professional Leadership Award
2007–2012	Member, board of directors, CACREP
2010–2012	Chair, board of directors, CACREP
	Fellow, American Counseling Association
2010	ACES Robert O. Stripling Award for Excellence in Standards
2014	CACREP Martin Ritchie Award for Excellence in Advocacy
2018–present	Martin Ritchie Endowed Scholarship in Counselor Education, University of Toledo

Chapter 16

Thomas J. Sweeney

Michael D. Brubaker

There is always room for another leader.
—Thomas J. Sweeney, April 7, 2020

Mentee's Introduction

I, Michael D. Brubaker, met Thomas J. Sweeney in 2008 when I was selected as a leadership fellow and intern (LFI) with Chi Sigma Iota (CSI). Tom had served as executive director since the founding of CSI in 1985, and I got to know him better through my work as CSI secretary and, later, as president. I also served on many committees and was fortunate enough to work with Tom often. Although I did not know this when I began my work for CSI, I was also connected to Tom through my own father, who was a professor of education at the University of North Carolina at Greensboro, where Tom's wife, Jane Myers, was on the faculty and where Tom briefly served in administration. Learning of this connection only caused me to grow closer in my friendship with Tom, and now I also call him one of my mentors.

Tom Sweeney is one of the pillars of the counseling profession and is, without question, an influential leader in the profession. Tom contributed his service during some of the most critical years of counseling's movement toward professionalization. It is important for students and new professionals to not only know of his contributions but also to know who he is as a leader, what shaped his leadership philosophy, and what insights he has for the future of the profession.

This profile is written with a certain familiarity but also with novelty; it comprises recent email and phone interviews, knowledge of Tom's career through my own training, and my personal experiences working with Tom. I hope to highlight

Tom's commitment to make things better, affiliate with the "doers," show respect for others, and mentor a new generation of leaders.

Thomas J. Sweeney's Journey

Early Years and Career Path

Tom Sweeney was born and raised in Akron, Ohio, by parents of Scottish immigrants who had arrived in the 1920s, just a few years before the Great Depression. His grandparents worked in the rubber factories, and after the 10th grade, his mother had to leave school to assume responsibilities at home and take care of her siblings. This did not stop her from excelling as a leader herself, however. "My mother was extraordinary," Tom noted. She was "low-key, not flashy," becoming president of the school Parent–Teachers Association (PTA), president of the city PTA, and then serving as a representative at the state level. She imbued a solution-oriented leadership sensibility, asking, "how do you make things better?"

Both of Tom's parents valued education, and even though neither attended college themselves, they made it clear that Tom and his older brother, Joe, could go anywhere they wanted—but they would have to pay their own way. Both Joe and Tom began work as rubber factory messengers while in high school and continued to work throughout college. Joe, 3 years Tom's senior, was the first to go to college. Popular in high school, Joe was elected in his senior year to be president of two key high school organizations and had to choose which one to serve. Joe seemed to do whatever he did effortlessly when they were children. A "natural" leader, Joe was chosen by his bosses at the rubber factory to become a regional manager after graduation from college and his return from mandatory military service. That was the plan for Joe.

Tom began volunteering for class representative for the Red Cross and other organizations just as he had seen his mother and brother volunteer. As an Adlerian, in good humor, Tom characterizes himself as a typical "second child" in classical terms: "We try harder!" Tom followed Joe, attending the University of Akron and also majoring in teacher education while continuing to work in the factory. Both of these first-generation students served in the military, Joe became an Air Force pilot and was killed when his engine failed immediately after takeoff while Tom was still at school in Akron. The family grieved, but Tom does not remember any bitterness or complaint from his parents over Joe's death. Their parents had instilled in both of them a respect for those who serve their country, whatever the cost. Devout Catholics, they turned instead to their faith for strength as they did for all matters of consequence including celebrations, grateful for their blessings.

Tom's parents had moved to a city suburb while he was a freshman, and in his sophomore year the university retroactively doubled his tuition because he lived outside of the city. Adding insult to this family tragedy, Tom's advisor made a mistake that left Tom one course shy of qualifying for a once-a-year graduation. These setbacks did not deter Tom's progress, however, and he used this extra time to take graduate courses while finishing up his required undergraduate coursework. Despite the many challenges Tom faced, he persevered, finding solutions and looking to the future.

Why did he start taking counseling courses? Tom could have taken many pathways to advance his career, but he wanted to improve his ability to understand

and connect with others, particularly the students in schools. He grew up in a working-class, multicultural, immigrant neighborhood where fist fights were one way young boys coped with their differences. Small in stature, Tom learned at an early age when he had to be physically proficient and when to negotiate or step aside. As a young, creative teacher, he was already inclined toward group work, setting aside time in class for students to talk about "what was on their minds." He understood that his students were experiencing challenges, but he remained frustrated because he could not connect with them, particularly because he did not have a lot of prior experiences with African American youth. He was intentional about expressing respect for his students, but he wanted more. Tom believed that counseling was a pathway to understanding his students and to instilling a greater purpose for school and beyond. School counseling was just the type of profession that would help him do this.

When one of his teachers announced that the University of Wisconsin (Madison) was accepting applications for its National Defense Education Act (NDEA) fellowships in the school counseling program, Tom jumped at the opportunity. In 1960, Tom received his orders to join the Army and left the cold Wisconsin winter for hot San Antonio, Texas. He was a trainer of Army medical instructors, and his commander wrote a letter of commendation to help him stay on active duty as an Active Reserve Officer. At that time, however, Army policy required that he leave before he was eligible to receive financial benefits that would have helped as he established himself in a new career. Tom retired from Active Army Reserve service after more than 11 years and looked forward to finding new opportunities for his future.

On his way back home, Tom stopped in Columbus, Ohio, to meet with Herman J. Peters at The Ohio State University (OSU). Peters had previously visited the counseling program at the University of Wisconsin over St. Patrick's Day and happened to ask if anyone was Irish, and classmates stated that Tom was a talented Irish singer. Peters took to Tom and encouraged him to apply to OSU for the doctoral program, and by the end of the day, Tom was invited to accept an NDEA fellowship. "Things fell in line," Tom remarked about this. He also noted that singing and amateur drama compensated for his being a "raging introvert." One of his part-time jobs while attending OSU was singing once a week on a live television morning show pitched to stay-at-home mothers. While working as a high school counselor and finishing his doctoral research, he sang the lead in *Carousel* for a local women's Catholic college annual fundraiser.

In addition to these early college experiences, Tom learned about leadership while being a member of his fraternity. He described this as the "working boys' fraternity," which was distinguished from fraternities for those who did not need to work while in college. During member meetings, he observed the strategies employed by house leaders to effectively move ideas into action. They would carefully listen, summarize, and conclude with a motion. He had earlier high school leadership roles, but this experience opened his eyes to effectively navigating parliamentary procedures. These lessons would prove invaluable in later years; for example, when he was president of the American Personnel and Guidance Association (APGA, now ACA).

Together, these experiences shaped Tom's leadership philosophy and practices. "Leadership for me is having a shared vision and helping to see it consummated." Whether this vision was his idea or the ideas of those around him, bringing them into action was an essential part of this work, and his career evidences the impact of this approach.

Pivotal Moments

Over the course of Tom's illustrious career, numerous key moments influenced him, including many that reinforced his early life lessons. These included early interactions with division leaders; advocating for state licensure, national preparation standards, and accreditation; serving as president of the ACA; and serving as founding executive director of CSI. These key moments are described in more detail in the following section.

Leadership and Advocacy

Tom's leadership experiences are many and varied. He learned to lead by following the doers, and he stepped up to advocate for clients and for the profession. He developed an effective style of parliamentary leadership and was an exemplar for servant leadership during his years of service to CSI.

Following the Doers

As Tom entered the profession, he attended conferences and began to meet the leaders of the profession. He was particularly influenced by the Southern Association of Counselor Education and Supervision (SACES) and as a recent graduate was impassioned by the reality that counseling was an occupation but not yet a true "profession." Counseling lacked accreditation and a code of ethics, standards that were common in other professions. At SACES, he heard Robert Stripling speak on a related topic, and Tom thought to himself, "I'm on it now. This man is my man." Stripling and other leaders, such as George Hill from Ohio University, "understood the big picture and wanted to help us move in that direction." Tom distinguished these leaders from others who appeared to be in leadership positions just for show. "These were the doers," and Tom was eager to follow them to raise the level of professionalism of the counseling field. These early moments fueled his passion for excellence in the field and would lead him to accept positions where he could support needed changes.

Professional and Client Advocacy

Tom provided leadership on other social issues of that time as well. Committed to the civil rights of women and persons of color, he was the first president of SACES (1972–1973) to financially support the Committee on Women, and he coauthored an ACES position paper on "Non-White Concerns in Counselor Education." Civil rights and professional advocacy intersected for Tom when he was the first chair of the SACES Committee on Licensure and subsequently the first chair of the ACA Committee on Licensure. In his role with ACA, he fought for counselors to have the right to serve their communities, advocating for professional counselors such as Culbreath Cook, an African American practitioner and community leader who was arrested for practicing psychology without a license. Understanding the relationship between professional and client advocacy, Tom noted how racism was a potential factor in Cook's case, making the committee's advocacy efforts all the more important.

In 1974, Tom documented his concerns with restrictive psychology laws that were criminalizing the careers of professional counselors, and he proposed a blueprint for the profession to establish policies and structures that would empower the counseling profession to have equal stature and representation with licensed psychologists. As a result of his advocacy, he was asked to draft a position paper for counselor licensure that was adopted in 1975. He then became the first ACA Licensure Committee chair, and these efforts guided this work for many years. Tom quickly noted the accomplishments and sacrifices of hundreds, if not thousands, of others throughout the states. He noted that Ohioans Bill Nemec, Susan Sears, and especially Melvin Witmer met faithfully for 8 years with Ohio legislators until the state counselor licensure law was passed. He also highlighted the lesson of patience because acting too quickly could have been costly. "We could have had a law much sooner had we been willing to sacrifice really important language, like treating emotional disorders and being able to diagnose." Being committed to a long-term vision helped Ohio have one of the strongest scope of practice laws for professional counselors in the United States.

Parliamentarian Leadership

Having served as president of SACES (1972–1973), ACES (1976–1977), and then ACA (1980–1981), Tom understood well how to work within an organization to get things done. Chuck Lewis, executive director from 1971 to 1983, wrote a letter to Tom sharing that he "was one of two presidents during his tenure who was truly politically effective." Tom attributes this success to fostering good interpersonal relationships and upholding the basic value of respect. Respect is a central value of Adlerian theory, and Tom aligns his own clinical and leadership practices with this value. Practically speaking, he strives to (1) establish mutual respect by acknowledging the legitimacy of each individual's feelings and concerns; (2) pinpoint the issue of "winning or losing"—there will be no losers such that all will have a voice in resolution of an issue; (3) focus on "what each of us can do" to reach a mutually satisfactory outcome and appropriate action; and (4) involve all participants in a democratic process of finding alternatives, problem solving, and discussion resulting in a new agreement based on mutual respect.

He offered an example from a time when he was ACA president, leading over 40 members of the governing council, including representatives from each of the regional and state counseling branches, as well as its divisions. Leading such a large group of people with differing interests and trying to get anything done is no easy feat. Each person represented a different constituency, and they would arrive with individual and sometimes competing agendas. In addition, some did not get along well with each other, making agreement even more difficult. Tom invested the time to get to know everyone, recognizing that "everyone has good ideas." Incorporating others' ideas into the larger goals of the group, he aimed to be sure that each person felt heard and respected. And when those ideas were not acted upon by motion or decision, everyone at least had the opportunity to be heard.

Getting to know these representatives was a top priority for Tom, and he spent many hours on the telephone and in the hallways talking with these leaders about their interests and needs. This also helped him plan for meetings, and he always came prepared, often with motions in hand to share with these other leaders. This can be very important for any leader in a professional association that follows Robert's Rules of Order; without a motion, the topic may never be fully discussed. To be an effective leader, Tom sought out good ideas and collaborated with his colleagues to ensure that they would be heard, all with the intention of moving the profession forward.

Known to his closest friends at the time, Tom's father died suddenly the month before he became president of APGA (ACA). His mother died some years later after 10 years of suffering from Alzheimer's. He and Jane Myers saw to her care during this time.

Honor, Excellence, and Servant Leadership

Tom expresses "shared" satisfaction for the many accomplishments he and his colleagues achieved during this period of counselor professionalization. Counselor credentialing, ethical standards, accreditation, and standards of preparation were highly important to the profession, and each has been advanced through his leadership along with that of many others, including some who are profiled in this book. With all of that said, Tom's greatest satisfaction comes through his leadership within CSI. With over 130,000 members initiated and 400 chapters chartered since its inception in 1985, CSI is the third largest counseling association in the world, and it arguably has had a great impact on the profession and on our society as a whole.

Tom shared a story known only to a few. Tom's inspiration for CSI came as a result of his observation of the benefits to students in the Ohio University program who joined the Rho Chi Sigma rehabilitation counseling honor society cofounded by Jane Myers. She was then serving as the Ohio University chapter faculty advisor. Jane, whose mentoring includes several of the profession's top scholars and leaders today, provided a unique mentoring relationship that exceeded anything Tom had witnessed before by a faculty member. Once Tom shared with Jane his vision for a new organization for professional counselors that embraced all specialties and was dedicated to excellence in both preparation and practice, Jane was a founding life member.

A few short years later, Rho Chi Sigma merged with CSI, and to this day, its chapters and members are on the CSI rolls. Jane eventually became CSI president and executive director and performed many other roles pro bono, including setting up CSI's first website and database. For all of us who knew her, her presence and contributions far exceed anything that could be found on her pages of accomplishments, awards, and leadership positions. She was a friend, a mentor, and a supporter to any who opened themselves to her counsel. In practice, Jane was nationally certified in rehabilitation counseling, gerontology counseling, and as a neurofeedback practitioner and was renowned as a wellness counseling scholar and teacher. At heart, however, she would tell you that she was first and foremost a professional counselor and proud of it. As Tom would tell it, then as well as now, her vision and passion were exactly what the profession needed.

CSI was formed during a time of striving for increased professionalism in the counseling field. Counselor legitimacy was continually challenged, and counselor identity was diffused throughout several disciplines that had diverse interests. As practitioners were adopting more generic terms such as "therapist" for their professional roles, Tom understood the need for counselors to understand their uniqueness as distinct from other mental health professions. Counselors needed a group that would identify the best of those trained in counseling and encourage them to excel with the ultimate goal found in the CSI vision statement: To "realize a healthy society by fostering wellness and human dignity."

CSI was founded as both an academic and a professional honor society and formed to nurture excellence among students and professionals in the field. The chapters are highly active in their communities and are financially supported by CSI headquarters staff and volunteer committees. In fact, CSI has reinvested over $1.6 million in rebates to its chapters (currently $125,000/year). Tom notes that "virtually every counseling association has within its leaders and members individuals who were mentored in CSI chapters under the tutelage of chapter faculty advisors (CFAs)." He emphasizes how important motives are for successful leaders. His close friend, Ed Herr, himself an extraordinary scholar and leader, helped CSI codify an essential ingredient of leadership. Service, not for one's benefit or advantage but as dedication to the mission and goals of a group, distinguishes the "servant leader." As CSI has adopted Greenleaf's philosophy of servant leadership, these CFAs and the members who will serve in other professional associations infuse this philosophy in their work as they serve the profession and the larger community. Tom adds that CSI and its chapters are also referred to as co-curricular partners with CACREP because they model servant leadership and promote strong counselor identity.

With 35 years of history with CSI, Tom has seen many of counseling's leaders throughout their development. "I've watched the neophyte become a mature leader, scholar, and teacher among other shakers and movers in our profession," and this gives him great satisfaction. He also sees the impact on the honor society's commitment to professional identity. "I feel the most satisfaction knowing that when asked by others what they do, CSI members can say confidently, 'I'm a professional counselor!'"

Some have identified Tom as a charismatic leader, a leader who actualized the vision he and others had to develop a thriving honor society for the counseling profession. Charismatic leaders are often visionary leaders, inspiriting creativity and healthy risk-taking, which is certainly true of Tom. The problem with applying this typology is that it suggests Tom's leadership was largely based on motivating others through charismatic means, whereas Tom had a desire to make things better, a very pragmatic aim. Also, given Tom's self-identification as an introvert, it seems unlikely that he would be inclined to see his own style as charismatic.

Indeed, by Tom's own account, he identifies as an Adlerian, and he is committed to the value of mutual respect and aligning with Greenleaf's idea of servant leadership whose aim was to serve first. These values are consistent with lessons Tom learned in childhood. In elementary school, he and other children were "buddies" of children with disabilities, and they would see to their safety during fire drills and attendance at school auditorium functions. Years later, he was responsible for establishing two rehabilitation counseling programs when he was department head. Later still, the rehabilitation counseling honor society was invited to merge with CSI, and they did so. One may also argue that such leaders instill greater trust because it is clear that their interests are in helping others to grow. Greenleaf also was highly interested in mentoring and promoting the wellness of followers, two areas that have been central in Tom's life work. Considering all of these perspectives, it is evident that Tom was driven by a servant leadership philosophy and that through this he inspired others to transform the profession.

Having an understanding of what drives us as leaders is the first step in professional and client advocacy. Tom's process appeared to begin even earlier and was perhaps less of a conscious choice. Becoming an advocate, and later a leader in professional advocacy, was more akin to having a fire lit within him. Rooted in his identity as a professional counselor, he was eager to join the cause of professionalization through newly formed connections with action-oriented leaders. In similar form, new leaders may better see their own calling within the profession by looking to their professional identity and the needs of the profession as well as the communities they serve.

In addition to finding their passion, adopting a service mentality, and mentoring others to do the same, leaders must be strategic. Tom has a keen sense of the contexts in which he is working; he does his homework and forges alliances with those who share common interests in advancing the profession. During our interview, he talked about periodically meeting with Carol Bobby and Tom Clawson, leaders of CACREP and the National Board of Certified Counselors, respectively, to discuss the current needs of the profession and what still needed to be done. Such alliances are natural, given the role of these organizations along with CSI, but they also are essential as these leaders strategically plan to successfully propel the counseling profession forward. As was true of his work as ACA president, Tom understands the importance of having effective working relationships based on mutual respect, shared values, and a commitment to action.

The Future of Counseling

Tom emphasizes the fact that no leader does this work alone; hundreds, if not thousands, of people are working on professional and client advocacy. He named dozens of leaders who have made our progress possible in standards, state and national credentialing, and accreditation. It is no surprise that Tom continues to call each of us forth to better the profession by remembering our counselor identity. He shared this vision along with a caution:

> I would like to see the profession build more upon its roots as a developmental, wellness-based profession. Due in large part to external factors, our focus on facilitating normal human development over the life span (e.g., assistance during normal life transitions), group work (e.g., developmental assistance facilitated through classroom meetings, parent education, intimate relationship enrichment), and career development (e.g., post–high school or retirement transitioning) has been underutilized. A whole host of explanations can be expounded upon as to why, but the essential point is, I believe that we risk losing sight of our reason for being a unique profession.

Many opportunities exist for the counseling profession to set itself apart and show its unique value. It is also true that counselors may be viewed as easily replaceable if we do not demonstrate our value. Tom provides three examples in which this challenge is most evident: career counseling, group counseling, and wellness.

Tom was a career consultant for the General Electric Foundation for 18 years, helping to establish educator in-service programs to raise consciousness of the career opportunities for young girls and minorities, particularly in technical and engineering fields. Literally thousands of educators participated in summer and year-long local industry employee shadowing programs. Federal legislation funded school career guidance programs under the leadership of an ACA past president and counselor educator, Ken Hoyt, who served in the U.S. Department of Education as head of its implementation. Since that time, career counseling has been replaced by career coaching, which requires less training on the holistic understanding of how one's career influences overall quality of life. He adds, "Now more than ever, our people and the economy need career counseling services." This is a leadership opportunity for those with the vision and commitment.

Similarly, counselor education standards long have required group work training. Originally derived from school counselor standards where large caseloads were common, the profession adopted group skills as a "core" area for all counselors when CACREP was established. Tom reflected on his work in the schools and later with marriage enrichment groups. "[There] are developmental needs that, when addressed, result in fewer more serious problems for everyone involved. By utilizing this training and perfecting this expertise, we can prove our practices more effective and efficient than other 'helping' practitioners. Aspiring leaders have another rich opportunity here!"

Given Tom's extensive scholarship in the areas of wellness and wellness counseling, he is concerned that this essential practice of the counseling profession has been neglected just as other professions are beginning to emphasize wellness more.

> Drawing on the outstanding scholarship of Jane Myers, we now have over 25+ years of research, an empirically derived holistic wellness model, and momentum is building for more research. Others from business, nursing, medicine, and psychology among others are citing our models, instruments, and literature not only for research tools but for practices and resources suitable for use in everyday settings. I am receiving daily notices of research citations and inquiries from individuals in different fields literally all over the country and abroad. Others think we have what they need.

If the counseling profession loses sight of these unique aspects of its identity, Tom believes others will assume them as their own, leaving counselors behind in research, practice, and value to our society as a whole.

Words of Wisdom

To seize the opportunities that lie ahead, counseling will require new leaders to step forward, just as Tom did in his early years as a new graduate from OSU. He leaves us with these words of wisdom: "There is always room for another leader." I asked Tom to clarify this, and he replied that his focus is largely on the person who has a "burn to see something done." He emphasized that there is always room for the good ideas of another person, and these leaders do not have to hold an elected office, although elected opportunities can bring out capabilities yet unrealized. He recalled:

> My first professional leadership opportunity was as a state branch president (South Carolina Personnel and Guidance Association [SCPGA]). For years, about 25 state supervisors, university faculty, and a few school counselors would meet in Columbia on a Saturday morning twice a year. When I became president, I started a newsletter to all counselors in addition to counseling faculty. Our officers agreed to try starting a conference at a Myrtle Beach hotel in the fall. I arranged to invite a top group expert at the time to lecture and demonstrate group processes. Over 200 counselors came from all over the state to the conference. SCPGA membership grew to over 300 the following year. New committees were formed out of new alliances across specialties, and a new life was breathed into the organization. In later years, they were champions of counselor licensure and other such initiatives. As a consequence, I still think strong state branches are essential to a healthy successful counseling profession. The internet with all its advantages cannot duplicate the human ingredients found in person-to-person contact.

I asked Tom what he wished someone had told him when he began his graduate studies in counseling. "I wish in graduate school that I had been encouraged to find a career mentor to whom I could look for advice, encouragement, honesty, correction, support, and celebration." Tom shared that many of his early attempts to seek advice were brief and without follow-up. Finding an authentic connection with someone who holds your best interests may make a key difference. "So my personal advice to students today is to cultivate a relationship with a mentor(s) with whom you can be yourself, and ask them to help you to become even better!"

Michael D. Brubaker's Final Reflections

As I reflect on Tom's statements about his own lack of mentorship, I can only imagine how much larger his influence might have been if he had found one or more key mentors in his early days. Frankly, I don't know how he did as much as he has done for the counseling profession. I feel fortunate to be one of those who has benefited from Tom's mentoring and support. I am grateful that I was able to build a connection with him and many other great leaders in Chi Sigma Iota, the organization he helped found, in part, to support others seeking guidance in their own leadership development.

In 2007, when I applied to become an LFI with CSI, I wrote, "I would like to see our honor society measure excellence with the yardstick of compassion and justice-making." When serving on the Strategic Planning Committee, it was evident that many chapters were engaging in community service and that we needed a way to support this work and promote excellence within it. I honestly do not know if Tom saw my original application, but he understood my passion, and I was soon asked to chair a CSI task force that would evolve into the Counselor Community Engagement Committee. I gladly agreed and was subsequently appointed the committee's first chair. Looking back on my interviews with Tom to prepare this profile, I now see how he instilled these core values within CSI: to appreciate the interests and ideas of others to better an organization and our profession as a whole. My ideas and passion to make things better were recognized, and Tom and the other leaders made room for me at the table. I cannot think of a more valuable lesson, and I hope to do the same for my students and colleagues who have such a passion to do good in the world.

Notable Accomplishments

1975	Author, APGA Adopted Positions on Counselor Licensure
1976–1977	President, Association for Counselor Education and Supervision
1980–1981	President, American Counseling Association
1980–1981	President, American Personnel and Guidance Association
1981	Author, APGA Adopted Positions on Counselor Accreditation
1981–1987	Founding chair, Council for Accreditation of Counseling and Related Educational Programs (CACREP)
1985–2012	Founding president and executive director, Chi Sigma Iota International
2019	Author of *Adlerian Counseling and Psychotherapy: A Practitioner's Wellness Approach* (6th edition) as well as more than 80 articles in national refereed journals

PART II: 2016 CACREP Standards Alignment

The Profiles

SECTION 2: PROFESSIONAL COUNSELING IDENTITY
COUNSELING CURRICULUM

1. PROFESSIONAL COUNSELING ORIENTATION AND ETHICAL PRACTICE
   b. the multiple professional roles and functions of counselors across specialty areas, and their relationships with human service and integrated behavioral health care systems, including interagency and interorganizational collaboration and consultation
   c. counselors' roles and responsibilities as members of interdisciplinary community outreach and emergency management response teams
   d. the role and process of the professional counselor advocating on behalf of the profession
   e. advocacy processes needed to address institutional and social barriers that impede access, equity, and success for clients
   g. professional counseling credentialing, including certification, licensure, and accreditation practices and standards, and the effects of public policy on these issues
   j. technology's impact on the counseling profession
2. SOCIAL AND CULTURAL DIVERSITY
   d. the impact of heritage, attitudes, beliefs, understandings, and acculturative experiences on an individual's views of others

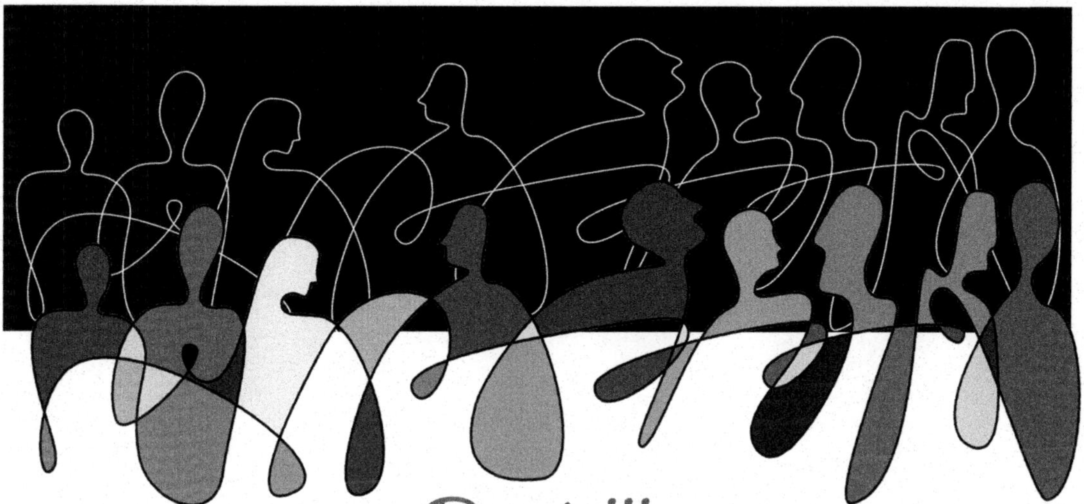

Part III

Synthesis & Concluding Thoughts

Chapter 17

Synthesis

Devon E. Romero, Madelyn Duffey, and Cassandra A. Storlie

The voices of the first two authors of this synthesis (Devon and Madelyn) are new to this book, so we begin by introducing ourselves. We were asked to create a synthesis of the stories shared by the leaders/advocates who were profiled in Part II. We want to be transparent about our positionality and further share that we work with and have been mentored by Barbara Herlihy, one of the leaders profiled in this book. At various points throughout this final chapter, you will find us asking you reflective questions. Through this reflection, we ask you to think strategically on how you can contribute to strengthening the future of the counseling profession.

I, Devon, am a counselor educator, daughter, sister, friend, and first-generation college student. I identify as a Cajun and Black biracial woman. Each of these identities influences my understanding of what it means to be a counselor, counselor educator, researcher, leader, and advocate. I am honored by the opportunities that have been extended to me, appreciative of the individuals I have met along the way, and lucky to have had extraordinary mentors. My past and current service roles have been instrumental in my own development as an aspiring servant leader. I hold various service positions within the department, college, and university; I serve as assistant editor of the Chi Sigma Iota (CSI) *Exemplar* newsletter, am a member of the CSI Awards Committee, and serve as chapter faculty advisor for our local CSI chapter.

I, Madelyn, am a counseling doctoral student, wife, volunteer, friend, and daughter. While I am new to the profession of counseling, I have assumed a number of leadership roles in nonprofit organizations in my community. Like many of the leaders profiled in this book, I did not seek leadership and am thankful that others recognized qualities in me that I had not seen in myself. I am grateful for the opportunities they provided. As a student, I have continued to develop my leadership skills as a member of the American Counseling Association (ACA) Professional Advocacy Task Force and the ACA Awards Committee and as an officer in my local chapter of CSI. I see leadership as an opportunity to contribute to a cause, form friendships, and work collaboratively on issues of great significance. At their best, I believe leaders raise up others.

As we developed this synthesis, we engaged in active dialogue to capture the essence of these profiles with authenticity. We separately engaged with each profile using an adaptation of thematic coding that included personal memos for reflexivity. We generated initial codes and established an audit trail to revisit and reflect upon. Then we moved into generating major themes through a fluid process that helped us view the convergence and divergence of themes across profiles and between us. We hope that we, a third-year assistant professor and a doctoral student with varied levels of leadership experience, have represented the perspectives of you, the reader. We also acknowledge the subjectivity of our interpretations through our unique worldviews.

Before we present our analysis, we share our overall impression. The stories in Part II are about people. People with passion. People with purpose. People who encountered doubt and persevered in the face of grief, loss, and adversity. Throughout the profiles, we read stories about counselors and community engagement, and professionals who made meaning out of their experiences. We followed their stories of risk-taking, of people who made mistakes and desired to learn from them. The profiled leaders and advocates spoke the language of equity and advocacy, carried the banner for feminism and social justice, left their mark in scholarship, and celebrated their relationships with others. As you reflect on these stories, we hope you will deepen your connections to leadership and advocacy in the field. Through our thematic analysis, we highlight how these individuals related to and differed from one another in the spirit of strengthening the future of the profession.

We identified four major themes: The Individual: Pathways to Leadership; Professional Identity and Action; Philosophy and Advocacy; and Wisdom to Strengthen the Counseling Profession. We also generated various subthemes under each of the four major themes. Some themes overlapped because we interpret counseling as a number of territories of knowledge that can move, touch, and intersect.

The Individual: Pathways to Leadership

Rising to leadership can feel daunting for the novice counselor, yet reading the stories of counselors whose trajectories have involved prominent leadership roles, it is clear that many did not begin their professional lives with a mission to lead, and several attribute happenstance and serendipity to paving their way to leadership and advocacy. All profiles illuminated unique beginnings that support professional identities as a counselor, leader, advocate, educator, researcher, and supervisor. As you have read, many of the professionals who are profiled are first-generation college students, military veterans, and some describe experiences of great loss. Leadership can begin in unexpected places and can develop throughout the life span. Leadership is a call to service; it can begin with a childhood experience, an early mentor relationship, or an unexpected opportunity.

Legacies and Traditions

As we reflected on the early years of the leaders/advocates, several formative influences emerged in our synthesis. Culture and family helped shape the leaders' personal values, belief systems, and identities. Mentors provided support, encouragement, opportunities, and personal and career wisdom. Early adversity contributed to leaders' personal development, professional and advocacy interests, and leadership styles. The leaders exhibited a number of personal characteristics that guided their leadership trajectory, and we offer thematic explorations of their journeys into leadership.

The Complexity of Identity

Identity is complex and core to our being. We support the idea that individuals carry a multiplicity of identities that intersect and may even compete with one another (Sue & Sue, 2019). Physical health and ability, race, gender, and socioeconomic status, among other factors, all influence identity development, and culture can influence our participation in activities and leadership. For example, some leaders noted that feeling a sense of "being different" inspired them to represent a group not always identified as leaders, showing the profession and the world their competency and cultural pride. Patricia Arredondo described how being a female Mexican American shaped her early leadership trajectory, and it felt like she "had to work twice as hard." Courtland C. Lee described the challenges of being the only Black student in his program and the profound impact of having a mentor who shared his racial background. We attest that remaining culturally responsive and deepening your multicultural competencies will expand your world in exponential ways and will enrich your connection with others and yourself.

Other profiles illuminated that privilege, rather than minority status, influenced how leaders perceived the world and grew in their understanding of advocacy. Still others noted an internal drive for leadership and the influence of strong parental figures who inspired their budding identities as leaders. For example, Thomas J. (Tom) Sweeney spoke of his mother's extraordinary leadership. Although she never attended college, she was always striving to "make things better."

Consider your own background and how it has helped frame your identity. What personal strengths drawn from your past will support your role as a counselor and leader? What practices do you undertake that help you reflect on your strengths and attributes?

Grief, Loss, and Adversity

Grief is commonly associated with bereavement and death, but the experience of grief and loss can take on many forms and come from a variety of situations. Some leaders experienced the death of a parent or spouse, separations, or family disconnections. Carol Bobby reflected on losing both of her parents at a young age, and through the power of counseling, she felt a strong "draw to the profession as a result of actually experiencing the profession." At some point, most leaders encountered career disappointments or setbacks. Because of legislative restrictions early in the school counseling profession, Martin Ritchie found himself initially unable to find a job as a school counselor despite having a master's degree. Others faced and witnessed prejudice, discrimination, and outsider treatment. The leaders' profiles highlight how experiences of adversity shaped who they are, how they lead, and what they value. For instance, Samuel Templeman (Sam) Gladding shared his childhood experiences with his language disability and how facing adversity helped him to work hard and stay flexible.

Each of us has faced forms of grief, loss, and adversity in our lifetimes. When considering your own losses, how might those experiences motivate you in your advocacy and leadership trajectories? How are you inspired by what you see, what you experience, and by those who have supported you along the way?

Mentorship

Mentoring relationships can arise at different points in our lives for different reasons. Sometimes we seek them out, and at other times, someone sees unrecognized potential within us. No matter how these relationships begin, the profiles highlight their deep impact and profundity. Each profile began and ended with thoughtful statements by the leaders' mentees, who described feeling humbled and honored to interview and write profiles for their mentors. The mentees wove sincere respect, appreciation, and regard into their reflections.

The leaders discussed many of their own meaningful experiences as both mentees and mentors. Many leaders had mentors who instilled confidence, highlighted unknown opportunities, and served as sounding boards. Casey A. Barrio Minton shared how Jane Myers mentored her leadership skills and provided direction on how to gain new experiences and develop relationships in the field of counseling. Over time, the leaders themselves became mentors, thus giving back to the profession by developing meaningful professional relationships and disseminating knowledge. As you have read, the mentees described their mentors' immense impact on their growth as they navigated graduate school and new family and career responsibilities.

Considering that many of the leaders felt like outsiders at one point or another, it makes sense that mentorship experiences were both powerful and empowering. How have you experienced mentorship at this point in your professional journey? Have your mentors inspired you to "pay it forward," as was expressed by several of the leaders?

Personal Characteristics

Resilience and Perseverance

Our understanding of the profiles suggested that resilience and perseverance were key to overcoming obstacles. Although resilience is often viewed as an inborn quality that people access in times of distress or adversity (Volk, 2014), current views speak to the relationality of resilience. We are resilient *because* we have, or have had, the support of one or more caring persons. This is known as *relational resilience* (Jordan, 2018). The leaders described a variety of tactics that helped them to persevere despite myriad obstacles. Sam Gladding and Craig Cashwell utilized humor. Patricia Arredondo focused on what it would mean for her community to see someone of Mexican heritage succeed professionally.

Many of us resonate with the feelings of doubt, uncertainty, and imposter syndrome that some of the leaders discussed. How did I get here? Do I belong? Will I be successful? It was heartening to read that others who have accomplished so much have navigated similar feelings. How, then, do we overcome these uncertainties and bounce back when at some point in our lives we inevitably fall short of our expectations or hopes? Have you struggled with uncertainties about your ability to succeed professionally? What strategies have you employed to overcome these obstacles?

Open, Optimistic, and Flexible

Remaining open allows for unseen options to come into view, and optimism offers the hope and desire to consider possibilities not yet known to us. Flexibility provides leaders with enough elasticity to consider the views of all involved, to make changes when necessary to existing plans, and to problem solve situations that invariably arise. Theodore P. (Ted) Remley was both flexible and confident in concurrently pursuing a JD and a PhD. He also exhibited the optimism necessary to undertake and achieve both goals.

The profession of counseling has evolved in numerous ways since its beginnings. As the leaders described, questions of licensure, board certification, accreditation, and portability require tremendous dialogue, negotiation, vision, and collaboration among leaders and stakeholders. Patricia Arredondo likened her professional flexibility to border crossing; she described how she intentionally positioned herself so that she could cross into several professional roles and ventures to enact meaningful change.

Throughout the history of the counseling profession, leaders have had to negotiate high-stakes endeavors and grapple with strategic challenges and concrete dilemmas. Remaining open, flexible, and optimistic, while remembering there will be times when we cannot muster any of these qualities, provides an opening for us to move through these situations. We strive for the good of the order *and* remember that sometimes our very best, even in the face of disappointment, has to be good enough. In those times, we must give ourselves that grace.

Can you think of times when your best didn't seem "good enough" and you felt disappointed and discouraged? Were you able to remain open, flexible, and optimistic in the face of those situations? How can you channel that experience to inspire continued strength and growth in the counseling profession?

Humility, Authenticity, Patience, and Empowerment

As the profiles illustrate, humility at its best describes leaders who do not need to take center stage and are comfortable sharing recognition for collaborative work, giving people voice in meetings and valuing teamwork. This can be particularly relevant to women, some men, and members of minority groups who may be socialized toward humility in ways that make it challenging to assert their needs or rights. Humility is not a virtue when we sell ourselves short or continuously stay in positions where others fail to value us.

Authenticity refers to a person's capacity for congruency and a willingness and ability to be oneself despite the risk of perceived failure or rejection (Jordan, 2018). Humility and authenticity in leadership create a climate in which people can feel safe to speak, make mistakes, and grow. This was evident in the countless hours Tom Sweeney spent investing in others by building authentic relationships among governing council members when he was president of APGA (now ACA).

Patience and empowerment both resonate with themes of authenticity and humility, and together they enable growth in a climate that empowers people without fear because they know they have the support of leadership. Authenticity is core to Carol Bobby as she shared the importance of creating a work-life balance, which can be challenging, and highlighted the importance of nurturing yourself and staying grounded.

When you think of your own role models of leadership and advocacy, do the words "humble" and "authentic" describe them? If you have striven for humility, authenticity, and patience as you traverse your professional path, have these traits empowered you?

Professional Identity and Action

Professional identity and action is the phrase we chose to represent how the profiled leaders perform and embody professional identity and the role of professional counselor and the components and collective actions that contribute to the larger identity of the counseling profession. At times, we have questioned our own ability to lead and have experienced imposter feelings. Like some of the leaders in this book, you also may find yourself questioning your ability to lead or thinking that "leader" is not one of your identified roles. You might wonder whether you can live up to the legacies of those profiled in this book. In addition to individual factors, we have learned that a strong professional counselor identity is at the core of each profile. When we peel back the layers of their achievements as leaders and advocates, we can see the importance of training as a counselor and learning how to use counseling skills. Leaders and advocates Barbara Herlihy and Martin Ritchie alluded to the parallel between counseling skills and leadership skills, and many others provided examples of these person-centered, relational, and culturally responsive skills in action.

Organizational Involvement

Professional organizations are a component of professional counselors' identity and their overall identity in the counseling profession. In addition to curricular standards for professional identity, national accreditation standards (Council for Accreditation of Counseling and Related Educational Programs [CACREP], 2015) identify active participation in professional counseling organizations as a foundational standard for entry-level and doctoral-level programs. Counseling organizations provide an avenue for networking, disseminating knowledge, and building on the legacy and traditions of the profession through memberships, activities, conferences, and leadership initiatives. Each leader discussed conference attendance and participation, scaffolded leadership experiences, and related their international and national presidential service and administrative leadership. Many of the profiles highlight exemplary leadership and advocacy efforts, such as Gerard Lawson's work in legislative advocacy. Within these profiles, we see organizational involvement at the highest levels.

There are many additional ways to lead and advocate within and outside of counseling organizations. We must acknowledge the inherent privilege in organizational involvement; barriers exist that can prevent some from accessing the national and regional associations, such as costly annual membership fees, conference registration rates, and other expenses associated with attending and contributing in the international, national, and regional arenas. If some of these barriers limit your involvement, we suggest looking to opportunities with state and local community organizations, which are also very valuable for networking, mentorship, and the exchange of knowledge—sometimes at no cost.

Engagement in counseling organizations strengthens the profession through collaborative actions. How would you describe your involvement in professional organizations? In what ways have you benefited from your involvement?

Advancing the Profession Through Action

Actions in the present moment are salient to moving the profession forward and adapting to our consistently changing world in light of systemic injustices and the current coronavirus pandemic. Every micromovement is directing the future of our field and creating a stronger understanding of our professional identity. The counseling profession can be thought of as a living organism that can be nurtured and, when needed, pruned. The collective efforts of counseling professionals (including those profiled here) have the power to steer the future of the profession. As leaders remain flexible and open to new perspectives and initiatives, they expand their potential to productively influence the growth of the profession.

The stories shared in this book describe individuals who have contributed to the professionalization of counseling. These leaders have enacted and continue to enact social justice change in times of inequalities and inequities in society and in the profession, such as Courtland C. Lee's pivotal work in multiculturalism, diversity, and the internationalization of counseling. Within the context of the counseling profession, advocacy efforts have resulted in third-party reimbursement, use of assessment instruments in counseling practice, global involvement, national standards for counselor preparation, and state licensure. Next, we present some subthemes that highlight additional ways we can advance the profession through action.

Nurturing Professional Identity

We are proud and honored to be counseling professionals. We recognize that we are members of a young profession that has made great strides in developing an identity distinct from other mental health professions. Counseling is a profession that emphasizes development throughout the life span, values relationships, and promotes wellness and human dignity. As we continue to consider the profession as an organic being, we do so with keen awareness that progress in the profession may expand the definition of what it means to have a professional counselor identity. Counselors must have a clear understanding of and the ability to fully articulate our professional identity to others (e.g., consumers, other professionals, public officials) to enhance our visibility. Counselors can nurture professional identity by choosing to use terms such as "professional counselor" rather than "therapist" and engage in opportunities to educate, inform, and promote our profession through professional advocacy (Sweeney, 2012).

Each professional counselor and counselor-in-training is a representative of the larger profession. Therefore, ensuring quality training programs, competence of counseling graduates, and client access to services are essential to the welfare and continued development of the profession. Counselor educators and supervisors have an ethical obligation to safeguard the progression of the profession by shaping the development of competent and ethically informed practitioners.

Take a moment to reflect on your own actions. When did your professional counselor identity begin to take root? The profiles illustrate that the health, integrity, and cultivation of the profession connects to the training of professional counselors. How has your training program affected your own professional development? What actions have you taken to educate, inform, and promote the profession of counseling to others?

Creating a Living Legacy

You might think of a legacy as something left behind and sustained beyond the individual. We challenge you to take an action-oriented approach and consider the legacy of your work. Define, plan, and live your legacy with authenticity, persistence, and intentionality. Leadership roles and even one's tenure in the counseling profession are temporal. Actions must transcend time. Many of the leaders profiled spoke of the need for leaders to consider those who will come after and how the organization will evolve beyond their own period of service.

Through our engagement with those profiled, we recognize that creating a living legacy involves professional generativity and promotion of the counseling profession through knowledge sharing, role-modeling for the next generation, and paying it forward through acts of service and mentorship. Mentorship is a mechanism for spreading oral traditions and is an oft-cited ingredient necessary to advance the profession. For example, Spencer G. (Skip) Niles reflected on the mentorship he received in his doctoral studies from Ed Herr specific to academic writing. Tom Sweeney shared how an influential mentor encouraged him to apply to Ohio State's doctoral program. These pivotal moments advance our profession in its development of scholars and advocates.

Creating a living legacy includes sharing knowledge through teaching, collaboration, and scholarship. It is also important to celebrate and recognize the achievements and accomplishments of counseling leaders and advocates. Through celebration and recognition comes awareness that empowers others to engage. The leader profiles describe prolific writers, book authors, and many who served in editorial roles with our top counseling journals. Knowledge sharing is one way to contribute to the preparation of future counselors and advance the profession.

You have the ability to create an impact. So we ask, what contributions do you want to make? Even if you don't consider yourself primarily to be a scholar or a teacher, how will you share your unique knowledge and experience? How will you define and live your legacy?

Philosophy and Advocacy

The establishment of the counseling profession and its evolution over time was not accidental. Transformations in the counseling profession over the past 60 to 70 years reflect the work of many inspirational counseling leaders and advocates who saw a need for change and took action. These leaders exemplified transparency, relationality, and creativity. The leaders profiled here are supportive of others, intentional in their roles, and strategic in their efforts.

Leading by Doing

Leading by doing represents leaders and advocates who were not afraid to roll up their sleeves, get in the trenches, and show up to do the work. Several leaders reminded us that leadership happens behind the scenes, in the community, and not always when serving in a formal position. Leadership is choosing to take action, to create a new path, and to inspire others to walk with you toward a common goal. These choices leave a mark and continue to contribute to and serve the profession.

Some profiles described supportive leadership and transformational leadership. Others reflected the role of dependability and mindfulness in leadership. Leaders who spoke their truth and understood their place in relation to others exhibited authentic leadership. Sam Gladding identified existentialism and Rogerian theory as important components of his leadership style, emphasizing the need to deeply understand your own place in relation to the client, the profession, and the world. Some profiles highlighted relational leadership and collaborative leadership, but servant leadership was a central and consistent theme across all profiles.

Servant Leadership

M. Sylvia Fernandez stated, "Who you are as a counselor and a leader is an embodiment of who you are as a person." Servant leadership represents the authentic expression of leadership qualities that are transformational, motivational, inspirational, and supportive of others. As highlighted in Chapter 3, servant leadership closely aligns with the values of, and is valued within, the counseling profession. Early in Gerard Lawson's counseling career, he pondered how he could be an agent of change and the person who is "helping move the process forward." The servant leader, whether in a formal leadership position or not, is a servant first. Courtland C. Lee described servant leadership as service to others and the ethical use of power and influence for the benefit of others.

We identified some overlap between servant leadership philosophy in action and other leadership styles. From Barbara Herlihy, we saw how social justice leadership is entwined with servant leadership. Martin Ritchie described leadership as an "honor and responsibility to advocate for others." We concur.

What does servant leadership mean to you? Does it differ from your previous ideas about leadership? Even if you haven't seen yourself as a leader, can you envision yourself engaging in servant leadership?

Forms of Advocacy

Advocacy is a function of effective leadership and a fundamental responsibility of professional counselors as agents of change and social justice. Advocacy is implemented in various forms (e.g., client advocacy, professional advocacy, legislative advocacy, community advocacy, systems advocacy), each of which is unique but also interrelated and may be pursued alongside other forms. Efforts that may benefit the self may also be to the benefit of the client, and by extension, to the overall profession. We identified client advocacy, professional advocacy, and systems advocacy as significant themes in these profiles.

Client Advocacy

Advocacy on behalf of a particular client or population is commonly discussed in counselor education programs and enacted by professional counselors. Many leaders discussed client advocacy in direct relation to leadership and professional advocacy. For example, Ted Remley was actively involved in the committee on TRICARE to benefit clients and to support counselors as providers of mental health services. Others spoke of the continued need for increased diversity and cultural competency within the profession to promote client advocacy and specialized training for professional counselors related to specific client populations.

In what ways do you advocate for your clients or the client population you intend to serve? It is likely that you are engaging in advocacy in your daily work without labeling or recognizing it as such.

Professional Advocacy

Professional advocacy refers to actions that promote the counseling profession and contribute to professional counselor identity. This form of advocacy is evident in many of the leader profiles. In our review of the 13 profiles, professional advocacy was among the most frequently occurring themes, and it encompassed a broad scope, from promoting national training standards, to engaging in research and scholarship, to lobbying for licensure, certification, and other legislative initiatives.

Although you may not have had opportunities to engage in organized advocacy efforts such as lobbying for legislative changes, you engage in professional advocacy every time your individual actions promote our profession and clarify our identity. Are you able to name some specific instances when you have enacted this type of advocacy? How can you continue to advocate for the counseling profession to strengthen our future and the futures of our clients?

Systems Advocacy

Professional counselors who engage in advocacy from a systemic perspective attempt systemic change with and for others. Skip Niles shared that he and colleagues navigated institutional systems in efforts to create the first CACREP-accredited program at Penn State. This effort had a direct impact on the professional identity and development of the students and faculty in the program, and by extension, on the clients they serve. The use of narrative storytelling by Barbara Herlihy helped to create mental health programs in schools after Hurricane Katrina, providing an example of the impact systemic advocacy can have at the community level.

No system is perfect, and every organization or university can be improved through joining with others to effect needed change. If you see a need for change within the system in which you work or study, how might you engage with others to advocate for change?

Wisdom to Strengthen the Counseling Profession

You are in a unique position to learn from the experiences of these exemplary leaders and advocates. Although the leaders profiled here took different personal, educational, and professional paths to becoming counselors and counselor educators, they all share a deep commitment for growing the profession. Throughout their journeys, these leaders learned valuable lessons that can help the next generation of counselors and counselor educators continue to craft a cohesive identity that leaves room for diverse interests, backgrounds, perspectives, and practices. They noted how technological and scientific advances are ushering in new possibilities and recognize the enduring challenges of licensure and portability (Bohecker & Eissenstat, 2020). In the midst of the global and societal reckonings brought on by the coronavirus pandemic and persistent systemic racism, the leaders also provided valuable words of wisdom regarding professional unity and identified opportunities for growth to meet today's challenges.

Professional Identity and Unity

Professional identity and unity do not mean we must all be of one mind-set (Woo et al., 2016). Unique perspectives and creative ideas greatly contribute to professional identity and keep counseling relevant. Different specialty areas and tracks shelter under the umbrella of counseling (CACREP, 2015), and divergent narratives are imperative to foster a professional identity that is inclusive, reflective, and responsive. Multiple leaders discussed the need for professional unity. If we want to continue to see positive movement and have a strong social and political impact, we must find a way to do so with a message that unifies the profession with a shared mission and vision (Kaplan et al., 2014).

Unifying the profession requires teamwork and collaboration. Several profiles identified the need for more interconnectedness and collaborative relationships between professional counseling organizations. As Carol Bobby noted, collaborative relationships that work well include those that exist among CACREP, CSI, and the National Board of Certified Counselors. Ted Remley spoke of a rift between counseling organizations that threatens the identity of the profession. He suggested that the American School Counseling Association (ASCA), the American Mental Health Counselors Association (AMHCA), and ACA need to come together and reunite. If that is not possible, ACA needs to create new divisions for school and mental health counseling. M. Sylvia Fernandez underscored an important message for the future of the counseling profession: "Fragmented we are weak and vulnerable to external threats." What ideas do you bring that can further unify our profession?

Opportunities for Growth

As we enter a new decade already marked by dramatic changes, the profession of counseling is ripe with opportunities. Historically important topics, such as licensure portability and parity, remain critical areas of focus for counseling leadership (Bohecker & Eissenstat, 2020). Distance counseling and telehealth are growing trends, made particularly salient during the coronavirus pandemic (Maurya et al., 2020). Integrated care, in which clinical mental health counselors collaborate with other health professionals to provide services to members of a community, continues to emerge as a valuable resource, and unfolding research in neuroscience creates unprecedented opportunities for counselors to offer clients neurofeedback and other brain-based services (Ivey & Zalaquett, 2011). Craig S. Cashwell voiced excitement about research in this emerging field and the potential of neuroscience to bring healing to clients with trauma. Professional counseling is expanding worldwide, bringing forth exciting international collaborations and opening pathways for the globalization of counseling.

Online/Telehealth and Distance Counseling

Online counseling has emerged as a viable practice in recent times, and the global pandemic has dramatically highlighted its value. Many counselors and counseling students who never anticipated offering distance counseling found themselves gaining new skills and certifications in a matter of days. Despite numerous benefits of distance counseling, such as access for those who might not otherwise have it, Gerard Lawson cautions us that counselors must study, research, and thoughtfully provide online counseling services. Casey A. Barrio Minton identified the rapid change in the counseling profession's service delivery and advises new leaders not to lose the "values and priorities the profession prides itself in holding" during this time. Several professional organizations, including ACA, offer specialized training and ethical guidelines (ACA, 2014) for telehealth and distance counseling. How are you and your programs embracing telehealth and distance counseling? How can your work using these new modalities continue to enhance the strength and unity of the counseling profession?

Licensure Portability

Licensure portability, which refers to the ability for an independently licensed counselor to transfer a professional counseling license from one state to another (Bayne & Doyle, 2019), is necessary to ensure that counselors can continue to do good work despite geographic relocations. Leaders, including the ones profiled here, have discussed the need for licensure portability over the years, and this continues to be an area of focus for the future. Yet numerous factors remain to be considered if we are to move forward with portability plans proposed by several counseling groups for states' consideration (Bohecker & Eissenstat, 2020). As leaders sought solutions, they discussed forming interstate compacts, and more recently, ACA contracted with the Council of State Governments' (CSG) National Center for Interstate Compact (NCIC) on a new initiative involving interstate contracts. Key stakeholders representing diverse organizations and state boards are currently involved in a multistaged process to explore the potential for interstate compact agreements between states (Meyers, 2020a). Having the freedom and opportunity to move and transfer licensure from one state to another is a reasonable request for independently licensed counselors. Leaders profiled in this book remarked that removing barriers to portability remains an important leadership goal and responsibility. In what ways can you contribute toward the goal of licensure portability? How will your actions help the counseling profession grow and develop to serve more clients?

Globalization of Counseling

It is difficult to read the profiles and not smile at the enthusiasm of some leaders for counseling's international prospects. Whether taking doctoral students to study abroad or presenting at international conferences, these leaders are dedicated to learning, engaging, and sharing thoughtfully and mutually around the globe. Multiculturally competent counselors remain open to being influenced by our international neighbors, which creates an opportunity for mutual learning and growing.

Reflective of this century, counseling's reach is spreading internationally and connecting individuals and groups across vast distances (Lorelle et al., 2012). The profession's deepening understanding of multicultural contexts both informs the internationalization of counseling and offers a framework for conceptualizing how counseling is applied and experienced internationally. Just as multicultural principles guide the profession in understanding and respecting that culture and context remain salient considerations in counseling practice, they help us recognize the value and human dignity in all people. As our world becomes increasingly interdependent, professional counselors must remain dedicated to mental health and wellness for each global citizen (Lorelle et al., 2012). How can you contribute to global wellness and cultural responsiveness on an international scale to combat marginalization and oppression everywhere?

Seize Opportunities

As we reflect on the leaders and their stories, several themes or words of wisdom come to the forefront. Many leaders discussed the importance of seizing opportunities and explained how we are optimally positioned to do so. Risk-taking also requires courage, as we have seen in each of the leaders profiled.

Take Risks and Don't Sweat the Small Stuff

M. Sylvia Fernandez described how taking risks can lead to personal and professional growth. As a young professional, Sylvia advocated for maternity leave, challenging departmental expectations. She risked the ire of those around her and those in positions of power to enact change and set a meaningful precedent. As her story illustrates, taking risks is necessary to advance the profession and to provide responsive care to our communities. Similarly, in recognizing the challenges and barriers that others face, profiled leaders identified that striving for authenticity contributes to balance and well-being.

In considering ways to best seize opportunities, leaders discussed the need to remain focused on what matters most to them. When Craig S. Cashwell was asked what lesson he wanted to share, he wished someone had told him, in ways that truly resonated, "not to sweat the small stuff" and just be himself. Being true to oneself is integral to authentic leadership and showcases congruence in our thoughts, words, and actions. Training to become a counselor and developing as a professional involve numerous challenges that can produce questions and doubts. "Not sweating the small stuff" can help students, counselors, and current leaders learn new skills, navigate challenges, and seize opportunities for growth without losing sight of who they are and the skills and gifts they have.

Recognize Courageous Opportunities

Casey A. Barrio Minton urged others not to shy away from opportunities that are different from what they expect, anticipate, or desire. These unexpected opportunities can lead to creative and unique paths. One unique path that may continue to be an opportunity for counselors in the future is our involvement in integrated health care. Integrated health care is a collaboration between medical and behavioral health practitioners to provide whole health services that are cost effective and convenient (National Institute of Health, 2017). Counseling positions within integrated care settings afford community members access to important physical and mental health services, representing a holistic health care approach for clients who may need it the most (Moe et al., 2018).

Recognizing opportunities can also help leaders bring about the evolution necessary for personal and professional growth and counselor well-being. Sometimes a person must have courage to meet an unexpected opportunity. Skip Niles suggested, "Stretch and learn. Don't focus on whether or not you will be successful as much as what each opportunity has to teach you about yourself and the world." Leadership involves grappling with challenging situations, and doing so calls for courage. In that respect, several leaders identified "bravery" as an important component of leadership. At times, the right decision is not the popular one, and it takes courage to stand for our principles, and for what we perceive as the greater good, with integrity and vision. Risk-taking, not "sweating the small stuff," and being brave occur when we are engaged in being our best selves. Be your best self!

Chapter 18

Concluding Thoughts

Cassandra A. Storlie and Barbara Herlihy

Chapter 17 illuminated the ideas on culturally responsive leadership and leadership and advocacy in the field presented in Part I, providing a synthesis of common themes found in the stories of the counseling profession's most prominent leaders. We were privileged to be the first to read the profiles of these leaders/advocates, and we were somewhat surprised that ethics did not emerge as a prominent theme in their leadership and advocacy stories. Perhaps these individuals felt no need to "state the obvious," that is, that good leadership is ethical leadership. Although some guiding documents on ethics and leadership exist, such as the ACA Code of Leadership (2019) and the Chi Sigma Iota *Principles and Practices of Leadership Excellence* (2009), empirical research seems to be lacking, and very little has been written about ethics in counselor leadership. Perhaps one of you will be inspired to pick up the mantle and conduct some needed research into this topic. Myers (2011) discussed leadership ethics in terms of Chi Sigma Iota's *Principles and Practices*, and several of those principles and practices are evident in the profiles. Certainly, service to others is a hallmark of effective leadership, and that is a consistent theme throughout the leaders' stories. Other principles that were illuminated in many profiles are having a vision for the future; mentoring, encouraging, and empowering others; recognizing the contributions of others; and engaging in self-reflection.

Leadership and advocacy in contemporary times will continue to be challenged by the coronavirus pandemic and the systemic racism that has historically permeated institutions and organizations in the United States. As we reflect on the leaders profiled here, we are inspired to see the growth of the counseling profession from humble beginnings and feel awakened to undertake the work that has yet to be accomplished to strengthen our profession. We recognize that these profiles provide a limited snapshot of the current state of counseling; our profession is blessed with many more exceptional leaders and advocates and many more who are "in the making." We hope future writings explore the narratives of scholars whose focus is specifically on research leadership in counseling. We are grateful to our own mentors who have inspired us to complete this book so that others can be inspired by these journeys.

We continue to be encouraged by our professional counseling organizations' culturally responsive statements that denounce racism in all of its forms. We encourage you to engage in efforts that illuminate the strength of our diversity as a society and to do so with passion and integrity. Although we used a systematic method in selecting leaders to be profiled, we recognize that this group of leaders does not reflect counseling as a female-majority profession, and these profiles represent too few people of color. As advocates for equity and equality, we call on the profession to nurture, mentor, and increase diversity among future leaders.

We were also struck by how many of the leaders/advocates identified each other as their mentors and role models. In that sense, counseling and counselor education and supervision really is a "small world." But this is by no means "a closed loop." Each of the leaders expressed gratitude to their own mentors and affirmed their commitment to "paying it forward" by mentoring others. As Thomas J. Sweeney so aptly pointed out, "there is always room for another leader." We hope you have heard the message that leadership and advocacy in the counseling profession are for everyone. One does not need to be in an elected position in a counseling organization to be a leader. Each of us can engage in leadership and advocacy within our families and communities, schools and colleges, institutions and organizations. Counseling leadership and advocacy offers a unique and valuable paradigm for training, practice, and research. Although space limitations preclude us from exploring the implications for practice, teaching, and supervision, we encourage you, as counseling professionals, to blaze the trail!

In conclusion, we offer some suggestions we hope you will find helpful as you step forward into leadership and advocacy in the counseling profession.

1. *Find a mentor.* Mentorship was invaluable to our profiled leaders, often launching them into arenas they hadn't seen as a place for them. If you don't currently have a mentoring relationship, seek one out. Don't assume that a leader is "too busy" or wouldn't be interested in talking with you. It never hurts to ask, and you may be pleasantly surprised.
2. *Start small.* Opportunities to engage in leadership and advocacy are right in front of you. If you are interested in the work of a local counseling association, volunteer to serve on a committee. If you are a student, get involved with your university's chapter of Chi Sigma Iota. If you see an injustice in your workplace or institution, speak up and advocate for change. As former Supreme Court Justice Ruth Bader Ginsberg notably stated, "real change comes in small steps."
3. *Keep your balance.* Students and early career professionals in the field of counseling can be passionate and driven to effect change. Although passion is necessary, so is a good life-work balance; remember to nurture yourself. Each small step you take will move you forward, but it takes time and sustained effort to produce lasting change.

4. *Lead to serve.* The servant leadership philosophy that underpins the counseling profession reminds us that leaders are not always "front and center stage." Effective leaders are motivated by a desire to improve the lives of others, not by personal gratification. If you are a counselor, you already have that desire, and you can harness it through advocacy for others.
5. *Trust yourself.* You have much to offer. If someone else sees something in you, it's because that "something" is already there. You are a member of the next generation of leaders and advocates for the counseling profession.

Onward!

• • •

PART III: 2016 CACREP Standards Alignment

Synthesis

SECTION 2: PROFESSIONAL COUNSELING IDENTITY
COUNSELING CURRICULUM

1. PROFESSIONAL COUNSELING ORIENTATION AND ETHICAL PRACTICE
   - b. the multiple professional roles and functions of counselors across specialty areas, and their relationships with human service and integrated behavioral health care systems, including interagency and interorganizational collaboration and consultation
   - c. counselors' roles and responsibilities as members of interdisciplinary community outreach and emergency management response teams
   - d. the role and process of the professional counselor advocating on behalf of the profession
   - e. advocacy processes needed to address institutional and social barriers that impede access, equity, and success for clients
   - g. professional counseling credentialing, including certification, licensure, and accreditation practices and standards, and the effects of public policy on these issues
   - j. technology's impact on the counseling profession

SECTION 6: DOCTORAL STANDARDS: COUNSELOR EDUCATION AND SUPERVISION

B. DOCTORAL PROFESSIONAL IDENTITY

5. LEADERSHIP AND ADVOCACY
   - h. current topical and political issues in counseling and how those issues affect the daily work of counselors and the counseling profession
   - i. role of counselors and counselor educators advocating on behalf of the profession and professional identity
   - j. models and competencies for advocating for clients at the individual, system, and policy levels
   - k. strategies of leadership in relation to current multicultural and social justice issues

Additional Readings on Leadership and Advocacy

We encourage you to broaden your knowledge about leadership by delving further into the literature. The following books may be helpful.

Bennis, W. (2009). *On becoming a leader: The leadership classic*. Basic Books.

Chang, C. Y., Barrio Minton, C. A., Dixon, A. L., Myers, J. E., & Sweeney, T. J. (2012). *Professional counseling excellence through leadership and advocacy*. Routledge.

Conyne, R. K., & Bemak, F. (2005). *Journeys to professional excellence: Lessons from leading counselor educators and practitioners*. American Counseling Association.

Marshall, C., & Oliva, M. (2010). *Leadership for social justice: Making revolutions in education*. Pearson.

McKee, A., Boyatzis, R., & Johnston, F. (2008). *Becoming a resonant leader*. Harvard Business Press.

Northouse, P. G. (2019). *Leadership: Theories and practices* (8th ed.). Sage.

West, J. D., Osborn, C. J., & Bubenzer, D. L. (Eds.). (2003). *Leaders and legacies: Contributions to the profession of counseling*. Routledge.

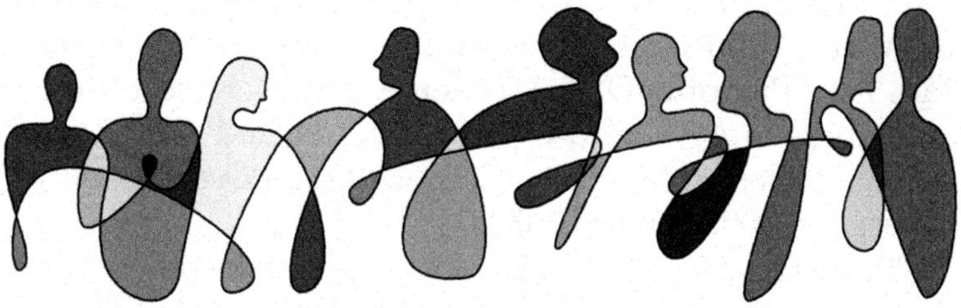

References

American Counseling Association (n.d.). *Our history.* https://www.counseling.org/about-us/about-aca/our-history

American Counseling Association. (2014). *ACA code of ethics.* https://www.counseling.org/resources/aca-code-of-ethics.pdf

American Counseling Association. (2015). *Multicultural and social justice counseling competencies.* https://www.counseling.org/docs/default-source/competencies/multicultural-and-social-justice-counseling-competencies.pdf?sfvrsn=20

American Counseling Association. (2019). *ACA code of leadership.* counseling.org/doc/default-source/leadership-resources/aca-code-of-leadership.pdf

American Counseling Association (2020a, February 18). *The American Counseling Association denounces immigrant youths' breach of confidentiality.* https://www.counseling.org/news/updates/2020/02/18/the-american-counseling-association-denounces-immigrant-youths-breach-of-confidentiality

American Counseling Association (2020b). *Antiracism statement.* https://www.counseling.org/news/updates/2020/06/22/aca-anti-racism-statement

American Psychiatric Association. (2013). *Diagnostic and statistical manual of mental disorders* (5th ed.).

American School Counselor Association. (2018, August 23). *ASCA issues statement opposing any proposal to use federal education funds to purchase firearms.* https://schoolcounselor.org/Standards-Positions/Position-Statements/ASCA-Position-Statements/The-School-Counselor-and-Prevention-of-School-Rela

Anderson, J., Hilert, A., Lara, M., Martinez, R., & Mavaneh, S.S. (2015). *The history of Counselors for Social Justice (CSJ).* https://www.counseling-csj.org/uploads/1/2/3/6/123630265/history_csj-history-final-version-january-3-2016.pdf

Arredondo, P., & Glauner, T. (1992). *Personal dimensions of identity model.* Empowerment Workshops.

Arredondo, P., Toporek, R., Brown, S. P., Jones, J., Locke, D. C., Sanchez, J., & Stadler, H. (1996). Operationalization of the multicultural counseling competencies. *Journal of Multicultural Counseling and Development, 24*(1), 42–78. https://doi.org/10.1002/j.2161-1912.1996.tb00288.x

Association for Multicultural Counseling and Development. (n.d.) *History.* https://www.multiculturalcounselingdevelopment.org/amcd-history

Baggerly, J., Tan, T. X., Pichotta, D., & Warner, A. (2017). Race, ethnicity, and gender of faculty members in APA- and CACREP-accredited programs: Changes over five decades. *Journal of Multicultural Counseling and Development, 45*(4), 292–303. https://doi.org/10.1002/jmcd.12079

Barfield, G. L. (2019). The evolution of person-centered encounter: Creating egalitarian environments for mattering, meaning & healing. *Person-Centered & Experiential Psychotherapies, 18*(3), 228–242. https://doi.org/10.1080/14779757.2019.1650809

Bartels, S. J., & Naslund, J. A. (2013). The underside of the silver tsunami—Older adults and mental health care. *New England Journal of Medicine, 368*, 493–496. https://doi.org/10.1056/nejmp1211456

Bayne, H. B., & Doyle, K. (2019). Licensure portability through an ethical lens: Considering multiple stakeholders. *Journal of Mental Health Counseling, 41*(2), 97–111. https://doi.org/10.17744/mehc.41.2.01

Beck, M. J., & Lane, E. M. D. (2019). Exploring effective practitioner advocacy: A study of ASCA's school counselor of the year finalists. *Journal of Counselor Leadership and Advocacy, 6*(2), 174–187. https://doi.org/10.1080/2326716X.2019.1601602

Beck, M. J., Rausch, M., Wikoff, H., & Gallo, L. (2018). Ecological considerations and school counselor advocacy with LGBT students. *Journal of Counselor Leadership and Advocacy, 5*(1), 45–55. https://doi.org/10.1080/2326716X.2017.1402393

Beers, C. (1908). *A mind that found itself: An autobiography*. Longmans, Green.

Behl, M., Laux, J. M., Roseman, C. P., Tiamiyu, M., & Spann, S. (2017). Needs and acculturative stress of international students in CACREP programs. *Counselor Education and Supervision, 56*(4), 305–318. https://doi.org/10.1002/ceas.12087

Bell, D. A. (1995). Who's afraid of critical race theory? *University of Illinois Law Review,* 893–910. http://heinonline.org

Black Lives Matter. (n.d.). *About.* https://blacklivesmatter.com

Bohecker, L., & Eissenstat, S. J. (2020). Five licensure portability models for the counseling profession to consider. *Journal of Counseling & Development, 98*(2), 220–229. https://doi.org/10.1002/jcad.12316

Bronfenbrenner, U. (1979). *The ecology of human development: Experiments by nature and design.* Harvard University Press.

Bronfenbrenner, U., & Morris, P. A. (1998). The ecology of developmental processes. In W. Damon & R. M. Lerner (Eds.), *Handbook of child psychology: Theoretical models of human development* (pp. 993–1028). Wiley.

Brubaker, M. D. (2020). Finding your professional niche: Getting involved in professional organizations and honor societies. In M. O. Adekson (Ed.), *Handbook of counseling and counselor education* (pp. 19–35). Routledge.

Bryant-Davis, T., Adams, T. Alejandre, A., & Gray, A. A. (2017). The trauma lens of police violence against racial and ethnic minorities. *Journal of Social Issues, 73*(4), 852–871. https://doi.org/10.1111/josi.12251

Buchmueller, T. C., Levinson, Z. M., Levy, H. G, & Wolfe, B. L. (2016). Effect of the Affordable Care Act on racial and ethnic disparities in health insurance coverage. *American Journal of Public Health, 106*(8), 1216–1421. https://doi.org/10.2105/AJPH.2016.303155

Capuzzi, D., & Gross, D. R. (2017). *Introduction to the counseling profession.* Routledge.

Cartwright, A. D., Avent-Harris, J. R., Munsey, R. B., & Lloyd-Hazlett, J. (2018). Interview experiences and diversity concerns of counselor education faculty from underrepresented groups. *Counselor Education and Supervision, 57*(2), 132–146. https://doi.org/10.1002/ceas.12098

Cashwell, C., & Barrio Minton, C. (2012). Leadership and advocacy in counselor education programs: Administration and culture. In C. Y. Chang, C. A. Barrio Minton, A. L. Dixon, J. E. Myers, & T. J. Sweeney (Eds.), *Professional counseling excellence through leadership and advocacy* (pp. 165–184). Routledge.

Cashwell, C. S., & Young, J. S. (Eds.). (2020). *Integrating spirituality in counseling: A guide to competent practice* (3rd ed.). American Counseling Association.

Center for Collegiate Mental Health. (2016, January). *2015 Annual Report* (Publication No. STA 15-108). https://sites.psu.edu/ccmh/files/2017/10/2015_CCMH_Report_1-18-2015-yq3vik.pdf

Centers for Disease Control and Prevention. (2020, December 10). *COVID-19 in racial and ethnic minority groups.* https://www.cdc.gov/coronavirus/2019-ncov/community/health-equity/racial-ethnic-disparities/index.html

Center for Servant Leadership. (2020). *The servant as leader.* https://www.greenleaf.org/what-is-servant-leadership/

Chan, C. D., Cor, D. N., & Band, M. P. (2018). Privilege and oppression in counselor education: An intersectionality framework. *Journal of Multicultural Counseling and Development, 46*(1), 58–73. https://doi.org/10.1002/jmcd.12092

Chan, C. D., DeDiego, A. C., & Band, M. P. (2019). Moving counselor educators to influential roles as advocates: An ecological systems approach to student-focused advocacy. *Journal of Counselor Leadership and Advocacy, 6*(1), 30–41. https://doi.org/10.1080/2326716X.2018.1545614

Chang, C. Y. (2012). Professional advocacy: A professional responsibility. In C. Y. Chang, C. A. Barrio Minton, A. L. Dixon, J. E. Myers, & T. J. Sweeney (Eds.), *Professional counseling excellence through leadership and advocacy* (pp. 95–107). Routledge.

Chang, E., & Kwon, P. (2013). Special issue on psychopathology in Asians and the DSM-5: Culture matters. *Asian Journal of Psychiatry, 7*(1), 66–77. https://doi.org/10.1016/j.ajp.2013.12.001

Chi Sigma Iota. (2009). *Principles and practices of leadership excellence.* www.csi-net.org/leadership

Cholewa, B., Burkhardt, C. K., & Hull, M. F. (2015). Are school counselors impacting underrepresented students' thinking about postsecondary education? A nationally representative study. *Professional School Counseling, 19*(1), 144–154. https://doi.org/10.5330/1096-2409-19.1.144

Chung, R., Bemak, F., & Grabosky, T. (2011). Multicultural social justice leadership strategies: Counseling and advocacy with immigrants. *Journal of Social Action in Counseling & Psychology, 3*(1), 86–102. https://doi.org/10.33043/jsacp.3.1.86-102

City of Cleveland, Ohio v. Cook, Municipal Court, Criminal Division, No. 75-CRB 111478, August 12, 1975.

Collins, P. H. (2015). Intersectionality's definitional dilemmas. *Annual Review of Sociology, 41*(1), 1–20. https://doi.org/10.1146/annurev-soc-073014-112142

Collins, P. H., & Bilge, S. (2020). *Intersectionality* (2nd ed.). Polity Press.

Cook, E. P. (2015). *Understanding people in context: The ecological perspective in counseling.* American Counseling Association.

Council for Accreditation of Counseling and Related Educational Programs. (n.d.). *About us*. https://www.cacrep.org/about-cacrep/

Council for Accreditation of Counseling and Related Educational Programs (CACREP). (2015). *2016 CACREP standards*. http://www.cacrep.org/wp-content/uploads/2017/08/2016-Standards-with-citations.pdf

Crenshaw, K. (1989). Demarginalizing the intersection of race and sex: A Black feminist critique of antidiscrimination, feminist theory, and antiracist politics. *University of Chicago Legal Forum.* https://chicagounbound.uchicago.edu/uclf/vol1989/iss1/8

Crowe, A., & Kim, T. (2020). Ethnicity, life satisfaction, stress, familiarity, and stigma toward mental health treatment. *Journal of Counseling & Development, 98*(1), 83–93. https://doi.org/10.1002/jcad.12302

David, E. J. R., Schroeder, T., & Fernandez, J. (2019). Internalized racism: A systematic review of the psychological literature on racism's most insidious consequence. *Journal of Social Issues, 75*(4), 1057–1086. https://doi.org/10.1111/josi.12350

Day-Vines, N. L., Booker Ammah, B., Steen, S., & Arnold, K. M. (2018). Getting comfortable with discomfort: Preparing counselor trainees to broach racial, ethnic, and cultural factors with clients during counseling. *International Journal for the Advancement of Counselling, 40*(2), 89–104. https://doi.org/10.1007/s10447-017-9308-9

Demanchick, S. P., & Kirschenbaum, H. (2008). Carl Rogers and the CIA. *Journal of Humanistic Psychology, 48*(1), 6–31. https://doi.org/10.1177/0022167807303005

Education Trust. (2019, February). *School counselors matter*. https://edtrust.org/resource/school-counselors-matter/

Eriksen, K. (1997). *Making an impact: A handbook on counselor advocacy*. Routledge.

Eva, N., Robin, M., Sendjaya, S., van Dierendonck, D., & Liden, R. C. (2019). Servant leadership: A systematic review and call for future research. *Leadership Quarterly, 30*(1), 111–132. https://doi.org/10.1016/j.leaqua.2018.07.004

Farrell, I. C., & Barrio Minton, C. A. (2019). Advocacy among counseling leaders: The three-tiered legislative professional advocacy model. *Journal of Counselor Leadership and Advocacy, 6*(2), 144–159. https://doi.org/10.1080/2326716X.2019.1644254

Fickling, M. J., & Gonzalez, L. M. (2016). Linking multicultural counseling and social justice through advocacy. *Journal of Counselor Leadership and Advocacy, 3*(2), 85–94. https://doi.org/10.1080/2326716X.2015.1124814

Fickling, M. J., Tangen, J. L., Graden, M. W., & Grays, D. (2019). Multicultural and social justice competence in clinical supervision. *Counselor Education & Supervision, 38*, 309–316. https://doi.org/10.1002/ceas.12159

Flynn, P. M., Betancourt, H., Emerson, N. D., Nunez, E. I., & Nance, C. M. (2020). Health professional cultural competence reduces the psychological and behavioral impact of negative healthcare encounters. *Cultural Diversity and Ethnic Minority Psychology, 26*(3), 271–279. https://doi.org/10.1037/cdp0000295

Fore, W. (2014). A joyful heart is good medicine: Sexuality conversion bans in the courts. *Michigan Journal of Gender & Law, 21*(2), 311–340. https://repository.law.umich.edu/mjgl/vol21/iss2/3

Fox, D., Prilleltensky, I., & Austin, S. (2009). *Critical psychology: An introduction.* Sage.

Foxx, S. P., Baker, S. B., & Gerler, E. R. (2017). *School counseling in the 21st century* (6th ed.). Routledge.

Freire, P. F. (2006). *Pedagogy of the oppressed.* Continuum International. (Original work published 1970)

Fullen, M. C. (2016). Medicare advocacy for the counselor advocate. *Adultspan Journal, 15*(1), 3–12. https://doi.org/10.1002/adsp.12015

Fullen, M. C., Wiley, J. D., & Morgan, A. A. (2019). The Medicare mental health coverage gap: How licensed professional counselors navigate Medicare-ineligible provider status. *The Professional Counselor, 9*(4), 310–323. https://doi.org/10.15241/mcf.9.4.310

Fye, H. J., Miller, L. G., & Rainey, J. S. (2018). Predicting school counselors' supports and challenges when implementing the ASCA national model. *Professional School Counseling, 21*(1), 1–11. https://doi.org/10.1177/2156759X18777671

George, B. (2003). *Authentic leadership: Rediscovering the secrets to creating lasting value.* Jossey-Bass.

Gibson, D., Dollarhide, C., Conley, A., & Lowe, C. (2020). The construction and validation of the school counseling transformational leadership inventory. *Journal of Counselor Leadership & Advocacy, 5*(1), 1–12. https://doi.org/10.1080/2326716X.2017.1399246

Gladding, S. T. (2011). Courtland Lee: A global advocate for counseling. *Journal of Counseling & Development, 89*(4), 493–499. https://doi.org/10.1002/j.1556-6676.2011.tb02847.x

Gladding, S. T. (2017). Professional involvement. In T. M. Kimbel & D. H. Levitt (Eds.), *A guide to graduate programs in counseling* (pp. 125–138). Oxford University Press.

Goodyear, R. K. (2000). An unwarranted escalation of counselor-counseling psychologist professional conflict: Comments on Weinrach, Lustig, Chan, and Thomas (1998). *Journal of Counseling & Development, 78*(1), 103–106. https://doi.org/10.1002/j.1556-6676.2000.tb02566.x

Greenleaf, R. K. (1970). *The servant as leader.* Greenleaf Center for Servant Leadership.

Guth, L. J., Nitza, A., Pollard, B., Puig, A., Chan, C. D., Singh, A., & Bailey, H. (2019). Ten strategies to intentionally use group work to transform hate, facilitate courageous conversations, and enhance community building. *Journal for Specialists in Group Work, 44*(1), 3–24. https://doi.org/10.1080/01933922.2018.1561778

Hacker, K., Chu, J., Arsenault, L., & Marlin, R. P. (2012). Provider's perspectives on the impact of Immigration and Customs Enforcement (ICE) activity on immigrant health. *Journal of Health Care for the Poor and Underserved, 23*(2), 651–665. https://doi.org/10.1353/hpu.2012.0052

Hargons, C., Mosley, D., Falconer, J., Faloughi, R., Singh, A., Stevens-Watkins, D., & Cokley, K. (2017). Black lives matter: A call to action for counseling psychology leaders. *The Counseling Psychologist, 45*(6), 873–901. https://doi.org/10.1177/0011000017733048

Haskins, N., & Singh, A. (2016). Advocacy competency of school counselors: An exploratory factor analysis. *Professional School Counseling, 20*(1), 149–158. https://doi.org/10.5330/1096-2409-20.1.149.

Hilert, A. J. (2020). Climate change and the international context of counseling. *Journal of Asia Pacific Counseling, 10*(1), 27–36. https://doi.org/10.18401/2020.10.1.3

Hines, E. M., Moore, J. L., Mayes, R. D., Harris, P. C., Vega, D., Robinson, D. V., Gray, C. N., & Jackson, C. E. (2020). Making student achievement a priority: The role of school counselors in turnaround schools. *Urban Education, 55*(2), 216–237. https://doi.org/10.1177/0042085916685761

Howell, P. B., Thomas, S., Sweeney, D., & Vanderhaar, J. (2019). Moving beyond schedules, testing and other duties as deemed necessary by the principal: The school counselor's role in trauma informed practices, *Middle School Journal, 50*(4), 26–34, htts://doi.org/10.1080/00940771.2019.1650548

Hyatt-Burkhart, D., & Lopez Levers, L. (2020). New frontiers for clinical mental health counselors. In L. Lopez Levers & D. Hyatt-Burkart (Eds.), *Clinical mental health counseling: Practicing in integrated systems of care.* (pp. 307–332). Springer.

Ilies, R. (2005). Authentic leadership and eudaemonic well-being: Understanding leader-follower outcomes. *The Leadership Quarterly, 16*(3), 373–394.

It's Going Down. (2018, July 11). *Winning phone zap campaigns: An interview with Oakland IWOC.* https://itsgoingdown.org/organizing-winning-phone-zap-campaigns-interview-with-oakland-iwoc/

Ivey, A., & Zalaquett, C. (2011). Neuroscience and counseling: Central issue for social justice leaders. *Journal for Social Action in Counseling & Psychology, 3*(1), 103–116. https://doi.org/10.33043/jsacp.3.1.103-116

Johnson, L. (2006). "Making her community a better place to live": Culturally responsive urban school leadership in historical context. *Leadership & Policy in Schools, 5*(1), 19–36. https://doi.org/10.1080/15700760500484019

Jordan, J. V. (2018). *Relational-cultural therapy* (2nd ed.). American Psychological Association.

Kaplan, D. M., & Gladding, S. T. (2011). A vision for the future of counseling: The 20/20 principles for unifying and strengthening the profession. *Journal of Counseling & Development, 89*(3), 367–372. https://doi.org/10.1002/j.1556-6678.2011.tb00101.x

Kaplan, D. M., & Kraus, K. L. (2018). Building block to portability: Culmination of the 20/20 initiative. *Journal of Counseling & Development, 96*(2), 223–228. https://doi.org/10.1002/j.1556-6676.2014.00164.x

Kaplan, D. M., Tarvydas, V. M., & Gladding, S. T. (2014). 20/20: A vision for the future of counseling: The new consensus definition of counseling. *Journal of Counseling & Development, 92*(3), 366–372. https://doi.org/10.1002/j.1556-6676.2014.00164.x

Kiselica, M. S., & Robinson, M. (2001). Bringing advocacy counseling to life: The history, issues, and human dramas of social justice work in counseling. *Journal of Counseling & Development, 79*(4), 387–397. https://doi.org/10.1002/j.1556-6676.2001.tb01985.x

La Roche, M., Fuentes, M., & Hinton, D. (2015). A cultural examination of the *DSM-5*: Research implications for cultural minorities. *Professional Psychology: Research and Practice, 46*(3), 183–189. https://doi.org/10.1037/a0039278

Lawson, G. (2016). On being a profession: A historical perspective on counselor licensure and accreditation. *Journal of Counselor Leadership and Advocacy, 3*(2), 71–84. https://doi.org/10.1080/2326716X.2016.1169955

Lawson, G., Trepal, H. C., Lee, R. W., & Kress, V. (2017). Advocating for educational standards in counselor licensure laws. *Counselor Education and Supervision, 56*(3), 162–176. https://doi.org/10.1002/ceas.12070

Lee, C. C. (2012). Social justice as the fifth force in counseling. In C.Y. Chang, C. A. Barrio Minton, A. L. Dixon, J. E. Myers, & T. J. Sweeney (Eds.), *Professional counseling excellence through leadership and advocacy* (pp. 109–120). Routledge.

Lee, C. C. (Ed.). (2019). *Multicultural issues in counseling: New approaches to diversity* (5th ed.). American Counseling Association.

Lenes, E., Swank, J. M., Hart, K. A., Machado, M. M., Darilus, S., Ardelt, M., & Puig, A. (2020). Color-conscious multicultural mindfulness training in the counseling field. *Journal of Counseling & Development, 98*(2), 147–158. https://doi.org/10.1002/jcad.12309

Lewis, J. A., Arnold, M. S., House, R., & Toporek, R. L. (2003). *ACA advocacy competencies.* https://www.counseling.org/docs/default-source/competencies/aca-advocacy-competencies-updated-may-2020.pdf?sfvrsn=f410212c_4

Lewis, J. A., Ratts, M., Paladino, D., & Toporek, R. (2011). Social justice counseling and advocacy: Developing new leadership roles and competencies. *Journal for Social Action in Counseling & Psychology, 3*(1), 5–16. https://doi.org/10.33043/jsacp.3.1.5-16

Lewis, T. F. (2012). Foundations of leadership: Theory, philosophy, and research. In C. Y. Chang, C. A. Barrio Minton, A. L. Dixon, J. E. Myers, & T. J. Sweeney (Eds.), *Professional counseling excellence through leadership and advocacy* (pp. 21–40). Routledge.

Lopez-Baez, S. I., & Paylo, M. J. (2009). Social justice advocacy: Community collaboration and systems advocacy. *Journal of Counseling & Development, 87*(3), 276–283. https://doi.org/10.1002/j.1556-6678.2009.tb00107.x

Lorelle, S., Byrd, R., & Crockett, S. (2012). Globalization and counseling: Professional issues for counselors. *Professional Counselor, 2*(2), 115–123. https://doi.org/10.15241/sll.2.2.115

Lykes, M. B., & Sibley, E. (2014). Liberation psychology and pragmatic solidarity: North-south collaborations through the Ignacio Martín-Baró Fund. *Peace and Conflict: Journal of Peace Psychology, 20*(3), 209–226. http://dx.doi.org/10.1037/pac0000045

Madhlangobe, L., & Gordon, S. (2012). Culturally responsive leadership in a diverse school: A case study of a high school leader. *NASSP Bulletin, 96*(3), 177–202. https://doi.org/10.1177/0192636512450909

Martin, S. L., Ashley, O. S., White, L., Axelson, S., Clark, M., & Burrus, B. (2017). Incorporating trauma-informed care into school-based programs. *Journal of School Health, 87*(12), 958–967. https://doi.org/10.1111/josh.12568

Martín-Baró, I. (1994). *Writings for a liberation psychology.* Harvard University Press.

Maurya, R., Bruce, M., & Therthani, S. (2020). Counselors' perceptions of distance counseling: A national survey. *Journal of Asia Pacific Counseling, 10*(2), 1–22. https://doi.org/10.18401/2020.10.2.3

Maxwell, L. A. (2020, May 7). School year closures now affect 50 million students. *Education Week*. https://www.edweek.org/education/school-year-closures-now-affect-50-million-students/2020/05

McGuire, T. G., & Miranda, J. (2008). New evidence regarding racial and ethnic disparities in mental health: Policy implications. *Health Affairs, 27*(2), 393–403. https://doi.org/10.1377/hlthaff.27.2.393

Mental Health America. (n.d.). *Our history*. https://www.mhanational.org/our-history

Meyers, L. (2020a). Interstate compact plan provides hope for portability. *Counseling Today, 62*(10). https://ct.counseling.org/2020/04/interstate-compact-plan-provides-hope-for-licensure-portability/

Meyers, L. (2020b, September 28). School counseling in the time of the coronavirus. *Counseling Today*. https://ct.counseling.org/2020/09/school-counseling-in-the-time-of-the-coronavirus/

Miller J. B. (1976). *Toward a new psychology of women*. Beacon Press.

Moe, J., Park, K., Johnson, K., & Finnerty, P. (2018). Integrated behavioral health and counseling gender and sexual minority populations. *Journal of LGBT Issues in Counseling, 12*(4), 215–229. https://doi.org/10.1080/15538605.2018.1526156

Morning, A., & Sabbagh, D. (2005). From sword to plowshare: Using race for discrimination and antidiscrimination in the United States. *International Social Science Journal, 57*(183), 57–73. https://doi.org/10.1111/j/0020-8701.2005.00531.x

Myers, J. E. (2011). Professional leadership, leading well: Characteristics, principles, and ethics of effective counseling leaders. In C. Y. Chang, C. A. B. Minton, A. L. Dixon, J. E. Myers, & T. J. Sweeney (Eds.), *Professional counseling excellence through leadership and advocacy* (pp. 41–61). Taylor & Francis.

Myers, J. E., & Sweeney, T. J. (2004). The indivisible self: An evidence-based model of wellness. *Journal of Individual Psychology, 60*(3), 234–244.

Myers, J. E., Sweeney, T. J., & White, V. E. (2002). Advocacy for counseling and counselors: A professional imperative. *Journal of Counseling & Development, 80*(4), 394–402. https://doi.org/10.1002/j.1556-6678.2002.tb00205.x

Na, G., & Fietzer, A. W. (2020). A national survey of social justice engagement among professional counselors. *Journal of Counseling & Development, 98*(3), 331–334. https://doi.org/10.1002/jcad.12326

Nassar-McMillan, S. C. (2001). Celebrating 50 years of service: A conversation with Mary Thomas Burke. *Journal of Counseling & Development, 79*(4), 497–504. https://doi.org/10.1002/j.1556-6676.2001.tb01997.x

National Institute of Mental Health. (2017). *Integrated care*. https://www.nimh.nih.gov/

Neukrug, E. (2016). *The world of the counselor: An introduction to the counseling profession* (5th ed.). Cengage Learning.

Newsome, D., & Gladding, S. (2014). *Clinical mental health counseling in community and agency settings* (4th ed.). Pearson.

Nichols, L. M., & Carney, J. V. (2013). Jane E. Myers: The evolution of an advocate. *Journal of Counseling & Development, 91*(2), 240–248. https://doi.org/10.1002/j.1556-6676.2013.00091.x

Northouse, P. G. (2016). *Leadership: Theories and practices* (7th ed.). Sage.

Northouse, P. G. (2019). *Leadership: Theories and practices* (8th ed.). Sage.

Pack-Brown, S. P., Thomas, T. L., & Seymour, J. M. (2008). Infusing professional ethics into counselor education programs: A multicultural/social justice perspective. *Journal of Counseling & Development, 86*(3), 296–302. https://doi.org/10.1002/j.1556-6678.2008.tb00512.x

Parry, M. (2010). From a patient's perspective: Clifford Whittingham Beers' work to reform mental health services. *American Journal of Public Health, 100*(12), 2356–2357. https://doi.org/10.2105/ajph.2010.191411

Peters, H., & Luke, M. (2021). Supervision of leadership model: An integration and extension of the discrimination model and socially just and culturally responsive counseling leadership model. *Journal of Counselor Leadership & Advocacy,* (Online first), 1–16. https://doi.org/10.1080/2326716x.2021.1875341.

Peters, H., Luke, M., Bernard, J., & Trepal, H. (2020). Socially just and culturally responsive leadership within counseling and counseling psychology: A grounded theory investigation. *The Counseling Psychologist, 48*(7), 953–985. https://doi.org/10.1177%2F0011000020937431

Pew Research Center. (2019). *Americans see advantages and challenges in country's growing racial and ethnic diversity*. https://www.pewsocialtrends.org/2019/05/08/americans-see-advantages-and-challenges-in-countrys-growing-racial-and-ethnic-diversity/

Pew Research Center. (2020). *Hispanics have accounted for more than half of total U.S. population growth since 2010*. https://pewrsr.ch/324NHu4

Piccolo, R. F., & Colquitt, J. A., (2006). Transformational leadership and job behaviors: The mediating roles of core job characteristics. *Academy of Management Journal, 49*(2), 327–340. https://doi.10.5465/AMJ.2006.20786079

Pollack, S. (2019, July). Interested in a VA career? *Counseling Today, 62*(1), 8–9. https://www.counseling.org/government-affairs/federal-issues/va-counselors

Ratts, M. (2009). Social justice counseling: Toward the development of a fifth force among counseling paradigms. *Journal of Humanistic Counseling, Education and Development, 48*(2), 160–172. https://doi.org/10.1002/j.2161-1939.2009.tb00076.x

Ratts, M. J. (2011). Multiculturalism and social justice: Two sides of the same coin. *Journal of Multicultural Counseling and Development, 39*(1), 24–37. https://doi.org/10.1002/j.2161-1912.2011.tb00137.x

Ratts, M., DeKruyf, L., & Chen-Hayes, S. (2007). The ACA advocacy competencies: A social justice advocacy framework for professional school counselors. *Professional School Counseling, 11*(2), 90–97.

Ratts, M., & Greenleaf, A. (2018). Counselor-advocate-scholar model: Changing the dominant discourse in counseling. *Journal of Multicultural Counseling and Development, 46*(2), 78–96. https://doi.org/10.1002/jmcd.12094

Ratts, M., & Hutchins, A. (2009). ACA advocacy competencies: Social justice advocacy at the client/student level. *Journal of Counseling & Development, 87*(3), 269–275. https://doi.org/10.1002/j.1556-6678.2009.tb00106.x

Ratts, M. J., & Pedersen, P. B. (2014). *Counseling for multiculturalism and social justice: Integration, theory, and application* (4th ed.). American Counseling Association.

Ratts, M. J., Singh, A. A., Nassar-McMillan, S., Butler, S. K., & McCullough, J. R. (2015). *Multicultural and social justice counseling competencies*. https://www.counseling.org/docs/default-source/competencies/multicultural-and-social-justice-counseling-competencies.pdf?sfvrsn=8573422c_22

Ratts, M. J., Singh, A. A., Nassar-McMillan, S., Butler, S. K., & McCullough, J. R. (2016). Multicultural and social justice counseling competencies: Guidelines for the counseling profession. *Journal of Multicultural Counseling and Development, 44*(1), 28–48. https://doi.org/10.1002/jmcd.12035

Remley, T. P., & Herlihy, B. (2020). *Ethical, legal, and professional issues in counseling* (6th ed.). Pearson Education.

Rogers, R., Eagle, T. F., Woodward, A., Leibowtiz, R. Song, M., Sylvester, R., Corriveau, N., Kline-Rogers, E., Jiang, Q., Jackson, E. A., & Eagle, K. A. (2015). The relationship between childhood obesity, low socioeconomic status, and race/ethnicity: Lessons from Massachusetts. *Childhood Obesity, 11*(6), 691–695. https://doi.org/10.1089/chi.2015.0029

Schriver, J. M. (2011). *Human behavior and the social environment: Shifting paradigms in essential knowledge for social work practice* (5th ed.). Allyn & Bacon.

Singh, A. A., Appling, B., & Trepal, H. (2020). Using the multicultural and social justice counseling competencies to decolonize counseling practice: The important roles of theory, power, and action. *Journal of Counseling & Development, 98*(3), 261–271. https://doi.org/10.1002/jcad.12321

Singh, A. A., & Nassar, S. C. (2020). Introduction to the special issue. *Journal of Counseling & Development, 98*(3), 235–237. https://doi.org/10.1002/jcad.12257

Singh, A. A., Nassar, S., Arredondo, P., &. Toporek, R. (2020). The past guides the future: Implementing the multicultural and social justice counseling competencies. *Journal of Counseling & Development, 98*(3), 238–252. https://doi.org/10.1002/jcad.12319

Storlie, C. A. (2016). Exploring school counselor advocacy in the career development of undocumented Latino youth. *Journal for Social Action in Counseling & Psychology, 8*(1), 70–88.

Storlie, C. A., Baltrinic, E., Aye, M., Wood, S. M., & Cox, J. (2019). Making room for leadership and advocacy in site supervision. *Journal of Counselor Leadership and Advocacy, 6*(1), 1–15. https://doi.org/10.1080/2326716X.2019.1575778

Storlie, C. A., & Jach, E. (2012). Social justice collaboration in schools: A model for working with undocumented Latino students. *Journal for Social Action in Counseling & Psychology, 4*(2), 99–116.

Storlie, C. A., Shannonhouse, L., Brubaker, M., Zavadil, A., & King, J. (2016). Exploring dimensions of advocacy in service: A content analysis extending the framework of counselor community engagement activities in Chi Sigma Iota chapters. *Journal of Counselor Leadership & Advocacy, 3*(1), 52–61.

Streed, C. G., Anderson, J. S., Babits, C., & Ferguson, M. A. (2019). Changing medical practice, not patients—Putting an end to conversion therapy. *New England Journal of Medicine, 381*(6), 500–502. https://doi.org/10.1056/NEJMp1903161

Stripling, R. O. (1978). Standards and accreditation in counselor education: A proposal. *The Personnel and Guidance Journal, 56*(10), 608–611. https://doi.org/10.1002/j.2164-4918.1978.tb05074.x

Sue, D., & Sue, D. W. (2019). *Counseling the culturally diverse* (8th ed.). Wiley.

Sue, D. W., Alsaidi, S., Awad, M. N., Glaeser, E., Calle, C. Z., & Mendez, N. (2019). Disarming racial microaggressions: Micro-intervention strategies for targets, White allies and bystanders. *American Psychologist, 74*(1), 128–142. https://doi.org/10.1037/amp0000296

Sue, D. W., Arredondo, P., & McDavis, R. J. (1992). Multicultural counseling competencies and standards: A call to the profession. *Journal of Multicultural Counseling and Development*, *20*(2), 64–88. https://doi.org/10.1002/j.2161-1912.1992.tb00563.x

Sweeney, T. J. (2012). Professional advocacy: Being allowed to do good. In C. Y. Chang, C. A. Barrio Minton, A. L. Dixon, J. E. Myers, & T. J. Sweeney (Eds.), *Professional counseling excellence through leadership and advocacy* (pp. 81–93). Routledge.

Tissington, L. D. (2008). A Bronfenbrenner ecological perspective on the transition to teaching for alternative certification. *Journal of Instructional Psychology, 35*(1), 106–110.

Toomey, R., & Storlie, C. A. (2016). School counselors' intervention in bias-related incidents among Latino students. *Journal of School Violence, 15*(3), 343–364. https://doi.org/10.1080/15388220.2015.1049354

Toporek, R. L., & Daniels, J. (2018). *2018 update and expansion of the 2003 ACA advocacy competencies: Honoring the work of the past and contextualizing the present.* https://www.counseling.org/docs/default-source/competencies/aca-advocacy-competencies-updated-may-2020.pdf?sfvrsn=f410212c_4

Toporek, R. L., Lewis, J. A., & Crethar, H. C. (2009). Promoting systemic change through the ACA advocacy competencies. *Journal of Counseling & Development, 87*(3), 260–268. https://doi.org/10.1002/j.1556-6678.2009.tb00105.x

TRICARE Certified Mental Health Counselors, 79 Fed. Reg. 41,636 (final rule, July 17, 2014) (to be codified at 32 C.F.R. pt. 199). http://www.gpo.gov/fdsys/pkg/FR-2014-07-17/pdf/2014-16702.pdf

Trusty, J., & Brown, D. (2005). Advocacy competencies for professional school counselors. *Professional School Counseling, 8*(3), 259–265. https://www.jstor.org/stable/42732467

Tuazon, V. E., Gonzalez, E., Gutierrez, D., & Nelson, L. (2019). Colonial mentality and mental health help seeking of Filipino Americans. *Journal of Counseling & Development, 97*(4), 352–363. https://doi.org/10.1002/jcad.12284

U.S. Department of Health and Human Services. (2020). *Designated health professional shortage areas statistics: First quarter of fiscal year 2020 designated HRSA quarterly summary*. https://data.hrsa.gov/data/fact-sheets.

Vereen, L., Hill, N., Sosa, G., & Kress, V. (2014). The synonymic nature of professional counseling and humanism: Presuppositions that guide our identities. *Journal of Humanistic Counseling, 53*(3), 191–202. https//doi.org/10.1002/j.2161-1939.2014.00056.x

Volk, K. (2014). *Childhood resilience.* https://www.samhsa.gov/homelessness-programs-resources/hpr-resources/childhood-resilience

Washington, A. R., & Henfield, M. S. (2019). What do the AMCD multicultural and social justice counseling competencies mean in the context of Black Lives Matter? *Journal of Multicultural Counseling and Development, 47*(3), 148–160. https://doi.org/10.1002/jmcd.12138

West, J., Osborn, C., & Bubenzer, D. (2003). *Leaders and legacies: Contributions to the profession of counseling*. Routledge.

Whaley, A. L. (2008). Cultural sensitivity and cultural competence: Toward clarity of definitions in cross cultural counselling and psychotherapy. *Counselling Psychology Quarterly, 21*(3), 215–222. https://doi.org/10.1080/09515070802334781

Woo, H., Storlie, C., & Baltrinic, E. (2016). Perceptions of professional identity development from counselor educators in leadership positions. *Counselor Education and Supervision, 55*(4), 278–293. https://doi.org/10.1002/ceas.12054

Wright, R. J. (2012). *Introduction to school counseling*. Sage.

Wright, G. W., & Reese, R. J. (2015). Strengthening cultural sensitivity in mental health counseling for deaf clients. *Journal of Multicultural Counseling and Development, 43*(4), 275–287. https://doi.org/10.1002/jmcd.12021

Zytowski, D. G. (2001). Frank Parsons and the progressive movement. *The Career Development Quarterly, 50*(1), 57. https://doi.org/10.1002/j.2161-0045.2001.tb00890.x